Reynard's Mirror
Reflections on Teaching Oppositional Adolescents; Letters to a British Psychoanalyst

Written and Illustrated by

CAROLYN J. CRAWFORD DAVIS

Reynard's Mirror is available at
Amazon.com and AmazonUK.com

ISBN: 978-0-692-83097-0

DEDICATION

First, to my caring, patient husband,
Zane;
then, to my parents,
bred on the hardscrabble plains
of the Texas Panhandle;
to Linda who left us way too soon,
to Marianna, Arloa, and Ruth who were my companions
in battle and finally,
to Rey,
who encouraged me to write

CONTENTS

ACKNOWLEDGMENTS

I want to thank all those who helped me with my teaching, especially Marianna, Arloa, Ruth, Linda, Joe, and Dick. Thanks especially to Paul who let me sit at the round table for a while, Larry Hedges who helped me understand, and Christopher Bollas who encouraged me to write. If there is any wisdom in these pages, it is because of what I learned from these people at Mountainview. I have only packaged it up with illustrations that my students provided.

I know I have left out many people who read my drafts over 30 years; please forgive me.

Most of all, I want to thank my students who put up with me.

Finally, I'd like to tip my hat to Walt Crawford Kelly, the brilliant cartoonist of the strip <u>Pogo</u>. His wit and whimsy were genius. Notice his middle name.

Preface

Christopher Bollas

Walking through the front doors of the Mountainview in 1983 was strangely familiar. Some twenty years before I had worked at The East Bay Activity Center (EBAC) in Oakland California, and Mountainview could have been its Southern California Sister Institution. But EBAC provided "education" and psychotherapy for children up to the age of 12 and then they had to go off into adolescence and to other institutions, including the state mental hospital. As they turned 10 we would bite our nails wondering whether our kid (we all had one child in particular to guide through the years at EBAC) would make it—to a special education school for adolescents—or whether he would be too disturbed to mix with ordinary children.

On the bad days when our kids were particularly disturbed and disturbing it was impossible not to imagine how they would be in mid adolescence. Our knees knocked, our minds fogged, and fear and trembling prompted us to ever greater therapeutic endeavors to "save them" from a dreadful fate.

Walking into Mountainview I entered a world I had always imagined but never visited. It was "the next stage"—the next good step—for a highly disturbed kid, but with the added dose of madness that we call adolescence. It is one thing to physically grapple with a robust ten year old, it is an entirely different matter to try to "hold" a ferociously angry fifteen year old who is threatening to kill you.

1

The staff were, however, very familiar to me although I had never met any of them. Places like Mountainview and EBAC tend to attract "off road" selves, people who are not afraid to leave the safer pathways of life; indeed, who rather enjoy the adventure of moving into unknown territories. An exception might be the Administrative Staff—the Principal or Head of the institution and the secretaries—who did indeed present the visage of confidence and normality that reassured the parents, visiting authorities, and fellow professionals. But once through the doors visitors were in a different setting; in that "milieu" (a favorite word of that era) where staff and their charges, moved in skewed geometric patterns driven by the fleeing adolescent and the pursuing therapist, all the while trying to create the semblance that this choreography was entirely natural.

And in a way it was.

And so, too, was it natural for differing members of staff to shriek at their charge, or get into their face with robust "interpretations" that might have gotten another adult killed on the streets, but within the therapeutic boundary of Mountainview those confrontations not only worked, they were very curious forms of love and care. No one who visited such a school could ever be otherwise than remarkably moved.

It was in that type of space that I met Carolyn, whose beaming face and welcoming smile set one immediately at ease. At the same time, there was a sort of "mess with me at your peril" stance, one quite specific to her task—having to work with frankly rather murderous adolescents—and if someone had told me that she had been in rodeos riding steers before her move to Mountainview I would not have been in the least surprised.

I was to visit Mountainview annually for many years and on each visit someone would present a "case". The first presentation was by Carolyn and I can still recall it.

2

She presented her work with a male adolescent who may have been in early training as a professional hit man. He was a cut above the ordinary terrorists in the school and had a certain eerie calm to him except when he felt it necessary to issue warnings to others, especially to Carolyn. He was to say the least not well liked. But as Carolyn presented him to the group the care with which she described the subtle nuances of his behavior and the evolving idiom of their exchanges was utterly absorbing and deeply moving. As she writes in this book, I did indeed comment that I thought she loved her patient. Love by a psychotherapist is understanding. It is the passion of enduring endless violations of the "rules" of relationship, of translating the bizarre into the ordinary, and of helping a kid move from the suicidality of a skewed adolescent process to the generativity of simply growing up.

Carolyn handed me a note about her work and it was immediately clear that she could write. I urged her to do this. Her unique verbal presentation was even more compelling in writing. I offered to read her work if she sent it to me in London but said I would not reply. In a way, I suppose, this was to offer my presence as something of a muse, but in a manner that could not possibly influence her own idiom and strength of mind which was so incredibly important. As the months and years passed and her packets would arrive at my home in London it was always a special thrill to open them up and walk through the doors of Mountainview once again and into the now literary world of Carolyn Crawford.

Read this book and you will see why she and it are so special.

June 2017

Forward

Lawrence E. Hedges, PhD.

You are about to encounter a series of remarkable experiences skillfully recorded for us by a master teacher whose desire is to show other teachers the many awful feelings that disturbed teenagers can stir up and the ways one can come to negotiate these feelings with oneself and the kids one works with. Kids are widely labeled, blamed and abused because of the confusing feelings that teachers have towards them. Carolyn's mission here is to help kids and teachers come to grips with the feelings and experiences that emerge as teens work through the traumatic experiences that interfere with learning and personal growth. My background as a clinical psychologist as well as a child and adolescent psychoanalyst prepared me to follow the painstakingly difficult and heart-wrenching work conducted by her at the Mountainview school in her special education classes over a fifteen year period.

I began in the early 1970's conducting bi-weekly teacher's conferences focusing on work with very difficult children and adolescents. Since all teachers and staff at the school worked together with whatever needs arose in each child and allowed each child to attach to whomever the child chose, I asked everyone involved in any way with the child to be discussed to be in attendance at the conferences—including a wide range of specialty therapists, the school psychologists, and the school administrators. I was amazed at the forthrightness and candor that came to characterize these meetings as we all struggled for a workable approach to helping each child overcome traumas they were carrying and to move forward in life. The most challenging work was that with the adolescents whose difficulties were mightily entrenched and who therefore required a great deal of skill, challenging, and cajoling to loosen as you will see in the chapters that follow.

When psychoanalyst Christopher Bollas began his annual visits for conferences and supervision with us at the Newport Psychoanalytic Institute I took him to Mountainview to witness the challenging work going on there and he immediately became interested in and followed Carolyn's remarkable work for a number of years in person and then later through reading her creative renditions of her work as they appeared and now by introducing this book.

It has been a pleasure and honor to be a part of Carolyn's work over the years and to be recognized as her consultant and mentor. But as always it is "from one's pupils one must be taught" and I can truly say I have learned a lifetime of lessons from watching Carolyn move among her children offering such amazing love and understanding in so many rich, strange, and strenuous ways as you will see. I too had the pleasure of hearing and reading these chapters as Carolyn produced them and thereby of feeling an ongoing part of her work.

This book stands as a tribute to special education teachers everywhere who give their life blood to helping children release the bonds of the past and find a life worth living. We have to be grateful to Carolyn not only for her beautiful and sensitive work but for her finding the energy, the courage, and the means to share it with us.

Introduction (2017)

Thirty years have passed since I first wrote this book and I find that now I need a second introduction. When I moved to my spectacular rural retreat I discovered that it was populated with citizens who, on the one hand, were dedicated conservationists defending the environment, and. on the other, were cautious conservatives.

I looked at my new beleaguered principal, running to and fro between students, parents and the school board, trying to placate all parties. Even here in this rural paradise, I thought, teaching is definitely a political activity. Being fresh from a recent sacking, I decided I'd better just keep a low profile. (Lacking tenure during the first two years meant I could be dismissed without due process for any unidentified frivolous reason.) Because I was so smitten with the beauty of my new home and fearful of reactions to my stories, I left my manuscript sitting in a cardboard box and went about the business of, first and foremost, joining a union, then learning how politics works in public schools, and trying to camouflage myself as a well-behaved school teacher.

After 36 years of teaching special ed I retired but I still wanted to share my stories with others who have suffered at the hands of adolescents, and received little to no support from administration, with the hope that my tales might offer them some comfort.

I spent a few years searching for a publisher or an agent. I received many rejections, mostly along lines of, "Who do we sell this to? Which shelf would it sit on in the book store?" I was about to give up when David Carle, a local author, told me about self-publishing. I like this much, much better. This book is mine, all mine. I get to put whatever *I* want into it, even my Pogo-esque drawings.

I sent the finished book to Rey (Christopher Bollas) and Mitchell (Lawrence Hedges). After so many years, protecting their identities no longer seemed very important. 'Reynard' offered to contribute a preface to the book and 'Mitchell' agreed to write a foreword. And finally, Paul, the Director of Mountainview, wrote an afterword.

Except for the epilogue, from this point on you will be reading the book I put in a cardboard box out of fear of political repercussions when I was a beginning public school teacher. I hope it offers you some comfort, relief or insight.

Carolyn

Introduction (1987)

Reynard the Fox was in trouble. He looked up at the King and Queen high above him on their royal thrones. King Nobel, the Lion, scowled down at him and bared his gleaming canines. His wife, the Queen, snarled her displeasure. Reynard, however, was a fellow who could improvise in a tight situation. He began telling them of his wondrous magical gifts for them…a ring with three jewels, a comb and a mirror. These gifts were imaginary, so naturally he could not produce them on the spot. But by raising his voice and embellishing his tale with a few more flourishes, he emphasized the gifts' astonishing powers and King Nobel halted mid-complaint. The King's anger was replaced by the glint of fascination and perhaps greed. Reynard's descriptions proceeded to his last gift, which was for the queen.

"Now ye shall hear of the mirror." Reynard leaned forward and spoke intently, "The glass is of such virtue that men might see therein all the things that you would desire to understand and know." Yes, smiled Reynard to himself, I think I hear the rumble of a royal purr.

The wily fox knew how much we all want to grasp the relief of closure, to escape the niggling anxiety of uncertainty, and so he offered his sovereigns the lure of knowledge. Armed with 'the answer' we can finally draw the warm comfortable cloak of righteousness around us. Then we can categorize ideas and people into dichotomies: the teacher who produces high test-scores and the low test-score teacher; the good student and the delinquent; and, the sane and the crazy. We can identify who is wrong or bad and mentally dismiss, blame or even eliminate them.

In my chosen field, special education, I am surrounded by authorities who regularly advocate some new technique they've concocted. These experts, with their bureaucratic adherents, who rarely spend much actual time in a classroom, make us apply their nostrums, and even evaluate us based on how well we use their brand new formulae. Wearily, I have watched program after program receive endorsement only to be replaced with another. While I disapprove of absolutism, I must admit that I, too, long for recipes and solutions, and crave the satisfaction of being positively in the right. However, when dealing with very unique adolescents, recipes are doomed to failure.

As you read my letters to a British psychoanalyst, who I shall call Rey, you will discover that I was confused about what I wanted from him. Mostly, I wanted to share my stories with him. He liked my writing, so he allowed me to ship many very long letters to him. At times though, I also wanted his wisdom and advice about my students which, of course, was not feasible by long distance. Rey, I hoped, really did have a magic mirror that could show me the truth.

This is not a book that offers answers, solutions or recipes. Instead of product, you will observe process, specifically, the process of coping with feelings of hatred, love, disgust and delight. You will find no demonstration of exemplary teaching or therapeutic sleuthing in these pages. In fact, you will see that I am frequently herded outside the boundaries of professional propriety by my wolfish adolescents as they snap at my tender nose and nip at my heels. This book illustrates the process of my own internal struggle to create relationships with very irritating and strong-willed students, my search to find my own writing voice, and my own image of knowledge in Reynard's magical mirror. As we would expect from the idiosyncrasies of a magical mirror, my image of knowledge will not be yours.

I am a special education teacher, but my particular situation was not at all typical of my breed. I worked in a small private school primarily with adolescents of normal to even superior intelligence who were performing far below their potential. They were usually acting-out adolescents ready to drop out of school, get into trouble with the law, or indulge in excesses of drugs, alcohol or sex. Some were on the verge of emotional breakdowns. Frequently they came to us after hospitalization, as a transition before returning to public school.

This book really began when I was asked to present a case study for Rey, who was visiting us from the UK. Unless you have attempted to teach a crowd of hostile adolescents for 30 hours a week for 15 years, you may have difficulty appreciating what Rey's approval did for me. My students' taxing behaviors had driven me on more than one occasion to excess. Rey was unique among many of the therapists I came into contact with because he knew immediately that I was a caring person and I was doing my best.

Rey was unique in another way as well. He loved writing. I was both appalled and delighted when he gave his presentations at the local psychoanalytical institute. To my mundane mind, whenever Rey was illuminating the daunting theoretical superstructure of psychoanalysis, I dragged my feet along behind him lumbered with frustration. Yet when he began to talk in concrete terms about the real interactions in his work with his patients, my mind would race along with his, darting about in anticipation of the next word, bubbling at a vivid image and grasping his internal trials. I knew this was a man who loved to write.

It may appear to you at times that I am idealizing Rey. This is true and it is not true. I was always well aware of his potential for flaw. Disorganization, blemishes, blots in his copybook and hints of clay about his feet did not escape my keen eye. Years of instantly sizing up adolescents had honed my capacity to recognize imperfection to razor-sharp acuity. Rather than

11

idealization, I think I accurately identified with that portion of Rey which reflected my own strengths. At last I had found a partner who enjoyed my tales, was able to understand what I grappled with daily, and most joyous of all, was willing to read and tolerate my writing.

At times you will find me begging Rey for help even though he had made it quite clear that he would not be replying as a supervisor of my work with my students. He knew very well that we had supervisory therapists on the staff at Mountainview, and that I also was working independently with Mitchell, another psychoanalyst, for supervision in my Masters in Psychology program. He knew these people and he knew I was in good hands.

Unknowingly, at least on my part, I made use of him in a very different way. I needed his silence and his absence. It would have been a mistake if he had ever attempted to recover me through the mail. I needed to discover my voice, and myself through my letters.

He wrote to me in the beginning that "Your accounts of your work are nothing short of remarkable...I think you should just write, write, and write some more." Throughout all the years his annual or biannual letters kept encouraging me to become a writer and to find my voice. Through his kindly silent support, he enriched my life immeasurably.

About once a year, Rey would come to town to give a lecture and if I was fortunate and could shove my way through the ranks of my competitors (therapists), I might spend half an hour in conversation with him. During those hurried moments, he would praise and encourage my writing, letting me know that my deluge of letters was not a burden to him. With each visit or letter from Rey, I would be caught up in another exultation of letter-writing.

The letters you see here represent a mere trifle compared to what Rey was subjected to from 1983 to about 1990. They are a condensation of those years. I must confess that I have removed the most blatant foolishness. As it is, I am a little worried about sharing this

12

with you, dear reader. In the world of education and mental health we don't speak about love, hatred and personal stupidity. I think we must, and so I am sharing my letters with you.

Mountainview is a private special ed school located in California in a middle to upper class, conservative community. Primarily because of our location, the school population of 80 to 100 kids was predominantly white. Our students came from frustrated and fed-up school districts who had tried everything their overcrowded and limited resources could supply. Faced with having to pay for the possible institutionalization of the student, they turned to us, a cheaper alternative. Our other source of students was parents who had given up on getting any help from their school district. They brought their sons and daughters to us, and mostly it was sons.

Just getting a child enrolled in Mountainview produced a certain winnowing effect upon the parents. If they were paying for the tuition themselves it was a considerable sacrifice, even though the school did provide a sliding scale based on the family's income. Often these parents did battle with their school district to get them to provide the funds, a very difficult task indeed. These were parents who had not given up. We rarely had apathetic parents. Sometimes they were maddening, exhibiting their own mental issues, but they were still trying to find help for their child.

I counted myself lucky that my failing students were not facing poverty and homelessness. My teacher training had shown me the extremes of conditions that could be found in a single school district. Half of my student teaching took place in luxurious Bel Air, and the other half was near the burned out riot torn shops of Watts. I vividly remember when my inner city L.A master teacher yanked me and my misbehaving student out of the classroom and shoved the three of us into a broom closet. Surrounded by mops and the sharp odor of disinfectant, she turned to the young 12 year old looking

13

anxiously up at her and asked him to tell me where he had spent the night.

"In a gas station toilet," he murmured. "My father was hunting us so he could kill us." As difficult as my Mountainview students were, they (and I) were buffered from the harsh reality of students facing poverty.

In reading these stories you may notice that I am usually more involved with my male rather than my female students. This is for two reasons. First, the percentage of females in our student population was about 15% which was generally typical of special education statewide at the time. Second, being the lead teacher with a credentialed 'aide', I felt it was my role to handle the hardcore, which usually meant that Brooke, my aide, handled the girls. I was the cop, while Brooke performed the role of the understanding teacher. The girls gravitated towards Brooke's sympathy and support and the boys squared off to do battle with the authority figure, me.

While I was at Mountainview, all the teachers had an aide in the classroom with them. How these aides were utilized was up to the discretion of the lead teacher. For me, my aide was my co-teacher; and, as far as was possible, she was my equal in managing the classroom. If I was ill, no substitute credentialed teacher was provided to cover for me, instead it was Brooke, who, happily, was also credentialed. However, this equality was often undermined by my students who knew good and well who the official teacher was.

Perhaps I should tell you more about the actual setting. Mountainview had purchased an old Spanish style stucco church. All of the younger students were housed in the building. Trailers were provided for the older students and those classrooms sat around the edges of an expansive backyard lawn. We were very close to a city park, which we often used for our physical education classes. We had no telephones in our trailers; if there was an emergency someone had to be sent to the main building. The building was also where the restrooms (teachers were not separated from students) and drinking water were located.

14

We had no curriculum, and very few appropriate books or materials. Frequently, I went over to a neighboring public school district warehouse to rummage through their dumpsters for books or I bought materials out of my meager salary.

We usually packed 12 or more adolescents into a 10' by 40' space and they spent the entire day with us except for those glorious moments when they went to physical education and their individual or group therapy. Brooke and I were responsible for teaching all the courses required for graduation from public high school as well as strengthening their basic skills in reading, writing and arithmetic. We were supposed to improve their vocational abilities so they could become productive adults and we were also responsible for their behavior and their social-emotional well-being. Let's face it...a Sisyphean task, rolling all those adolescent boulders uphill.

For myself, the main building held three refuges of comfort and support: the office of Paul, the director of the school; the office of Julia, a therapist, my friend and supervisor; and of course, the teachers' lounge. The staff also, offered remarkable comfort because they were all tough, caring and experienced. We were all going through the same things and found solace in our common plight. With them and in these three rooms I could regain my strength to return to my trailer for another round with hostile, oppositional students.

When I speak of the many therapists I dealt with who did not understand me, I am speaking of the private practitioners who were tangential to the school. Often a student came to us through the referral of his therapist. Of the 11 students included in this book, five had separate and private psychotherapists of their own. I was also exposed to other therapists in outside supervision groups. Frequently I was the only person in the group who was able to identify the hatred or anger buried in the therapist's presentation. I began to view myself as an emotional shill for the supervisor, who allowed me to be the person to point this out. I found this denial or lack of awareness in practicing therapists to be quite alarming. Teachers, on the other hand, generally know very well who they hate.

Nevertheless, I looked with envy at those therapists who were pulling in much greater wages than I and were only exposed to the harassment of a particular client for one or perhaps two hours a week. I decided that life had to be a lot easier as a therapist. Generally, the odds for survival are much greater in a therapy room than in a special ed. classroom...one to one rather than twelve to one. Besides, I had already been attacked and beaten to the floor by a hulking 6'6" adolescent. At the time of these stories I had decided to return to college to obtain my Master's degree in Psychology and obtain a Marriage, Family and Child Counseling license.   I had already started working as a co-counselor in group sessions at the school, and as an individual counselor with two students for an hour each week.

During the time I worked at Mountainview, our director, Paul, believed in allowing teachers and therapists to work, with supervision, in any reasonable style suited to their temperament. As a consequence, we used no recipes, and each situation was open-ended, with an evolving style that changed as we grew and adapted to the populations passing through our hands.[1]

As far as the kind of style I developed in this open and experimental environment, I tended to adapt bits and pieces from insights which Mitchell and his psychoanalytical institute brought to us. Mitchell, the analyst who really did all the scut work in helping me to understand my students, often told me that I have never been that concerned with making kids well-behaved or knowledgeable. Instead, he said, I try to show them something about themselves. He worries that people will

---

[1] Like any institution, Mountainview has evolved into a different school. My old way of coping with adolescents would not be appropriate there today. The Mountainview, which I have fondly recorded here, is gone.

only see the success of my craftiness and my manipulative side without understanding my capacity to work with each situation to 'mirror' or reflect my student's dynamics. According to him, I wait and watch for each student's style of interacting. Once I have absorbed that, a moment will come when I re-act. It may be a confrontation, a journal entry, or my own confession, but the goal is to look with the student into the mirror of my eyes at who he is.

All that sounds pretty good now, but when I began working at Mountainview, it was a different story entirely. My adolescents tampered with my sanity and threatened my capacity to find any human decency in their behavior. I was overwhelmed. I found myself acting in ways and feeling emotions that no right-minded teacher would want to see in herself. I completely understood teachers who had been fired for injuring a student. Strangulation seemed too good for some of my students; torture was more to my taste.

This brings us to the subject of transference and countertransference. In psychoanalysis, when dealing with patients who can function at a symbolic verbal level, the analyst can take a stance with the patient which might be called benevolent equanimity. Because of the analyst's neutrality, the patient is forced to create a relationship with the analyst out of his own repertoire of styles. This relationship he creates with the analyst is called transference. It is this that the two, patient and analyst look at together.

When dealing with individuals like my students, who function mostly at the pre-verbal level, their issues are not calmly verbalized but acted out upon the analyst (or in this case, the teacher) and generally the chosen behavior is accurately aimed for the Achilles' heel of the hapless professional. This may take many forms, for example, physical abuse, passivity, intrusion, seduction, substance abuse or suicide attempts. The responses called up in the analyst are called countertransference. Countertransference, of course, exists in the analyst, therapist or teacher for all patients, but it is remarkably more pronounced as the patient is more troubled.

Paul, our director, often had speakers come to the school and once when Mitchell came, he used the following imagery to explain transference.

When an infant, who carries certain genetic predispositions, is nurtured by significant figures, the interplay between these individuals will produce a molding or shaping of the infant. He brings that mold to other significant figures, a teacher perhaps, and instinctively tries to get her to remold herself into a good fit with him as he tries to replicate and work through his early childhood injuries with her.

An adolescent, however, may behave differently. Instead of replaying old scenarios of childhood, he may intuitively react against those experiences. Rather than play the role of the victim, he may take an active role and identify with the aggressor. Examples of the child replaying the role of the victim are: an abused child will try to get his teacher to abuse him, or; a pampered, overprotected child will try to get his teacher to take very good care of him. Examples of an adolescent identifying with the aggressor are: an adolescent who was abused as a child will abuse his teacher; or an adolescent who was emotionally seduced as a child will try to seduce his teacher.

Often countertransference appears as alien or confusing emotions within the teacher. As she translates these feelings through her own history, she will be shocked to discover that she has become abusive towards a student, or that she feels an alien affection towards an adolescent lad.

Countertransference then, is very subtle. Mitchell taught me to recognize it and understand that it was less about my own private life than it was the nature of my student. He helped me through those early years when I was certain that I was not fit to teach. In my supervision sessions with Mitchell, he showed me that by paying close attention to the kinds of feelings students aroused in me, I learned much about their early infancy, childhood and the

18

interplay between themselves and their parents.

The longer I was supervised by Mitchell, and came to understand countertransference, the calmer and less violent my classroom became. As I learned to feel empathy, to discover the child in each of my adolescents, they had less reason to behave in such outrageous ways.

These letters to Rey really extended over seven years, during which I worked with about 60 students. For narrative's sake and to avoid burying you, dear reader, under an avalanche of students, I have created one cast of characters. All of the events I describe to you are true, as true as my memory will allow. The individuals who perpetrate the action however, are disguised and composite characters. All names have been changed. I have also tampered with the timeline, wedging events together which took much longer to unfold in the real world.

Well, hopefully that's enough background, except of course, I need to introduce you to my students. In the manner of old-time mystery writers, I will include a description of our cast of characters.

Just remember, the confusion you feel, the emotions that their tales create in you, are what it's like to be a special education teacher working with them. Pay attention to those feelings. That's countertransference, perhaps the most powerful tool a teacher or a therapist can wield when working with troubled kids.

Charlie

A chronic liar overextended in his pose as a hard-ass

Charlie was one of my students who I never really got to know. He was tall and wiry with shockingly near-white blonde hair. His dark roots explained his bushy black eyebrows but not his vivid blue eyes. He could talk circles around me when he was on one of his favorite topics - politics or religion. Whenever he thought I was being unfair or wrong he would yell and preach at me with the fervor of a true believer. He was a very confusing boy. He lied constantly and dressed rebelliously in torn t-shirts and jeans.

His parents had divorced after his mother left the family. He lived with his paternal grandmother and his father. His father did not appear to play much of a role in his life, but Charlie was tightly bonded to his grandmother. He was completely unable to speak about anything personal. When he had an argument with his kindly grandmother, he became extremely depressed and mute. I knew when grandmother and grandson had a falling out because the next day he would disappear and I would have to find him, behind the building or under my desk, his knees drawn up to his chin, rocking back and forth. As we sat together, he was rarely able to tell me what was wrong. Charlie had been hospitalized twice for attempting suicide.

One of his journal entries:

This would be a very good school if the Dictator would throw out a few of the assholes who shall remain anonomous. Ive learned that one of the most important things in this place is self controle along with another special talent called kissing ass. Thanks to Carolyn and Brooke and others hear at Mountainview I have a very good chance of making it out in the BIG BAD WORLD.

Dawson

A heavy-metaled thorn in my side

Dawson was over 6 ft. tall and proud of his muscles. He spent a great amount of his school day flexing his biceps and asking others to admire the results. He had a long, narrow face, thin lips, and straggly, mousey blonde hair which he held back from his face with a black headband or a rubber band at the nape of his neck. Generally his dark blue eyes glared at me. He was always dressed in a black t-shirt decorated with a concert he'd allegedly attended.

Dawson's father, Marty, was a truck driver and the owner of several large transport trucks. Dad was often on the road, but when he was in town he was extremely demanding towards his son. At Mountainview, among ourselves, we described Marty as a helicopter father; he hovered. Marty was very overprotective, both frustrating and spoiling Dawson at the same time. He probably had good reason to be careful. Dawson's older brother was already in jail. Dawson's mother was passive, overwhelmed and helpless. Dawson had been hospitalized three times for nervous breakdowns.

From Dawson's journal:

last night my dad came home drunk and stard yeling at my mom and after he got dun yeling he barfed and I Loved it.

Tusday nite I had a big fite with him and that was the final stral the next time he start yeling at me for no fuckin reson Im just going to leve and Im not gona go bak for as long as I live.

Deborah

Mature, intelligent young woman

While Deborah had been at our school for four years, she had only been in my class for a year. It was impossible to visualize the silent, reluctant child who had entered our school in the poised young teenager who attended my class. She lived with her mother who was generally unable to take care of herself. Deborah was of Greek heritage with large deep brown eyes and a mane of dark wavy hair. She had a quiet pensive look about her which belied the quick acerbic wit hidden behind those gentle eyes. Her school district sent her to us because she simply refused to go to public school and she had made several suicide attempts. Deborah, with the support of the school, decided to do something with her life. She turned herself into a self-confidant young woman.

Her journal entry:

Nothing happened this weekend. I stayed home and sanded and painted the cabinets in the kitchen. I'm really looking forward to graduating and getting an apartment of my own. My teacher says that I am doing very well in my vocational class and she knows a medical office or two that will probably take me on. I can hardly wait!

Gillian

Compulsively tidy, driven and masculine young woman

Gillian was tall, athletic and lean. She wore her dark-brown hair cropped very close to her head. Her close-set serious brown eyes were perpetually vigilant above her tightly set lips. Gillian came from a military family and her bearing reflected her rearing. She had no mother and her father and older brother were both in the Marines and were stationed at a nearby naval base.

She held herself separate from her peers. She was critical and rigid, yet she could analyze how her behavior kept her from having friends. She would size up her personal flaws and set out to cure them with dogged determination. She was in our class for only four months before she graduated. She had been hospitalized on several occasions for violent behavior.

Her journal entry:

This is a very different sort of class. Everybody is so different from Adriane's class. I miss her a lot but I'm really glad to get away from her crazy, stupid infants. I don't like your students much either because they all seem to use drugs and they don't like me – especialy Nat. We did not get along in Adriane's class. But I only have 4 more months to put up with them and then I'll go to community college. Then I can forget I ever went to this school for the insane.

Kent

My skittish and cunning opponent

Kent was with us for about six months. He was a small lad for a 17 year-old. He was dark-haired with tan skin. His dark brown eyes had very long eyelashes. Kent's mother had three children when she was very young. His father abandoned the family. Because of his mother's neglect, the family was broken up and the kids were sent to foster homes. Kent was adopted at age 10. His sister was adopted by another family. Kent's older brother eventually moved back in with his mother. Kent's present family was very caring and well-intentioned.

Kent was inaccessible and oppositional. He was unable to speak his anger, instead he would sneak and cheat. He did the absolute minimum asked of him in school. He destroyed all his graded work and anything about himself that he could get his hands on. This included rifling my desk. Kent came to us after he had been hospitalized.

There is no journal entry from Kent. He destroyed his journals.

Kingsley

My shadow

Kingsley appeared chubby and well-fed, but that appearance was misleading. Under that puppy fat were muscular thighs, the result of skateboarding three miles to and from school every day. He also lifted weights regularly at home. He was very blonde with a round face and chubby cheeks. He went to church regularly, and except for his temper and his drinking, he was an upright clean-living lad.

His father was a wealthy lawyer, who had divorced his mother, but was taking financial care of his ex-wife and only son. Kingsley had become the center of his mother's life, but she was a passive and overwhelmed woman. Kingsley had observed his father's rages towards his mother and he too, on rare occasions had hit her. Kingsley was exceedingly stubborn and oppositional. Like Gillian, he did not socialize well with his peers. He was highly critical of his classmates and instead, considered himself to be a peer of his teachers, especially me. I was his favorite. He had been hospitalized with a nervous breakdown. He was somewhat school phobic, and he could bully his mother into letting him have his way and stay home from school whenever he wanted.

Here is his journal entry; He is writing to my partner Brooke.

If its not one thing bothering me its always something else bugging me. Carolyn yelled at me and I am not writing to her for a while. OK. Would you mind writing to me. I don't want to write to her until she starts treating me right. I feel lousy. Carolyn's pissed at me and I'm sure a little irked. I hope you understand! Carolyn doesn't – either that or she enjoys fighting. She's always in control – she's calling the shots – she's a hard nosed woman – pretty tough at times. I wonder what the weather is like in Mexico right now? If you can find out please let me know.

Nat

A small con man with a mean mouth

Nat was a small street urchin who was in charge of his own life. His mother had abandoned Nat, leaving his alcoholic and rarely present father in charge. Nat became the most responsible person in the family. He took care of himself and his younger brother. He has had to raise himself.

He was lean and wiry and in spite of his small size, he was one of the best athletes in the school. Instead of coming to class, his tanned body and sun-streaked brown hair could often be seen bobbing on his surfboard among the waves down at the beach. He had practically no academic skills at all. His reading and writing were rudimentary but give him a broken machine and he would probably fix it. When it came to mechanics, he was brilliant. His worse trait was his cruel mouth.

His journal entry:

I thik I am duing beter then you think. I am reding mor then I yous to. Dad was druk agin last nit. I mite be going to frisco to veset relativs.

Randy

Easy-going country lad

Randy was a large, lean, placid fellow. He had red hair, freckles and blue eyes. His parents were good solid folks; a patient father, and a mother who was a bit over-protective. Randy had three older brothers and he would be the last one to leave the nest. He spoke with a country-flavored accent, generally slowly and often containing mild barbs directed at Brooke or myself. He wasn't interested in school, or producing. Mostly, he just bided his time, did the minimum, amusedly watched the show that we put on for him daily, and entertained himself with pulling my leg.

His journal entry:

I had a boring weekend we went camping. You know one of those family get together things. Its not camping with my folks that is such a bore, its when they all get together and all they like to do is sit and bull shit. Even the women They just tell the same old stories over and over again.

Shaun

My seductive beauty

Shaun was part of our class for just six months. He was over six feet tall, fair skinned with raven-black hair and dark eyes. Shaun was irrepressibly charming. He was quick-witted and responsive with a wonderfully crooked smile. Shaun's father was wealthy and was preoccupied with his business. Shaun had two older sisters who were grown and out of the house. His mother, out of loneliness because Shaun was the last child in the nest, and the only male left in her life, turned to him for companionship. He was alternatively, devoted to and furious with his mother. His parents wanted a quick inexpensive fix for Shaun's inability to function and produce at school. He came to us after being yanked prematurely out of hospitalization.

Here is his journal entry when I asked him to describe a photo I had taken of him.

> This guy must really be cool. He really shows a good outward apperence. What a very sincere smile. He looks like one of those guys you'd meet on the street and go get stoned with, and then you'd realy like him sooo much. Look at those rugged outdoorsy macho features. That strong but kind face, that stern jaw, those piercing eyes and sensuous lips. Any girl would be so lucky. He's the type of guy that could drive faster, drink more, and play chess longer than anybody, why he's almost super human yes he's a god yes! Yes! Ye gods he's Jesus coming back to earth yes I can see it all. Oh Jesus!

Sissy

A small needy bundle of affect

Sissy was the second daughter of a wealthy businessman by his first marriage. He was now in his third marriage. Sissy's stepmother had children of her own and was preoccupied with them. Sissy had never felt mothered. During the school year depicted here, she moved in with her older sister because her stepmother had had enough. Sissy was highly emotional, finding daily crises that required my aide's special attention. She considered Brooke to be the mother she should have had. Brooke understood this and tried to give her as much care and attention as she could. Sissy was very narcissistic and could be verbally quite abusive towards me. (Brooke was the good mother; I was the bad stepmother.)

Sissy had short light brown hair, always arranged in a stylish tangle over one eye. She was tiny, fair and delicate. She had been hospitalized and had made more than one suicide attempt.

Her journal entry:

In the beginning of the year I came to Mountainview like a stubburn bull. I never wanted to cooperate with anyone. I hated it hear and I thought this was a mental ill school. So anyway I got used to the school hear at Mountainview. I learned a lot with the paitience of Carolyn and her endering smile and Brooke has been like my real mom. There are a few people hear that I could live without. Not to be rude, but some people upset me so much that I wake up every morning and say YUK! But a lot of the time I know this school has helped me improve. Something I am glad of hear at school is the closeness between our class. We treat each other as a family and defend one another.

I find the administration a bunch of unprofesional hippies who have nothing to do except yell at kids.

Sonny

My shocking infant

Sonny had been adopted when he was three years of age. His adopted family divorced and he moved in with his adopted mother, her new husband and his two sons. His mother was a mild quiet woman. Sonny's new dad tried to be an authoritarian with him and Sonny was rebelling against him.

Sonny dressed the part of a punk teenager. He had a mop of curly black hair that made him look a bit like an English sheepdog. Beneath his bangs, his dark eyes, lined with thick black mascara, exhibited many moods: glazing over with boredom at his schoolwork; anticipation at the thought of his next victim; or, beaming at me with the eagerness of a toddler.

His eyes and hairstyle required constant preening in front of a mirror, which hung on the wall over his desk. He dressed in white or black t-shirts and black jeans, torn or decorated to offend; alarming tattoos; steel-toed boots; and chains, studs, and enough rings on both hands to serve as dangerous weapons. It's hard to believe, but in spite of his shocking dress and behavior, which included acting flamboyantly gay, bullying small children and driving a safety pin through the loose skin of his neck while sitting quietly at his desk, there was something quite childlike and appealing about him. I had to be careful about recognizing his sweet side because it often produced outbursts of heightened offensiveness.

From one of his later journal entries when I asked Sonny to describe a person in the class.

There are days when I walk into the cold misty class room with hatred and gloom. At the warmest end of Mountainviews classroom sits a smiling blond with a stake of multicolored folders taller than her head. She shouts with infinite glee, Snookums! How's my pudgy little baby! In doom for another day with Shay's Rebellion I answer, Shitty! I later finish the Gernail when I just happen to turn around with glorious relief and theres Carolyn with a twikle in those blue eyes and the meanest frown and scowl on that face. On those wiked nails sits my pea green folder. I with a bitter feeling in the pit of my stomak pleed for mercy. My teacher says, Ah, but Snookums I filled everything out for you to do today. I said In all do respect I don't care. She smiles with great exitment and pinches my pudgy little belly.

P.S. Please no math test today.

29

Well, dear reader, there you have it, the background information. As I said this book is about coping with love and hate. These are feelings we all have for our students (or clients) and because we have them we must live at best with guilt, or at worst, denial. I have warned you that this book offers no recipes, but it is my fondest hope that by reading of my own failings, you too, will give yourself the same absolution and understanding that my students struggled to receive from me and that Rey gave to me on the first day I met him.

Chapter One

Rey

Dear Rey,

The rain woke me up. The racket on the roof, and the plops and splats coming from the dining room made it impossible to sleep. It was time get up and empty the pots and pans again. If you know anything about private schools in America, you must know they pay their teachers penurious salaries. I cannot afford to put a new roof on my leaky 40 year-old home. Americans still view teaching as women's work, an extension of the little homemaker, just a hair's breadth away from being a motel maid.

There are days, and nights, when I hate this hovel of a house I inherited from mother and my pauperizing profession. This was definitely one of those nights. I lay in my sagging bed staring into the darkness, and felt my fury grow. I looked over at my husband Zane, lying irksomely inert next to me, snoring with bulldog determination. The numbers on the clock glowed greenishly in the darkness. Three o'clock in the morning and I was hopelessly wide awake. I had to start teaching in five hours. I would be in great shape for today's battle.

It was more than the rain that was keeping me

awake. My mind has been a turmoil of ideas ever since yesterday when I had my supervision session with you. Waves of questions, opinions and confessions keep roiling through my head. There was no hope of sleep. Both you and the rain were being too insistent. There was nothing for it but to get up and face the both of you.

I climbed out of my warm bed and pulled on my jeans and a cranberry sweater. I went into the bathroom to brush my teeth. I looked in the mirror. This job is certainly taking it out of you, I thought. I'm 47 years old and the wrinkles are obvious. My blue eyes are bloodshot and my plain peasant face looks worn and tired. Only my blonde hair offers me comfort; it still turns golden and streaky in the summer. I peered out of the small rectangle of a window over the bathtub. It was pitch black outside. I knew the streets in front of my house would be curb deep in running water.

I emptied all the pots that were collecting rust-colored rainwater at an alarming rate throughout the house. I hoped they wouldn't overflow before my husband got up to go to grad school. I put on my red down jacket and waded out to my '65 VW bus. I climbed up behind the steering wheel, and wished once again that the bus had a functioning heater. I love my bus. I had overhauled the engine all by myself before I married Zane and we traveled in it all the way to Mt. Denali, Alaska and back again.

I started the engine and splashed my way down the white line in the center of the street, the only place where the pavement was still visible under the ripples. I arrived at an all-night coffee shop near my school without once stalling my ancient engine.

Now I am sitting in a booth, steaming moistly and drinking coffee. I am hypnotized by the rain as it pelts against the windows. My mind pulls me back to you and my supervision session. I want to relive those moments of finally being understood. I want to share my stories with you...like shells from a tide pool, collected and brought to you with grubby sandy fingers for your paternal

32

inspection. I'm not sure whether I want you to be analytical with my treasures or not, dissecting them with your formidable mind. Perhaps I just want you to look at them.

You do remember me, don't you? Yesterday, you visited Mountainview, our private special education school. I'm the desperate teacher trapped in the trailer with emotionally disturbed adolescents. At the supervision session you gave me advice about Dawson. Remember? And you also said you'd like to see some of my writing. Hah! Foolish man.

You will be leaving tomorrow. Maybe I will have the courage to give this letter to you before you go, but more likely, I will not. I hope that I will at least have the audacity to send it to you when you are safely out of town, back in London where you belong, and far enough away so I can risk embarrassment without a face-to-face encounter.

I've been teaching special ed. for 14 years now, and except for Mitchell, who I go to for private supervision, I've never met a shrink I could trust. I was certain that you were going to be just another one of those god-like therapists who act as if they are privy to great secrets yet cannot understand me and what I struggle with. Mitchell is really a psychoanalyst, just as you are. It's unnerving that I should choose to rely on you two, members of a highly suspect group.

When Paul, our director, told me that Mitchell had asked me to present a case to you, I did so, not for myself but because Mitchell has been such a help with my teaching that I could not refuse him. I would put myself under the scalpel once more, reporting what I was sure would be too alienating for you. No doubt you would be entrenched in the comfy frame of reference of the therapy *hour* and clients who come to you *voluntarily*, even paying for the privilege. Surely, like your peers, you would be arrogant towards teachers who must struggle for six hours a day, five days a week with emotionally disturbed

33

adolescents who are trapped in an educational purgatory they want no part of.

I remember my first sight of you. It was the end of the school day and I saw a moderately sized man with tousled hair and beard standing quietly in the front lobby with a bemused smile on his face. You looked as if you had just waded into a shallow pool and were quite content to just stand in the current watching the flow of children pouring around you as they escaped out of their classrooms to freedom.

I also vividly remember the case conference that followed. Our director, the therapists, the teachers and the aides all sat snugly together in a circle in the narrow confines of one of the classroom trailers. Mitchell introduced me by telling you that, "Psychoanalytically, Carolyn does everything wrong, but she also does everything right." Irritated, I looked at you. You nodded your head, apparently understanding all the implications. What the hell does that mean? Oh well, let's just get it over with, and so I began my party piece.

You were certainly different. Other therapists' faces would grow slack and glassy-eyed as my description of the anger in my classroom grew to near-violence. Instead, you kept making friendly eye contact. You even laughed with me as I described the outflanking maneuvers of Dawson, a truly horrible student. Still, I was sure that the best advice you would offer would be to blandly tell me how brave I was to work with such disturbed children and utter a few warning notes about my tendency to become too emotionally involved. As if I had any choice in the matter!

But you did not react as the others had. Instead, you removed the pipe which you had been smiling around and said in your lovely British accent, "Well, it's clear to me that you love this boy."

I gaped at you. I goggled! Inwardly, I was screaming. I what...? Me! Love! Dawson! I had no awareness of any such feeling lying dormant in me for the monster who tortured me daily. Finally in the presence of your sublime confidence I was able to locate some traces of affection for my hostile, hardheaded student. Well, maybe some of those feelings could even qualify as love, but this was a notion that would certainly take some getting used to.

You went on to tell me of how it was necessary to descend into the rage of Dawson's trauma to relive it with him. Experiencing it, we two could examine it together and by understanding our struggle, he would be able to grow past it. You recognized that my anger and resentment had purpose to them and even saw beyond them to the caring that lay beneath it all. I looked with astonishment at you, sitting comfortably in your chair, waving your pipe to punctuate all the things I had been doing right. My mind was pedaling furiously to keep up with you. You understood! You could even help me to grasp what drives me and my students. You weren't making me feel guilty!

For the rest of the time while you visited and lectured at the psychoanalytical institute, I prowled around the edges, wading through wannabe analysts and listening to everything you had to say.

What I could understand of your talks rang true. Much of it was relieving. It was as if I had been toiling up a rocky slope for my entire teaching career and had at last pulled myself over the edge at the top. I rested in soft meadowland grasses, ignoring the mosquitoes, and breathed deeply the fresh, heady air of a new perspective.

My sudden adolescent zeal was due to more than just being understood. You also had the strength to take me on. My students and I have much in common. Few shrinks can withstand our raw and savage natures. I needed someone who could handle the unbridled behavior that my students produce in me. I would not be writing to you if you had only shown an understanding maternal side. You managed to combine both a mother's

35

compassion and a father's power to set limits, to yank me up by the scruff of my neck and set me straight.

That paternal side of you is marvelously worrisome. I watched you lounging in your padded chair, looking every inch as safe as a teddy bear, a speculative yarn smile stitched onto your fuzzy face. Then, in the midst of your observations, rolling out amongst all of the heretofore gentle and soothing words, there escapes a slashing comment, lancing across the room couched in humor and startlingly graphic, jerking me to blinking wakefulness. What a delight! Someone to challenge me!

You have no idea of the hours I have spent in supervision sessions with sappy chrysalis-like therapists, stretching their crumpled damp wings as they emerge from their cocoon of idealism into the real world. Their clients are clasped suffocatingly to their professional bosoms. Caution and concern mask their every word. They make me want to throw up.

I hate my students. I love my students. They are disgusting, horrible people. They are lost and overwhelmed children. They make me want to quit this fruitless job of mine. Their affectionate eyes tell me I could never find a more fulfilling career. I hate my incompetence. I marvel at my skill.

You (and Mitchell) are the first therapists I've ever met who really understand the role of hatred in the therapy room. It does not frighten you. You can withstand me just as I can withstand my students. At last a shrink who can contain us!

Little did you know what you were unleashing when you said you'd like to see some of my stories. I am including one of them. I hope this is not too much of an imposition. While a response would be nice...no let's rephrase that...while a response would be fantastic, I guess I really don't expect one with the kind of schedule you keep. (That's to give you space for failure to be empathic.)

I am sending you a story that covers a couple of

days about a week ago. It will give you a better picture of what life is like for me. It includes the latest intrusion by my students. I cannot escape them. They are foremost in my mind when I drag myself from bed every morning. They ruin my breakfast, a bacon-cheeseburger at a fast-food chain. I am miserable as I sip my coffee, dully wondering what they will do to me today.

Carolyn

Chapter Two

A Day in the Life of a Special Ed Teacher

Part One

Envy

Dear Rey,

I thought I might share with you what one day is like for a special ed. teacher at Mountainview.

One of the peculiarities of teaching special ed. which makes it different from most jobs is that one is dragged into a land of stark extremes. It is not a realm of gentle undulating foothills where the patient traveler may, with perseverance, eventually reach the castle at the top of the mountain. There the traveler might reside in comfort, toasting herself with the knowledge of a bit of business well done and new luxuries to be enjoyed as part of the bargain.

I live in a far more unstable landscape, fluxing with transitoriness. Everywhere there are quivering, precipitous cliffs, dark yawning chasms and lurking feral beasts. Nothing is anchored in permanence. Whenever I manage to drag myself to a sunlit summit, my moments of celebration are nervous ones. Facial tics appear as my fingers clutch at the granite of my competence. I shout to the blue skies. "I know what I'm doing! I am a good teacher! I have some control over the situation!"

By tomorrow my rocky confidence may melt away in the heat of a defiant class, a hostile district official, or an outraged parent. My grip will fail and soon will come the shrieking plunge into despondency.

I must relish these few precious moments before it is too late and I have forgotten about life at the top. I rush to write to you before their dewiness dissipates into the parched earth of the vacant lots of my students' minds.

My most recent fleeting sense of competence began last night when Paul, my boss, made the entire staff go over to the foothills to visit Seaview, a wealthy upper-class private school. We drove through elaborately manicured and gated neighborhoods and arrived at sunset to find the school for the elite perched on the edge of a hill overlooking a blaze of city lights. We walked into a multileveled ski lodge complete with a flagstone fireplace and redwood beamed ceilings. We continued past the computer literacy classroom to an elegant receptionist who directed us to where the wine and cheese were being served.

Self-consciousness enveloped me as I padded through the thick carpet in my aged sandals. I was certain the whole swank assembly had turned to calculatingly scan my person from my bare toes to my uncoiffured hair straggling down upon the lapels of my best business-like jacket, a half-hearted attempt at professionalism.

I contemplated the other school's staff. Mostly females, yet with a surprising number of men (the pay must be good); they outnumbered us three to one. I knew these women. They were the same bunch who had pressed me into claustrophobia in my horrible education classes at the university so long, long ago. Worse than the tedium of listening to alleged experts in the art of teaching, who could barely make a point with university students, were the svelte sorority girls I had to co-exist with in that purgatory.

I was re-immersed into my old envy and resentment. So this was where they went! They looked older, but any one of them could still be riding on their sorority float in the homecoming parade. I looked at their shiny pumps, their elegant layered hair and their ruby and diamond engagement rings and thought, "Won't I ever escape these females?"

While I tried to blend into the crowd and hide my membership among the great unwashed peasantry, we were taken on a tour of the school. It was a showplace all right. I listened to the 'headmaster' (we have a director; they have a headmaster, a word rarely heard among the lower classes on this side of the Atlantic) tell us that he refused to have any of his classrooms smaller than 600 sq. ft. I felt agoraphobic as I surveyed these roomy and open vistas. I thought of my little sardine tin of a trailer packed with odoriferous adolescents, sweating and farting with glee.

After a while the passing parade of educational amenities became cloying: a huge library; woodshop; pottery shop; art studio; gymnasium complete with a basketball court, stands and a stage; tennis and volleyball courts; especially hired instructors in art, music, science and physical education; and, of course, supplies and equipment up the Wazoo.

I began to grow irritated at the advantages the offspring of the rich enjoy. I have always been impatient with people who need to claim more than their share of the world's resources.

We returned to the lecture hall. We sat in rows facing a lectern flanked on both sides by a wall covered with fanciful masks, irksome in themselves because they represented the efforts of an art specialist with access to preparation time, materials and the efforts of children selected for their intelligence and tractability. At Mountainview, we only try to sort out the addicts, parent abusers and most of the paranoid schizophrenics.

41

I put my scruffy toes as far out of sight as possible and looked at the welcoming, open faces of my neighbors. How annoying! One would hope that they could at least appear smug and superior so I could keep my envy at a rolling boil. But no, in spite of my long history of aversion to the polished and well-groomed, it looked as if I didn't have to dislike these people. They were being very friendly and accessible. An attractive lady with a label attached to her rose silk blouse which read, 'Sixth Grade: Literature Appreciation and Music" began to chat with

me. While I was paying polite attention, my mind began to tally up the classes that a card pinned to my blouse would list. Seventh, Eighth, Ninth, Tenth, Eleventh, and Twelfth Grade: Remedial Reading and Math; English, U.S. History, World History, California History, Geography, Civics, Earth Science, Physical Science, Biological Science, Algebra, Geometry, Vocational Skills; and finally the class' unquestioned favorites, Driver's Ed and Sex Ed. I paused and let my mind racket about in the uncluttered confines of what it might be like to be Sixth Grade: Literature Appreciation and Music.

I was interrupted from my intoxicating reverie by the headmaster. He was presenting the history of his school. Then Paul, my boss, had his turn. Both wanted their staffs to get to know each other. Paul attempted to encourage dialogue by asking his staff to tell the others about what it was like to work in a special ed. school. Not a good idea, I thought. I hunkered down in my seat and avoided his eye, but finally, he caught me. He asked me to describe what it is like to work with the biggest and the oldest kids at our school.

I am always getting into trouble for talking without

42

thinking. As I began I thought, "Oh dear, I wonder what on earth I am going to say." I was being asked to summarize a very complex situation in just a few sentences.

"Well, my trusty sidekick, Brooke, and I spend a great deal of time being detectives because our class is a very slippery one. If we don't stay on our toes all the time things really get out of hand. What this means is that we spend a great amount of time talking to students: class discussions, group therapy, individual therapy, on the phone to parents, parent conferences and a lot of sessions in Paul's office."

"I work with the 15 to 18 year olds. We are jammed together in a very small trailer. Basically they are a shifty and tricksy bunch but in spite of their general nastiness, I usually end up being very fond of each of them."

"In one respect I identify with them very strongly and I suspect that most of the staff does as well. In fact, it may well be the reason why we all continue to work there. Our students are all a bunch of rebels who can't fit into the public school system. I think the fact that they don't is somehow very admirable."

Good grief, people seemed to be enjoying what I was saying. Evidently, I was the ice-breaker. People began to shout out questions to me. Then finally, I was asked, "So your goal is what...a diploma?" Goal? Goal? Am I supposed to have a goal? I thought it was my job just to survive.

"Uhmm, a diploma's nice, but my goal is emotional health. Each one of these kids has learned behavioral patterns that have, in some respects, paid off for them but in the long run these behaviors do not make life better for them. They are repetitive, almost cyclical, so that when I see a student doing something to, for example, the teacher of the 13 and 14 year olds, I know that when he is enrolled in my class he will soon be doing the same things to me. These patterns have to be interrupted and healthier ones substituted. Otherwise when they become adults they will be doing the same unpleasant things to their employers, wives and children, and suffering as a consequence."

"I think one of the hardest parts about being the teacher of the high school class is that they come back to see me as adults and I must face my failures. There is no support system for them after they leave us. Few will have counseling. Some end up on welfare or the penal system..." Oops. This was probably not the image Paul wanted me to convey. I staggered to a halt as I found myself mired down in the dismal futures of my students and those perfectly groomed people staring uncomprehendingly at me and what I face.

Paul interrupted me and salvaged the situation by saying that if we can get our students at a younger age, they can often perform excellently in academics, even graduating with honors from universities.

In spite of my gaffe at presenting such a disturbingly bleak prospect, I came away feeling exuberant and wondering why. A day later, during my supervision tea with Adriane and Julia, they helped me to realize that when I had to explain myself to these old symbols of my envious youth, I was making a statement for the entire staff. Our rag-tag bunch had climbed grudgingly up the hill to have our noses rubbed in how the rich guys lived. Everywhere we looked, we saw the epitome of the wealthy private school. In my impromptu speech I waved a banner that displayed the courage and sacrifice of the path we've chosen. We accepted pitiful salaries for the freedom to fight for the underdog unentangled by bureaucratic shackles. We face battles both inwardly and outwardly that the rich guys ran from. We saw admiration in their eyes and we knew our worth. Paul had created a school that allowed us freedom to explore so that we could find new and innovative ways to help our lost kids. We all sit at a round table and we're given the autonomy and support to do our job. Some might even call it Camelot.

Basically, I'm feeling unbearably pompous. I think I should have those feelings occasionally before my students strike the smirk off my face. And while we are

44

speaking of how quickly they can knock me to my knees, my students had thoughtfully prepared a situation for me even before I left work to go up to the land of milk and honey on the hill. During the whole evening it had been nibbling away at any stores of complacency I might have squirreled away.

The bastards had stolen from me.

Chapter Two

A Day in the Life of a Special Ed Teacher

Part Two

Dawson's Dad

At least they didn't take money out of my wallet, although I always check daily before I make a purchase to see if one of them has ripped me off again. I expect to be emotionally maimed by them, but somehow stealing from me is a terrible betrayal, probably because I sacrifice so much to work with them. No decent salary, no contract, laughable health benefits, and finally, the most irksome of all...no union. The very least they can do is leave me what little I have, especially when most of them live far more comfortably than I do.

So I drew some comfort from the fact that instead of raiding my purse, they had stolen cards for a free lunch which a neighboring chain of fast food restaurants had generously given us. We had been given 14 cards and we had just handed out 4 cards to two students: Deborah, and surprisingly, Nat who had valiantly produced the best research paper on an early civilization his limited skills could manage.

The afternoon before Brooke and I were about to leave for the rich private school on the hill, we were both seated at the desk we share. Brooke decided she'd better check to see if the ten gift cards were still in their hiding place. She pulled out the center drawer and...they were gone! As we both stared blankly down at emptiness, our minds were working as one, furiously and simultaneously processing the same chain of events. We remembered who had been playing around at our desk during the day, teasing that he would steal from us. Brooke and I looked at each other and we both said just one word, "Dawson!"

You remember Dawson, don't you Rey? He was the student I presented to you during my case conference. Remember what you said when I finished? You said, "Well it's clear to me that you love this boy." Let me now demonstrate to you the depth of my love. As Brooke and I looked at each other, I pictured his smug, cocky face, and my next words were, "I'll kill that son of a bitch!"

Brooke despaired, "He'll have those cards spent as soon as he gets home. We'll never get them back."

Visions of my arch enemy getting away with it forced me into action. I jumped out of my chair and strode to the door. "I'm calling his folks right now. Maybe they'll be willing to search him as soon as he gets home."

I fumed as I trekked across to the main building with the dark cubby-hole and the one phone reserved for the entire teaching staff. Why the hell do I stay in teaching when all I get for trying to help my students is betrayal? I could imagine Dawson clearly, riding the school bus home. He'd be stretched out in the back of the bus, hogging the whole back seat. His long dishwater blonde hair would be hanging in limp strands upon his black heavy metal t-shirt. He wears steel-toed boots as a defensive measure and would like to wear metal studs as well, but the school draws the line there. I wondered if he'd have enough sense to keep his theft a secret, or if he'd brag about it. I prayed he'd want to boast.

Dawson is the result of Dad's iron-willed determination that only he will retain sole control of his son. No one else may interfere. To be sure, his attitude is somewhat understandable, having already lost Dawson's brother to prison, but I seriously questioned his approach, which on the face of it, seemed to be producing another little sociopath in the family.

48

In our cash-strapped school, if we want to take field trips into the cultural riches of California, we have to do it with our own automobiles, with our personal insurance, and buying our own gas. Some of the school districts provide transportation for their students to and from our school, but the school itself has no transportation services. As a result, Dad does not want me to take his son on field trips. A camping trip is completely out of the question. Even a short, local field trip is too risky. I might take him into a dangerous part of town, such as the museums downtown. I might not provide enough supervision. My car isn't roadworthy. My driving is questionable.

So whenever I require a field trip for the class, such as spending an afternoon with a Navajo artist, if Dawson doesn't want to attend, Dad is more than willing to let him stay at home. Dawson's freedom to participate according to his whim both undermines the willingness of his peers to attend and reduces Dawson's opportunities to explore the terrifying unknown, or more specifically in the example just given, to come to terms with his rampant bigotry.

Dad has effectively prevented me from using on Dawson the same pressures we use on the rest of the high school students. While other misbehaving adolescents can be asked to stay after school, being old enough to take the public bus home, Dawson is not allowed such a consequence. Since I have often used the bus system in this white, upper class community without ever having any problems, I find it incomprehensible that this muscular six-foot 16 year-old cannot be allowed to take the same risks I take.

Once, when I somehow managed to get permission on the phone to take Dawson to the San Onofre nuclear power plant, I listened in amazement while Dad threatened me. "If you ever cause my boy to miss the district school bus, my dear, you'll be responsible for driving him home yourself (about a two hour round trip). I will not have my son on the public bus system in

49

this county! You can be sure that I am notifying your boss of this as well, so you'd better be careful. I'm a hard man if I'm crossed."

At the last school district meeting for Dawson, I tried to get him enrolled back in public school on a part-time basis, primarily because Dawson had begged me for this boon. Dad arrived with boots, silver belt buckle and bolo tie and sat menacingly across the table from me. In the middle of the discussion about placement for next year, he rudely interrupted and declared that a return to public school would not even be a possibility. He jabbed his forefinger at me and announced, "If any teacher in this room (I was the only possible candidate), leaves this meeting and tells Dawson that the reason he isn't going back to public school is because of me, well, she's going to have to deal with me!" He finished with three final finger-pointing jabs at me.

While the entire table-full of stupefied administrators sat in stunned silence waiting for my response, I fought an internal battle over what I would say to the monster I had locked eyes with in mutual furious glares. I knew that if I began speaking I would not be able to stop before my reputation as an educator was in tatters. Behind my distended nostrils and the crimson flush on my face, it occurred to me with remarkable clarity that this bastard was ordering me around as if I was a second-class citizen (female) and that I was supposed to be obedient. All of my male sexist prejudices rocketed to the surface.

Then I remembered that Dawson had frequently shared his dreams in which he wanted to creep into his father's bedroom in the dark of night and attack him with his Bowie knife. Right now I would gladly join with Dawson in carving little patterns in this good ole boy's hide. I experienced a rare flash of satisfaction in knowing that at last, Dawson and I agreed on something. I was flooded with sympathy for Dawson. I kept my mouth shut.

As the year progressed and Dawson's technique for harassment blossomed, Brooke and I developed less and less tolerance for his behavior. With each incident, I pressed my case that Dawson's actions were serving as a role model for the other burgeoning little imitator bullies at the school. Dawson's behavior had to be confronted. Finally Paul agreed to have it out with papa.

There were two satisfying moments during that meeting in Paul's small office when I was able to sip the honeyed wine of revenge. The first occurred after I had outlined to both parents Dawson's many bullying crimes. Mother, apparently overwhelmed, slouched mutely in a chair in the corner. Dad sprawled on the couch across from Paul and his desk. When I finished, Dad looked at me accusingly and complained, "Well if all this is true, why is it that I'm only just hearing 'bout it now? Why haven't you called me about this before?" He looked over at Paul with comradely concern, as if to remind him that I was not doing my job. Paul remained inscrutable. Dad had no recourse but to return to the arena with me.

"Now you know my dear, that I would certainly support you if (and that was a very big if) Dawson has truly been misbehavin' in this way. Why haven't you called me?"

Apparently my many futile phone calls had been wiped clean from his mind. "I never call you anymore," I enunciated slowly and clearly, hoping that this time he would actually hear me, "because when I do, you blame me, not Dawson. And, if you don't get your way, you threaten me. It's useless asking for your help and I just don't want to put up with your abuse."

Shock appeared on his face. "Why when have I ever abused you?"

I gave him a couple of exact quotes and finished with the last district meeting. "Frankly, you embarrassed the hell out of me and I would just rather have nothing to do with you at all."

My second satisfying moment came later in the meeting when Dad thought he was playing his trump

51

card. He figured that because our school is so hard up for paying students we would never risk losing Dawson. However, I knew that Dad's worst fear was sending Dawson to public school where he could be exposed to all kinds of danger and temptation. Besides, the school district was paying the tab to keep Dawson as far away from them as possible, and there was no guarantee they would do so with another school, even if they could find one that would take his bad-tempered son. Dad had tried this maneuver on me before and it hadn't worked then, but tyrants are apt to be forgetful of how others feel about things. I knew he would threaten us with removing Dawson. I had discussed this in advance with Paul. We were ready for him.

We tried to spell out how indulging Dawson and always letting him have his way with no consequences was not good for him. We wrangled over which possible expectations and punishments we could give Dawson in the future. None was acceptable to Dad. Finally he snipped, "Well, if you don't like the way I'm raisin' my boy, perhaps I'd just better take him out of this school."

Like a gleaming trout leaping for a clumsy fat fly,

I surged high into the air, wriggling in delight and snapped, "Fine!" I looked over at Paul, "How about you?"

Paul's bland face showed no concern at all. He waved his hand dismissively, "Sure. It's all right with me." I thought he was going to yawn.

I looked across the room to mother, still cowering in her corner, "And you?" I asked. She cast an anguished glance at her husband and said nothing.

"Right," I said, and began making terminating movements. I collected my purse, my clipboard, my coffee cup and stood up. "Well since that's settled, there's no need to continue this meeting." I was walking to the door when gratifyingly, Dad yelped. "Well wait a minute!

Surely we can discuss this some more!"

Having gained some leverage with Dad at that meeting, he and I were presently in a very tenuous state of alliance. Dawson's possible theft of the cards would be Dad's first test. Unfortunately, when I phoned the house, it was overwhelmed mother who answered the phone. I explained my reasons for suspecting Dawson and even though I knew it was hopeless, I asked her if she would confront him when he arrived home. Of course, she wanted nothing to do with the problem. She would only agree to search his school backpack after he left the house. I knew then that the cards were lost because Dawson would take them with him to the park where he habitually goes to meet his friends. Today, instead of just pooling their money for beer and dope, they would have hamburgers as well. Feeling quite pissed at Dawson and his entire family, I hung up the phone and left for the land of educational milk and honey up on the hill.

REYNARD'S MIRROR

January 1986

Chapter Two

One Day in the Life of a Special Education Teacher

Part Three

Cornering the Thieves and Welcoming Shaun

The theft loomed in my mind as I returned to work the next day. To make matters worse, I was getting a new student, something I also dreaded. One student, especially our kind of student, can change the entire behavior of a class. As I drove to school in my bus, with the radio and my $20 speakers blaring gravelly tunes, I fretted and fumed.

Miraculously, by the time I arrived at school the culprits had been caught. Paul met me at the glass double doors of the entrance to the school and gave me the news. He was beaming. Paul loves to catch the villains. Dawson, it seemed, had made the mistake of assuming home meant refuge. As soon as he walked in the door, he asked his mother where the nearest hamburger stand was that would accept his gift certificates! Hah!

When he was questioned by his father, Dawson confessed, but only to being an innocent dupe. "I didn't steal them. Nat gave two to me." Nat had been one of the prize winners, a skinny little fellow with a mouth that kept him out of public school.

Later that night, Nat called Dawson on the phone to ask him not to rat on him. Dad eavesdropped on the extension. He heard Nat begging Dawson not to tell. Just like the gangster movies of the 40's, Dawson warned Nat, "Listen, I'm not taking the rap for this. You'd better get it taken care of yourself." In spite of this conversation, Dawson's dad continued to see him as Nat's victim, rather than a co-conspirator and a knowing recipient of stolen goods.

I was stunned to find that the primary villain had been Nat. As a prize winner he already had two cards. I had eliminated him as a possible culprit. My naiveté is one of my greatest stumbling blocks in this job.

I thought about Nat as I headed for the teacher's lounge. His mother had abandoned him long ago. He is small and wiry. His brown hair is sun-streaked from spending so much time down at the beach. He is an excellent athlete. He surfs and is usually a star performer at any of our team meets. He eels his way through any opposition.

He is 16 years old with extremely limited reading and writing skills, but he is a wizard with a broken machine. He is a child of the streets, having had to raise himself. He is a calculating con man who seems to be constantly sizing me up to see what advantage he can pry out of me. Generally, he is trustworthy. If he makes a promise or gives me his word, he'll keep it. Of course, I may have a hell of a time getting him to make a promise.

He hates authority and has been known to be quite verbally abusive towards teachers who get 'uppity' with him. He will not cooperate with authority at all unless he receives some acknowledgement of the legitimacy of his view of things. He cannot allow the control of his life to slip from his fingers.

I finally made it to the teachers' lounge and hopefully, a cup of coffee. I opened the refrigerator and stuffed my sack lunch into a jumble of other brown bags, some of which were weeks old. Then I noticed that Brooke was leaning over the sink, her long blonde hair hiding her face and concentrating with an excessive amount of attention on the task of dipping her teabag in and out of her mug of hot water. She looked up at me. I saw her bloodshot eyes and knew she was sick.

"I should have stayed in bed today," she croaked, "but I couldn't leave you to face a new student and this stealing mess on your own."

Noble woman! I grabbed her, gave her a kiss on the cheek and said, "Bless you, my child!" Brooke and I only take sick leave when we are at death's door. Neither one of us can bear the thought of forsaking the other to face the many-headed monster of our class alone.

Let me take a few moments to tell you about Brooke. Three years ago, when she was first assigned to work with me, I was told she was very good with kids, yet she hardly ever spoke. Young, tall and slim with masses of curly blonde hair, she was a cooperative, hard worker, but with very little to say. I wondered if she was just taking her time sizing me up. In those first few weeks when I was appraising this silent enigma, I found myself wishing I could kick her in the butt to see if there was any sign of life. Finally, on a hot summer day during an afternoon field trip I was gratified to discover that there was more to her than quiet competence.

We were sitting in the patio of a hamburger stand down on Pacific Coast Highway. Brooke sat next to me and beside her was Toby, a new 17 year-old who suffered from the same affliction as Brooke...taciturnity. Since it was a hot day, Brooke and Toby were both wearing shorts. I reached across the table for a napkin and knocked over a cup of ice water. I watched hypnotically and perhaps with subconscious delight as the water relentlessly tracked its way across the white catsup-speckled surface to pour into the bare laps of Brooke and Toby.

She let out a yowl and grabbed my shoulder. She

jumped up, with a whoop and a grin, and began to laugh. "Wow! What a sensation! That certainly cooled me off!" Toby, on the other hand, leaped up and frowned, irked at this inconvenience.

Humming to myself that this was certainly better than a kick in the butt, I thought, this one's going to work out after all. She isn't angry or embarrassed. She's even enjoying herself. It looks like she's going to be able to play. Very promising. Flexibility and an ability to laugh at yourself even in the face of adversity is a major requirement for anyone working with these kinds of kids.

Three years later, Brooke is a complete delight to work with. It is a marvelous thing when my aide and I complement each other well. I am not alone pitted against the guerillas masquerading as students in my classroom. I have a friend, a fellow-sufferer with me in our sniper-infested jungle. There is comfort to be drawn from mutual support when we can find a germ of humor in even the most miserable, devastating events. Just to look in the sympathetic eyes of another human being when one of my little beauties has done it to me again, helps me pull myself back together. Our silent messages flew back and forth across students' heads as a slight lift of one eyebrow, a hint of a smirk, or a shadow of resignation flashed across our faces. There was a give and take between us, a mutual responsiveness that had a modeling effect for our students.

When the weather is cold, our normal pattern every morning, is to unlock the trailer, turn on the heater, get some coffee, collect the kids and start class. This morning, in spite of her weakened condition, wily Brooke had come early, opened the trailer and then slipped back to the warmth of the teachers' lounge where she could spy through the window at the trailer. Sure enough, she soon saw Nat tippy-toeing to the trailer, entering, then immediately reappearing, hot-footing it across the playing field and trying his damnedest to look nonchalant.

Brooke, who is by far the better sleuth of the two of us, knew exactly what Nat was doing. She returned to the trailer, checked the desk drawer and found the missing cards right where they were supposed to be. Then she removed them for safekeeping. She was certain that Nat's ploy would be to claim that they had been there all along. By being vigilant she had him where she wanted him, and we had our cards back. Score one for our side!

I was busy searching for my coffee cup and wondering why there was no coffee in the pot when Paul came to tell me that Dawson's father was on the phone and wanted to speak to me. Evidently he was determined that I should hear the facts from him personally and not from any other source who might be subject to all kinds of defamatory errors. I went to the phone and listened patiently while he retold the story to me. Then I subjected him to a flood of compliments about how pleased I was with his cooperation, how admirably he had handled things, and how this was just the kind of back-up we needed with Dawson. Then he subjected me to many variations and repetitions of what a minor part Dawson had played in the whole affair. His son was an innocent victim of Nat's perfidy.

I headed out to the trailer, still without my cup of coffee and found Brooke just leaving the trailer. "Except for Randy, who's at the dentist, every single one of them is in there. You'd think that some of them would at least get sick or ditch once in a while."

While Brooke and I stood outside the trailer bemoaning near-perfect attendance, Nick, who is a sort of vice-principal at the school, delivered Shaun, the new variable for the classroom. Over six feet of dark curly-haired apathy, Brooke and I leaned him up against the trailer while we decided who would handle which chore. Although I am quite good at sizing up people, she is the better detective. We decided that she would follow through on Nat and the mystery of the reappearing gift certificates with Paul and Nick in the office. I would manage the rest of the class and introduce Shaun to our ways. I would also be stuck with a fuming Dawson for the time being, so that Nat could be confronted first, partly to determine Dawson's participation in this little crime.

Each year I let the class rearrange the trailer and my salvaged thrift store furniture to suit themselves. Our 40 ft. trailer is white with two doors and a set of stairs and banisters at each end. Inside, we have two old couches, bookshelves, students' desks, and a teacher's desk which Brooke and I share. One of the couches is a small flowered two-seater and the other is long, plastic and an acidic orange. The orange couch fits against the length of one wall between the two doors. The smaller couch sits at right angles to the orange couch across the width of the trailer, leaving just enough space for clumsy adolescent passage. The students also left a place behind the small sofa at the far end of the trailer for a bookcase, a small cabinet and a cubbyhole for odds and ends of pillows where they can retreat to hide from the vexations of being in school. On top of the small cabinet is an electric coffeepot which we use to heat up water for tea and hot chocolate. The desk that Brooke and I share is at the opposite end of the trailer. The students' desks are individual, easily moved and lined up along any available wall space. The wall above each desk is used to post any appropriate material the student wants near him. Sonny, for example, keeps a mirror above his desk.

I invited Shaun into the room. He spotted the long orange couch and collapsed upon it. I told him there was some hot chocolate down at the other end of the room if he was interested. He came upright and peered at the coffeepot. "Yeah, that might help a lot." He tottered off to the fixings.

I waited until the class had gotten their drinks and left another sludgey mess for me to clean up. I asked them to bring their chairs and form a discussion circle by the couches. Sonny, at the risk of mussing his inky-black sheepdog hairdo, laid down on the two-seater for a morning nap. I told him to sit up. About 10 times.

I looked at them all, wondering what Shaun would think of them and how well he would fit in. He was promising kid with dark hair, blue eyes and fair skin. He was clean and neat, apparently not needing to advertise his adolescent role models on black t-shirts as Dawson, Sonny and Charlie did. Dawson periodically glowered at me, and at the newcomer as well. Yes, the new kid did look as if he might become a possible challenger to Dawson's reign of bullying.

Sonny, gazing intently at Shaun, decided to move over and sit down next to him. Oh dear, he's going to try to intimidate Shaun by acting gay. Sonny simpered as he scooched his hips as close to Shaun's as he could. Then, he put his arm on the couch behind Shaun's head, and boldly fluttered his eyelashes at him, which were heavily coated with mascara. Shaun looked over at him and chuckled dismissively. Deflated at Shaun's reaction, Sonny put both arms back in his lap and daintily crossed his legs, both hands posed upon his knee. He was wearing black fingernail polish, a rare fashion statement in the early 80's.

A stolid and pestering Kingsley, instead of bringing a chair and sitting where I asked him to, persisted in cross-examining me about whether I had read his journal entry yet and if I had looked over his lesson plans for his church study group that evening. I told him I couldn't discuss it with him right at the moment. "Give me a break, Kingsley. I've got to get class started. I'll try to get to you as soon as I can. OK?" It was not good enough. He sat down with his chubby face averted from the group and sulked.

Sissy, small and tawny with hazel eyes, was busy checking Shaun out through her light brown curls. Evidently, she too, thought he looked promising. Charlie was not happy about this new addition. While he and Sissy had never quite become a couple, he still viewed her with a modicum of ownership. Charlie was tall, with gold-white hair and pitch-black eyebrows. He was slim and clumped around in combat boots that outweighed his thin body. He was very quick witted, but close-mouthed about personal feelings. Charlie often preached libertarian politics at me, with the fervor of a revolutionary. He was a self-proclaimed expert on any political subject and it only took a glancing blow at the mention of politics for him to launch into lecturing me. Right now, his blue eyes were scowling at Shaun.

Deborah seemed to view Shaun with the same aplomb that she handles most things. Like Nat, she had also raised herself. She had changed from a school-phobic, suicidal thirteen year-old who had come reluctantly to us, into a young woman, determined to have a professional career. She ran her fingers through her long wavy hair and regarded Shaun thoughtfully. She would wait and see how this one handled himself in the classroom. She had been at this school long enough to watch plenty come and go.

Mentally, I went over the attendance list. Nat was in the office. Randy was at the dentist's. Dawson, Sonny, Kingsley, Sissy, Charlie, Deborah and now Shaun were present. That made nine. I was counting my blessings that this year I had a small class. Usually, I have twelve or thirteen. I know, it doesn't sound like much, does it, especially when I think of those poor teachers in public school with 30-35 students in their classes. Let's face it though, that's not teaching, that's warehousing. Overcrowded classrooms were a major reason why I had turned to special education where hopefully I could actually teach and develop relationships with my students.

Well, it was time that I actually started teaching. First I needed to begin Shaun's orientation to Mountainview. After introducing everyone, I looked at

Shaun and asked him how long it had been since he'd gotten up this early in the morning.

"A long time."

"How long is that?"

He shrugged his shoulders. "Long time."

I pushed for something more specific, "Surely, you can…"

"You might as well tell her." Dawson, sitting on one of the student's desks, leaned over and barged in, "She won't leave you alone until you do. Next thing you know she'll be accusing you of things like she did to me!" His pasty face sneered down at me.

Well, so much for a positive beginning. I sneered back at Dawson and snapped, "Yeah and I was right too! I caught you and that's why you're mad at me this morning." Struggling to achieve a better first impression for Shaun, I continued, "However, as mad as you might be with me, Dawson, we are trying to greet Shaun and introduce him to our school. I'm hoping that we can set aside our feelings for now. We can argue later." Little did I know that he would hold me to my promise. I was hoping that his upcoming session with Paul, Brooke and Nick would let me off the hook.

I looked back at Shaun, slumped on the couch, hot chocolate clutched to his chest, and Sonny still trying to rattle him by curling one of his long black locks of hair around one finger while eyeing him coquettishly. I ignored Sonny and asked Shaun, "You really have no idea how long it's been since you were in school?"

"About four months."

"Four months! Then this is worse than coming back from summer vacation. I can understand how terrible you must be feeling this morning." I looked around at the rest of the class. "Do you all remember how awful you felt on your first day of school?" They groaned sympathetically.

"How many of you are here against your will?" All

of them raised their hands except Kingsley and Sonny. Those two much prefer my mothering. School is an escape for them. If I wasn't careful, they'd be in my lap all day.

"Can those of you who don't want to be here offer any hope for Shaun? Is coming here going to be terrible for him? Is there anything at all positive for him to look forward to?" Stupid question. What was I thinking?

Dawson, eager to be as upsetting as possible to the new kid said, "They won't let you go off campus on your own. The teacher has to go with you."

That woke Shaun up. He straightened up, stared at me and asked, "How come?"

I explained that this was for the protection of the school, since so many schools that let students roam freely during lunch were being sued. "Kids go off campus, get into trouble, and because they are legally under the care of the school until they reach home, the school is responsible."

Dawson introduced a critical problem with this rule. "Cause the teacher's always around, you can't get away with smoking pot during the day. The only thing you can do is smoke it before you get here. They can't get you for that."

I said, "At least that way, you only lose out on learning in the morning, rather than not learning all day long."

Shaun persisted with this topic. Not a good sign. "What happens if you get caught?"

"Let me put it to you this way, Shaun. If we do not catch you with hard evidence, but we are able to tell that you are loaded all the time, we will call in administration and your parents to deal with it. On the other hand, if I catch you with any illegal substance on this campus, I make you a personal promise that I will call the police myself."

Sonny, my pussycat in disguise as a gay punker, sat

up in his seat, flapped a hand at me and said, "Well, that's not very nice."

"I know, it seems like I'm breaking a trust, doesn't it? But that's the law. Bring it on campus and I have to call the police."

I looked around at a very enervated group and said, "You are all painting a pretty bleak picture for Shaun. It looks as if you want to just tell him about how awful the rules are. Are there any others you've left out?"

"You can't be in the classroom without a teacher."

Shaun looked at me as if I were really being impossible. "Why not?"

"Anybody want to tell Shaun how that rule came about?" I asked.

Deborah, adult and disapproving with snapping dark eyes said, "Well some of these idiots decided to have a fight in here when Carolyn was out of the classroom, so now she has to be here and babysit these infants."

I added, "We did not start out with that rule. I wanted you to have a place where you could get away from the teachers for a while, relax and listen to music, but there was a fight and things were stolen. Now I have no choice. Is there anything else that Shaun needs to know?

"Watch out for Nick," Sissy offered helpfully.

"Who's Nick?"

Charlie, the libertarian, began describing the school administrator in highly unflattering terms. He could not pass up a chance to preach on the tyranny of authority.

"Wait a minute! Nick's a good friend of mine (and has been for longer than you've been alive, I silently added). I won't sit here and listen to you talk about him like this. If you don't want any problems with me, you'd better find a more polite way to describe him to Shaun. Or perhaps we'll need to discuss Nick during lunch, here in the trailer?"

Pause. Silence.

"Nick's the guy who yells at you when you get into

trouble," Deborah suggested diplomatically.

"Anybody want to tell Shaun about ditching and being tardy?"

"If you're late you've got to make up the time and if you ditch, you have to make up the whole day, six hours!" Shaun looked at me in astonishment and groaned.

"I'd also like you to know that we're not beyond going to a student's home and getting him out of bed." I once took the entire class to help me wake up one of my reluctant learners. His mother, exhausted with the morning ritual of prying her son out of bed, was very pleased to have our help. The student was a little shocked to wake up and find his teacher and classmates peering down at him. He came to school regularly after that.

"Well, I think we've covered just about all of the rules. You still have not offered Shaun any hope about being here. I think he must be pretty depressed by now. Isn't there anything good about being here?"

Sonny, who had given up pressing his body close to Shaun's and was now able to act normal said, "The work's not hard."

"The hell it isn't!" Dawson leaped up and leaned menacingly over Sonny. "There's too much of it as it is. You'd better shut your mouth before she gets any ideas!"

Sissy cut through Dawson's efforts to intimidate, "You get lots of help with your problems here." Sissy was an expert at finding crises for us to help her with...love affairs, pregnancy scares, running away from home and threats of suicide.

Kingsley, suddenly stung by a novel thought said, "Oh yeah, the teachers are nice!"...Finally, I thought someone has something nice to say about me, their very own teacher. Alas, it was not to be..."They tell some interesting stories."

Sonny joined in enthusiastically. "You should hear the stories Sam tells about Vietnam! He gets real gory and..."

"Never mind, Sonny. I think Shaun has gotten the idea."

Then Brooke opened the trailer door and told Dawson it was time for his interview in the director's office. The interrogation had progressed beyond Nat to his accomplice.

As soon as Dawson left, Sonny leaned over to Shaun and hissed at him. "Watch out for Dawson. He likes to get his way."

At 9:30 it was time for nearly half the class to go to group therapy. I put Deborah in her math book, gave Shaun a math evaluation test and ran a World Civilization group with the rest. We studied Mesopotamia and the Nile Delta. Deborah worked diligently. I looked over at Shaun. He had moved to the couch to work on his math. He had dozed off, his mouth hanging agape, a slight snore issuing forth. I made a serious mistake. I let him sleep.

Break time arrived. I never have time to take a full break, or lunch, or even prep time when the kids go to P.E. This break would be no different. It was time for Dawson to start a fight with me.

I headed for the front lobby and the only restrooms in the school. There I found half of my class leaning on the front counter admiring our beautiful secretary, Shelly. She is slim and tan, with a Scuba diver's body. She laughs all the time and treats her adoring adolescents with great kindness and patience. My boys are entranced by her. Shaun had found at least one pleasant aspect to being here. I heard him ask her, "Have you got a younger sister?"

I would have left them in peace except that Dawson, fresh from his inquisition with Paul and Nick had taken a feather duster from behind the front counter and was chasing Sonny and his jet-black sheepdog hairdo around the lobby with it. "Here," he yelled, "that hair needs a little dusting!" I told Dawson to stop, took the duster away from him, and returned it to its place behind the counter.

Leaving the restroom, I found Dawson at it again. Once more I told him to quit. He ignored me. I raised my voice and told him to "Take it outside!" Of course, that was stupid of me. You'd have thought that by now I would have learned never to confront an adolescent in front of his peers. Still, he started to leave, then thought better of it, spun on his heel and pushed right by me, insolently brushing my restraining arm aside, saying, "I have to get a drink."

Rey, I can't tell you how many times that one has been used on me. A seemingly reasonable request, yet one that serves to thumb one's nose at the teacher...nay, of even making an obscene gesture at the teacher. As he returned, sauntering and wiping drips from his mouth with the back of his hand, I said, "Well you've just upped the ante. Now you've lost your break. Go to the detention room." Surprising the hell out of me he turned and walked right into the detention room.

Suspicious of such sudden obedience, I went back a few moments later and found him once again at the front counter. His fellow classmates were having a difficult time deciding which was the most entertaining, Shelly's nubile charms or Dawson vs. Teacher.

Once again, I herded Dawson back to his place of keeping, threatening him with, "It's up to you. You can keep this up and the situation will get a lot worse, or you can do what I'm asking and finish this. You can be sure that I will keep checking on you." As soon as I left, he returned to the lobby and his admiring fans. I knew I would have to pull in extra help or this contest would go on all day.

I found Nick and asked him for help. Nick, having spent the entire morning confronting Nat and Dawson, was on his way over to the nearby market to buy coffee for the staff. At that moment Nick was consumed with getting his cup of coffee, something that I, too, was missing. I caught him just as he had opened one of the glass double doors and told him I needed help with Dawson. He managed to focus on me and frowned irritably. "Well, what is it you expect me to do?"

This was very unlike Nick, but I recognized his mood. It occurs whenever his multiple chores descend upon him all at once. Generally he is very patient with these interruptions...crawling out from under the sink, off the ladder, pushing his computer aside, or hanging up the phone. Today, however, there was real urgency in his voice.

I looked at his weathered tan face, his receding brown hair tied in a ponytail, and his frowning brown eyes with concern. "You're telling me that you don't want to bother with this right now and that you really need your cup of coffee."

He sighed, scowled at me and then tracked Dawson down and ordered him into the office.

"Good ole Nick," I thought warmly. He is a comfortable substantial force at the school. He's expert at managing our budding criminals. One of the major reasons I keep working here with a salary that could qualify me for food stamps is because of the extraordinary backup each teacher has with their students. Paul has made it a point to keep the student population down to somewhere around 80 students. This is because he wants to personally know every student in his school. All of the administration is well aware of each student's personal history and quirks and can be counted on to drop whatever they are doing to help us whenever one of them runs amuck. We know we will never be left in the lurch.

The Director's office is small, square, windowless, and brick walled. Nick told Dawson to take a seat and he chose the chair in the right outside corner of the square. I sat next to him on his left and Nick sat in the director's chair, opposite him. After I had described Dawson's antics, Nick cocked one bushy brown eyebrow at my opponent and asked, "Do you know what a cheap shot is?"

"Of course I know what a cheap shot is."

"Tell me."

"It's when you hit someone and they aren't looking."

"No. A cheap shot is when you do something to someone and you know they are helpless to fight back. A cheap shot involves no risk to yourself. You've been taking cheap shots at Carolyn."

"I have not!"

"If you went up and hit a little kid, would that be a cheap shot?"

"Yes."

"If I attacked you verbally, would that be a cheap shot?"

Dawson, confident that administrators can't cuss at students, scoffed, "I'd outclass you any day with my mouth."

"Is that so? Well listen to this. You're just a punk kid who thinks he's tough, but you're really antithetic, sophomoric and malevolent."

Pause.

"Well?"

"Well what?"

"I'm waiting for you to outclass me with your mouth."

With one ankle resting on his knee, he glumly inspected the sole of his black boot and said, "Yeah, right."

I have always believed that all students want to achieve mastery; they do want to learn. However, this can only happen if they are willing. Too often, the game of 'beating the teacher' becomes the only thing they strive for, the only reason to go to school.

I joined in, "You do see the point, don't you Dawson? You know I can't physically make you behave. You know you can push me around and show off to your classmates. You can be the best bully. You win. But is beating the teacher all you want from school? Why bother to come? I know you could just refuse to come…or could you?"

"My father makes me come."

"How?" Nick asked, "Does he force you on the district bus in the mornings?"

"He watches me and makes sure I get on the bus."

I persisted, "I still don't understand why that gets you here. Exactly what does he do to get you on the bus? We'll call home if you're absent so whether he watches or not doesn't really make a difference."

"Money. I do what he wants for money. I never talk to him unless he gives me what I want."

That sounds right, I thought. I remembered his father telling me that he gives Dawson plenty of money because if he didn't, Dawson would steal.

"I bet that's very true Dawson. I expect you have the upper hand with him in many ways."

Nick continued, "Still you must have to think ahead to get what you want out of your father. Do you ever plan ahead? If you want money for the weekend, don't you have to think about cooperating with your dad ahead of time?"

"Nope, I can get money anytime I want it."

Nick persevered, "What about your birthday? Is there anything you want for your birthday?"

"Yeah, I want a motorcycle."

"Well, what do you have to do in order to get it?"

"I have to stay out of trouble."

"Aha!" Nick pounced, grinning. "So you do have to plan ahead. You have to make choices that will keep you out of trouble. How about getting ready for the adult world? Do you have to plan ahead for that?

71

"Nope. I already know what I'm going to do."

"What's that?"

"I'll be working for my father. He's going to start me at $20 an hour."

"But I bet you could make your father mad enough so that he wouldn't even arrange that."

Dawson was now fascinated by the sole of his boot. His mousey blonde hair hung over his face as he leaned over to pick at some diverting imperfection. Still, he was paying attention because he sat up straight and solemnly nodded his head at the truth of Nick's statement.

"So you have to plan ahead in order to keep your dad happy. You have to let him have some degree of control over you for your own benefit. And Dawson, you have to learn to let others besides your father control you for your own benefit.

I said, "Right now your father is trying to control you with some success, but how are you going to handle some supervisor at work telling you what to do. What if he said to you, 'You idiot. You're so stupid. You never do anything right. I don't know why I put up with you.'"

Nick took over. "What are you going to do with that Dawson? You've got two options. You can satisfy yourself and show him who's the toughest and end up being a dishwasher at minimum wage, or you can take the heat and keep your good-paying job. What do you think Dawson? Which choice will you make?"

"Well it'd be stupid to give up $20 an hour to be a dishwasher," Dawson admitted.

"But Dawson," I asked, "the question is, are you going to let your teachers control your behavior so that you can benefit from your education?"

Nick had softened him up enough for me to begin discussing why he was a really angry at me. Nick left to get coffee at the supermarket. I continued. "The reason you're showing me I can't control you is because this is the first time your dad and I have teamed up against you. You are really angry that you couldn't play the two of us against each other like you usually do. When I accused you, he checked into it and found out I was right. You couldn't convince him that this was just another case of my unfairness. Today you are trying to show me how powerless I am and things haven't changed at all.

There was a knock at the door. I opened it about two inches. Sonny was on the other side, pushing to get a good look at the classroom bully in trouble. I pushed back so he couldn't peek. He squawked when I trapped his curly black mop in the crack.

"Uh, Brooke wants to know what she's supposed to be doing with the kids that don't go to group therapy."

I rummaged around in my brain trying to recall what on earth I had planned to do. Ah yes, "Tell her to wake Shaun up and get him to finish his math evaluation and to hand out the math test to the rest of you."

"Do I have to?" he whined.

"You'd better."

I shut the door on a still snooping Sonny and turned again to Dawson. "You are probably the single most important person in your father's life. He loves you very much, perhaps too much. I know how he makes you crazy because he limits every little thing you want to do, but everything he does is because he thinks it will keep you out of trouble or from being hurt. He told me he's trying his best to keep you from ending up in prison like your older brother. I'm afraid that includes teaming up with me to manage you.

Another knock at the door. This time it was the director, Paul. "I wanted to notify Dawson that I have just had a long talk with his father. Somehow his dad had the wrong impression. He thought Dawson didn't understand when he took those cards from Nat that they were stolen." Looking pointedly at Dawson, he said, "I made it very clear that you did know they were stolen and that you were an accomplice in the theft.

Dawson, forgetting his boot for the moment, looked up at Paul and said dolefully, "Thanks a lot."

I was feeling enormous satisfaction with Paul for tackling Dad's denial. Suddenly, I was brimming with well-being. "Well, you'd better go to class. I know you and Nat have trash detail after school and your dad will be driving down here to pick you up. Beyond that though, you still owe me 15 minutes for ignoring me during break. You can do them at lunch. That will give you about 20 minutes left to eat and have a break."

"All right, all right, I'll do them. Just let me out of this damned office. I've been in here all day."

I sent him back to Brooke and a math test. I finally managed to get my cup of coffee. On my way back to class I found Nat, the other card culprit, lurking out back when he should have been in his group therapy session.

I reminded Nat of where he was supposed to be. He just scowled defiantly at me. I scowled back at him. Good grief, I thought, was I going to have to have a session with Nat too! After a few moments of mutual glares, he went off to his appointment.

January 1986

ChapterTwo

One Day in the Life of a Special Ed Teacher

Part Four

A Class Meeting with Paul

Lunchtime arrived. Wednesday was my turn to walk them down to a nearby food stand for lunch. I went out to the adolescent hangout at the side of the school to gather the big spenders together for the trip. Sometime long ago landscapers had placed a large boulder there under some trees. Nat was sitting on top of the boulder and seemed to be waiting for me. He approached me scowlessly and humbly asked for a loan. He looked so apologetic and forlorn standing there empty-handed that I gave in. I knew he had a very long day in front of him with trash detail added onto his afternoon. I never loan money to my students if I can help it because I have a very hard time getting it back. Being surrogate mother, it is my role to be completely giving. Reciprocity in the relationship is rarely acknowledged and as a consequence, attempting to get my money back is viewed with amused tolerance.

My refusal to participate in such pauperizing exchanges forces my students to spread their business out among the rest of the staff, most of whom keep tally sheets or notebooks for this charitable endeavor. It also serves to

75

establish relationships between my boys and the authorities. They must present their most winning sides, make dutiful promises while the lender questions the worthiness of their reputations and establishes due dates. I have often seen one of them begging two dollars from Paul so that he can pay off the dollar he owes Nick, who has become huffy about his outstanding accounts. That leaves our debtor with enough left over for a burrito. Sometimes when I ask who will be walking down to the taco stand I'll get replies such as, "Give me five minutes and I'll go."

"Why do you need five minutes?" I ask.

"Because I need to borrow some money first. I'm gonna hit up Shelly. She likes me a lot. She always loans me money."

They usually obtain their objective.

Today however, I looked at motherless Nat who had just been interrogated in the director's office and scrutinized in group therapy. More to the point, he was asking me, which he never does, to trust him with a loan. This was a test. It was time to let him know that I really did not hate him. Could I still take care of him in spite of his betrayal? I decided to be a forgiving mother. I made a great fuss about how broke I was, what a sacrifice this would be and how I never loan money but that just this once, I would give him whatever change I had in the bottom of my purse. Together we rummaged through its depths and discovered a bountiful two dollars. He paid half of it back 30 minutes later. I suspect this quick response was due to his sale of a single cigarette for a dollar. Quite an entrepreneur is our Nat. He understands a tight market.

Sonny, ever alert, sized me up as a likely pigeon since he had just seen me shelling out for Nat. He came over and asked for a loan too.

"What! You just saw me give Nat the last of my change! You vultures wouldn't even leave me enough money to make a phone call!"

"OK, OK, I was just asking. You don't need to make a federal case out of it."

Good. I had re-established my boundaries. Like an Australian sheepdog nudging at my lambs to speed up, I herded them over to the food stand and back.

By the time I made it back to the teachers' lounge to eat my lunch, there was five minutes left, well fifteen if I stretched it and gave us all an extra ten for lunch. I decided to indulge and give myself enough time to eat my sandwich.

I poked and pried among the trash heap of brown paper bags in the refrigerator until I squeezed one that felt as if the lump inside could be my dolphin-free tuna fish sandwich. I collapsed and let the coffee room chatter wash over me. I used to think that I suffered from hypoglycemia, mononucleosis or some other enfeebling disease, because the moment I stopped teaching and found a moment to relax, my brain congealed, my eyes went glassy, and my body became flaccid. I know now that it is only the normal response to the overload of working with nine to thirteen of these creatures all at once, much like being caged with tigers. It requires constant vigilance and over the years it erodes the mind into quasi-paranoia. I have become certain that at least some of them are out to get me, and I am right.

Before I knew it, the time had slipped past. I looked over at Brooke, her feverish head hung over the remains of her soup. Unfeelingly, and selfishly thinking only of my own survival, I said, "I don't remember what we planned for after lunch."

Like the champ she is, she rallied. "Don't you remember? I have a video tape on mental health in the family. Then Paul is coming in to confront the class on their tardiness."

"That's right, which means all I've got to manage is a follow-up discussion on the film. Why don't you go on home?"

"How about instead, I just take a nap on the sofa in here?"

While I was collecting the students from their hangout spot, I told them we were going to watch a video and I described the subject matter. Charlie suddenly became very hostile.

"I've seen that already and I'm not watching it again. My grandmother made me watch it with her when it was on TV last week. Once is enough!" He turned on his heel and clumped on his combat boots into the main building. I followed him to the front lobby where he folded his arms on his chest and plopped down on one of the naugahyde couches. I left him for the moment, to go to the classroom to set up the video and to roust Brooke from her nap so that she could monitor the class while I talked with Charlie.

After settling the class down to watch the video with Brooke, I returned to Charlie in the front lobby. He appeared very depressed and would make very little eye contact.

I asked him, "Why are you so alarmed about watching this video a second time. There must be something about it that upsets you?"

"Nothing! I just don't want to waste my time doing things twice. It was a stupid video and I don't want to see it again."

"I don't believe you. There's something about it that really bothers you."

"I already told you! Nothing in that film upsets me. I just refuse to watch it over and over. It was bad enough the first time!"

I had seen the video. It was about parental causes of mental health problems in their children. I wanted my class to see it because we had been working on understanding how personalities develop. For example, we had watched "Death of a Salesman" and we studied all the characters, trying to determine what in their histories had caused them to act the way they did. This was part of my campaign against viewing life in black and white terms. If I could help them understand what drives people to be mean, negligent, alcoholic, etc. and to find sympathy for them, then perhaps one day they would be able to look at their own parents with greater compassion. Maybe, eventually, they could even find compassion for themselves.

It upset me a lot that Charlie was having such a reaction to this film, mostly because it demonstrated how much Charlie was in flight. I couldn't demand he watch it, and he was so adamant about it that I feared it might even do him some harm.

"All right, Charlie, I give up. I won't force you to watch it. Are you sure you won't reconsider?"

He looked away from me and shook his head no.

I asked Shelly to keep an eye on him and returned to the classroom. I told Brooke to return to her couch in the teachers' lounge and then noticed, much to my irritation, that Kingsley was back in form. He had his eyes averted from the screen, notifying me that he would not pay attention to anything I wanted him to watch. He was punishing me because I still had not read his journal or his plans for his church lesson.

We finished the film and discussed it while we waited for Paul to come to the classroom. I collected Charlie from the front lobby, returned with him, and had the class arrange themselves in a circle for Paul. Usually they attempt to find a prone position but I told them that while they might get away with such disrespect for Brooke and me, they could not lounge in front of the director. After all the fuss and bother of the day, they were in remarkably good spirits, except for Kingsley, chafing under my neglect, and Charlie who was still withdrawn. I was arguing them all into upright positions when Paul arrived at the door of the trailer.

Dawson, surprisingly chipper with a newly cleaned

conscience, jumped up and grabbed an olive couch-length foam pad from the pillow collection and threw it down on the floor in front of Paul. "The green carpet treatment for the boss!" Paul grasped the play, pranced his way down the length of the foam cushion with royal nods and bows to his subjects. Everyone cheered.

I settled them down again and since there was no more room for another chair, I sat in the only remaining available space, on the floor next to Randy. He was sitting in a chair and towered over me. Randy had missed the morning's entertainments because of a dentist appointment. Randy is a tall, placid lad with red hair and freckles. He's from Oklahoma and has a slight drawl. He is never tardy, which was the topic of the meeting. I looked up at him and he grinned speculatively down on me, like a Cheshire cat with canary feathers leaking out of his mouth. He likes to lay traps for me. He finds great satisfaction in pulling the teacher's leg.

Paul confronted the class about their tardiness, and Randy, innocent of such behavior, grew bored and restless. He became so fidgety that it began to interfere with my concentration. He gathered up a beanbag pillow for his lap and was pounding on it with his fist. I tried to pull it away from him. He leaned over and spoke very paternally to me.

"Now Carolyn," looking down at me, he frowned warningly, and hissed, "don't you try and take my pillow."

I pulled harder making executive noises.

"I told you Carolyn," he hissed again, "leave my pillow alone." He yanked it out of my reach.

I switched tactics. I whispered up at him, "Does Randy Wandy need his little pillow-willow?"

He chuckled at my blatant maneuver. "Yes Carolyn, I do. This is your face I'm pounding on. See." He demonstrated. In spite of our exchanges, the class was unaware of our quiet battle. The director still had the attention of the rest of the class. I began to wonder if

Randy had sampled some drugs before arriving at school.

I grabbed the arm doing the punching and asked him, "Is all this restlessness due to some stimulant taken between the dentist's chair and here?"

"No, Carolyn. Don't you worry your little head about things like that." He began punching again.

I turned to Paul who was busy telling the chronically tardy that they must sign in with him every morning. I interrupted him and asked, "Paul, do you think Randy's restlessness could be explained because he is feeling left out? Everyone except Randy and Shaun, who started only this morning, is in trouble. Perhaps he'd like to be added to your list to check in with you every morning."

Paul, ever the accommodating one, asked, "Is that right Randy? Would you like to be included?"

"No thanks, Paul." He waved his hand dismissively. "I'm just fine as I am. I'll pass on that." The pounding stopped.

The next time I looked in his direction, he had discovered the zipper, opened it up, and plunged his hand into the depths of the snow white pellet-filled interior. His canary-feathered smile widened.

With real menace, I said, "You'd better not, Randy.

I'll have you picking up every single one of them by hand if it takes the rest of the day."

"OK, OK, Carolyn. Just let me get my hand outa here without making a mess."

The punching started again. Finally, I looked him in the eye and shook my finger under his nose, raising my voice and interrupting Paul's discussion. "Now listen here, Randy Thompson, you've been bad all day long and I want you to shape up right this minute!"

He stopped and looked down at me. Silence. Paul and the class waited for his answer.

Nodding his head in affirmation, he said, "Thanks a lot Carolyn. I needed that."

Paul stood up to leave. Dawson leaped up and pushed everyone aside, shouting. "Out of the way, peasants!" He snatched up the foam cushion again, banged open the trailer door, and laid it down on top of the trailer steps for another green carpet treatment. Oh no, I thought, if Paul tries to climb down those cushion-covered steps, he'll break his neck.

"Make way! Make way!" Dawson shouted to the world outside the trailer. He turned back to Paul and presented the steps to him with a royal bow.

Somehow Paul managed to find his footing under all that foam. He swaggered down the stairs like a champion boxer, both arms raised and fists clinched in victory. Once Paul reached the lawn, Dawson leaped over the pillow covered stairs and began to prance around back and forth behind Paul, carrying an imaginary cape. I watched them disappear into the building, both of them having a great time with their play-acting.

Dawson returned jubilant. Brooke returned and we made them get back to work, completing their unfinished assignments. They succeeded in concentrating for a solid twenty minutes. Then, with their antennae quivering in accurate estimates of their next release from paperwork, they sensed it was time for their afternoon break and after that they would go to P.E. They began to poke assignments under our noses as justification for escaping to break early. Brooke was checking their production and accuracy while I told an outraged Kingsley that I wanted him to stay in for a discussion during break.

Nat warned me, "You better not try to keep Kingsley. He looks mad enough to smack you."

"He won't do that. Kingsley should know that if he did such a thing, I would both throw him out of the class for good and call the police on him."

"Oh yeah, that's right," Nat remembered helpfully, "you called the cops on Freddy when he went berserk on you, didn't you?"

"Very true." I neglected to mention that the police were overwhelmed by the hulking 6 ft. 6 in. adolescent and didn't want to take him on. They released him an hour later when he had calmed himself down. He was clearly a mental case and they wanted nothing to do with him. However, he was never permitted back on campus again.

The students all left for break and then P.E., except for Kingsley. Brooke returned and was looking very tired by now. "Why don't you just call it a day? I can handle them for the half-hour that's left after P.E." She still didn't want to go home, but she did agree to continue with her nap in the teachers' lounge.

After Brooke left, I turned back to Kingsley who was sitting at his desk in rigid fury. Once again I was being unjust and callous with his feelings.

I sat down at the next desk and said, "You're mad at me."

"Where do you get a ridiculous notion like that?" he snorted.

"Because you wouldn't turn your little head thirty degrees to the left and look at the video."

"I didn't need to see it. I was listening."

"And only got half the input."

"Why would I be mad at you?" His voice was getting louder. "I'm not even mad!" He stabbed at his desk repeatedly with his ball point pen.

"You're mad because I didn't give you enough attention this morning. You tried to show me your lesson plan for church tonight and I didn't have time to pay attention to something that was very important to you. Furthermore, I haven't read your journal entry either, so I am doubly guilty."

Pause. Silence. He smiled and looked away from me. "I wouldn't wish being a teacher on anyone. Imagine someone having to go around all the time thinking up ridiculous excuses like that for me not watching a video." He laughed and shook his head at such a ludicrous notion.

His body was no longer rigid. He was relaxed and comfortable. I patted him on the shoulders and sent him out to break.

At last everyone was gone. Now I could get some correcting and planning done. But it was not to be. Naturally I was interrupted. Betsy, another teacher, brought an old student of hers to come and see me. I remembered her as a freckle-faced little blonde who used to play with Flash, my Labrador, in the days when I brought him to work every day. She had been about eight at the time. Now she was a very pregnant 17, and of course, single. Last night's words were being dismally illustrated by this anxious full-bellied woman. My mind fleetingly recalled the beaming knobby-kneed youngster who fearlessly tugged tennis balls out of the jaws of my stubborn but patient Lab. Inwardly I sighed.

We discussed how she was handling her pregnancy. I gave her advice and admonitions. I told her what a good mother she was being towards her unborn child. She did not want to leave, but Betsy picked up on my hints that the class would be returning any minute and ushered her out. I quickly graded Shaun's math evaluation, read Kingsley's lesson plan and journal entry and wrote comments on both of them, dashed across the lawn to the bathroom and organized myself for the next onslaught.

As they dawdled their way back to class from P.E. (Paul's demand that they should strive for punctuality being immediately discarded), I told each one what they had to finish before they could be released for the day. Some were all caught up with their work and I gave those efficient ones an early dismissal. Kingsley read my comments about his lesson plans and journal entry, chuckled and smiled at me, packed up his stuff and left. Finally, only Shaun and Sonny remained.

I told Shaun, sitting on the couch (he seemed unable to sit at a desk), to look at his math errors, read the comments, and let me know where we should start with his math.

I was standing near Shaun, helping Sonny with the last bits of his vocabulary unit. Sonny was trying his best to hold it all together. He was having fits that vocabulary was keeping him from freedom and the hangout by the rock with the rest of the guys.

I noticed that Shaun had finished reading my comments. I asked him, "Well, what do you think?"

"About what?"

"About where we should start on your math."

"I don't know. It's up to you. I learned a long time ago that there are three kinds of people who are never wrong: parents, lawyers, and teachers. You know it all. You decide."

There it was; as I was to find out later, this was what we would battle about. He did not want to take control of his life. He wanted me to be in charge and then he would delay, avoid and obstruct whatever I gave him...mostly by lying down and sleeping.

"I'm giving you a chance to have some control over your math. If you give that control away to me, you may regret it."

Sonny, awakened from the ordeal of figuring out Latin roots, interrupted. "Don't let her have her way. If she's giving you a choice, take it! You'll be sorry if you don't."

Shaun reconsidered. "All right. I'll start on multiplication."

"What! Baby math! That's all you want to do? With that fine brain of yours?"

"She lets me do baby math," Sonny offered

helpfully.

"Yep, I'll only do multiplication."

"Well, I don't like it but if that's what you really want..."

"Remember," he said, wagging his finger at me, "only multiplication."

"Yes, Shaun, I think I can see your preference for multiplication."

Rey, I've been around you psychoanalysts far too long. I've even reached the point where I see hidden symbolism in math for these kids. They hate subtraction...loss. Even more hateful is division...splitting apart, separation, remainders. Fractions are worse...things that aren't whole. Adding is acceptable. Multiplying is tolerable, unless there are zeros, empty spaces. Now here was Shaun, certainly the most sexually advanced in the class telling me that he will only multiply.

I told him he could go and that I was glad to have him in the class. "You're going to be fun to work with, even though I'm sure that you'll cause me some trouble, like getting you off the couch."

"I will not cause trouble." He looked insulted.

"Well I didn't mean a lot of trouble," I hedged.

"I do not cause trouble," he declared, turned and walked out the door.

Oh dear, I've blundered into a sensitive area. Perhaps that is how he is viewed at home. The problem. I walked over to my desk and sat down.

Brooke returned from her nap feeling better. She sat down next to me at our desk to correct papers. Sonny, whom I had forgotten, was silently suffering, his black mop bent dutifully over his work. He could stand it no longer. He let out a howl, "Can I go now?" He walked over and poked his papers at me.

I checked his work and told him yes.

"Good!" he announced, grinning at us, and walked

to the door. He opened the door and stepped outside, turned and looked back at us and said, "Now I can pick off my black fingernail polish."

Sonny's primary goal is to shock. He had tried to scandalize Shaun by acting gay this morning, and his parting shot at us was to remind us that he had been wearing black fingernail polish. Deciding to shock back, I said, "Oh don't do that. Pick your nose instead."

He paused, standing on the trailer steps and thought. Then he said, "Now that's not a bad idea!" and slammed the door shut, sending shock waves through the flimsy trailer walls.

I looked at Brooke and was just about to say something to her when the door banged open again. Sonny stood there grinning like a small expectant child. "I heard that," he yelled.

"Do you really want to know what I was just about to say to Brooke?"

"Yeah, what?" Serious interest replaced the grin.

"I was just about to say that for such a horrid, shocking kid, he always makes me want to give him a hug."

Brooke gasped in mock surprise. "Carolyn! Don't tell him that! You know that he'll have to be even more disgusting now."

"Oh no! Is that true? Are you going to have to be even more shocking now?" We both looked worriedly at him.

Sonny assumed his most proper attitude and said, "Thank you." Then he closed the door with tidy precision.

By 3:30 I finally got my first break of the day. My fellow teacher and good friend, Adriane, drove Julia and me out of the parking lot to a neighborhood coffee shop. I made her stop and honk at the chastened and glaring pair, Nat and Dawson, as they picked up trash.

Once a week we three, Adriane, Julia and I have tea. Officially these teas are Julia's supervision sessions of Adriane and me. I could not survive without them. We ordered tea and well-earned apple cinnamon muffins.

Adriane announced that she had something to say to me. I looked at her short black grey-streaked hair and open smile. She is about the same age as I am. I glowed when she told me how much she had enjoyed what I said to the teachers of the rich the night before and what it had meant for the staff. That was all, but it was just what I needed, a positive ending for a hard day's work.

Well, enough of this. I shall quit now. I do hope that two or three pounds of letter are not too upsetting for you. I shall have to send this by cargo freighter. You may receive it in a few months. It does say something about your impact on me, doesn't it?

Carolyn

February, 1986

Chapter Three

Kingsley

Dear Rey,

I can't believe that you liked my story so much! And you even wrote back! I am in a complete gloat. Since your letter arrived my fingers itch for a typewriter, preferably electric. Right now the shape and form of an IBM Selectric is as satisfying to me as a Henry Moore sculpture. When I drive to work in my old VW bus, witty phrases slide through my mind, mostly to be lost in freeway traffic. Your enthusiastic reply lets me splash barefoot in the mud puddles of my mind. I delight in the mud squishing between my toes.

You told me I should just write, write and write some more while setting the psychoanalytic perspective to one side. After all, you said, I am a teacher and not an analyst...which is code for psychoanalytically speaking, you are clueless.

I must confess though...it's too bad you can't see how I relish using the word confess with you...that for a person who is as suspicious of shrinks as I am, my willingness to expose my teacherly misdeeds to you is amazing. I marvel. I boggle. I hope you have bad breath

89

or untidy fingernails, because so far you are too good to be true. My jaded sense of self-preservation is alerted. Surely he can't be trusted if he says, "I feel privileged to read anything you want to share with me."

I agree with you when you said you won't comment on my stories. I want to be able to write to you without fear of criticism. I don't want to have to worry about exposing my ignorance.

On the other hand there is a small part of me who wishes you were here to give me advice. I have Mitchell, Paul, Julia, Adriane and Brooke, if I need help. They are all well equipped to help me understand the adolescent mind. Still it is a great loss, not to be able to learn from you.

In my last letter, you may have wondered why Kingsley was so angry with me. He and I had just had a major confrontation the previous week and he was not convinced yet that I could be trusted. I thought you might like to read his story.

The image Kingsley evokes as he sits gloating in the corridors of my mind is rigid muscular oppositionality. On the surface, Kingsley may appear to be an overweight chubby-cheeked child, but underneath he is very strong. He is also horribly obstinate. So far, he has never behaved threateningly towards me; he just obstructs me. Yet, there is always the sense that he is inwardly seething and if I push him too hard, I could become an outlet for his emotions. He has attacked his mother more than once.

There have only been a few times in my teaching career when I have 'snapped'. Something actually seems to pop near the top of my spine and my consciousness slips into a state of disassociation. My body and any possible harm that might befall it simply do not matter anymore. My anger pours out in a flood upon the contemptible specimen of pubescence who has driven me to this madness.

Kingsley had me there last Tuesday afternoon.

My aide, Brooke, and I were alone in the classroom after school, confronting him with the detention he owed us for choosing to come to school two hours late that morning. Besides tardiness, which is his chronic notification to us that we cannot control him, he had not turned in any homework, which was overdue as well.

When gentle, soft-spoken Brooke asked him for his homework he jumped up and began shouting at both of us, yelling that we always, always, leap to conclusions about him. "You never have the consideration to ask politely. Oh no, you always think the worst!" He pulled his homework out of his backpack and flung it, ripping some of the sheets in half, on the floor at his feet. "Here's your precious homework! Now get off my back! And don't even think that you're going to get me to do any detention today!"

I had to get away from him, from the homework papers I was supposed to pick up at his feet, and from the surge of rage that had washed over me. I walked away from him and stood behind my desk. With Brooke by my side and the desk in front of me, I hoped they would provide a barrier to dam up the torrent of emotions that were carrying me away. I stood there pondering the arrogant adolescent who continued to berate me for my behavior and I knew I had reached my breaking point. I was also vaguely aware that there was some maneuvering room left, because in that hair-trigger split-second moment before I acted, I found myself wondering in schizoid detachment. OK, what'll it be this time? Shall I go wading once again through the quicksand of his irrational logic – which will take limitless time and energy – or shall I just give him what he is asking for, an intense reaction. Then he will finally be sure he has been seen and felt. Yes…I think I'll go with anger.

I slid into it with joy and exultation. Yes, yes, this is what I want to do! I've wanted this moment of rage from the first week he entered my class. How I hate this son of a bitch!

I slammed my hand down on the empty metal 'In" bin for homework. It made a wonderfully satisfying pistol-like crack. Doe-eyed Brooke jerked in surprise. It caught the bastard's attention because he stopped mid-harangue to evaluate this unexpected turn of events.

"Don't you give me anymore of your crap about my always assuming the worst about you!" I yelled. "You know that you are supposed to turn in your homework first thing in the morning. How long have you been in this class? An absolute eternity...a year and a half! And how many times have I told you to get your homework in as soon as your arrive? Hundreds! Thousands! But every day you make me ask for it. Every day you set me up for a confrontation because on that rare occasion when you do have it then you can accuse me of being unfair and fling it on the floor for me to pick up for you like the good servant you'd like me to be. Well I'm fed up and this had damn well better stop!"

I was taking a big chance with this kid because as I have already told you, he is a parent abuser. I have learned from bitter experience that teachers' identities can easily be fused with parents' by very angry and not too discriminating adolescents. In Kingsley I was facing a powerful adversary. He is pale and very blonde, and nearly six feet tall. In spite of his puppy fat, his strength is the one source of pride in him.

He tried to renew his stale attack, but by now my anger had carried me to the point where I had 'snapped'. I didn't care anymore about anything. I left the protection of my desk and strode up to his desk. He sat down, but continued his complaints. I bent over and jammed my face right up to his, my eyes riveted on his. My voice trumpeted several decibels above his, yet I had the good sense to take a different tack in my argument.

"I try my damnedest for you, Kingsley. I support you, listen to your troubles, give up a lunch break every week to spend with you, and bear up under all of your garbage. When you didn't show up again this morning and you were already 45 minutes late, I phoned your home and patiently encouraged you to rush so that you could salvage your day with a minimum of guilt and breast-beating. But no, you ignored me and said, 'Sorry, I can't hear a thing you're saying,' and hung up on me. Then you ate a leisurely breakfast, took a long hot shower and strolled in here two hours late. And now you have the unmitigated gall to tell me you refuse to take your detention!"

The detached portion of my mind which seemed to still be functioning noted that instead of escalating his fury as I had feared, my anger appeared to have calmed him down. He had stopped yelling. He seemed upset, possibly hurt. That's a good sign. He was just listening, head down, staring at his desk. I continued my rampage.

"I try Kingsley. I try every day for you and what do I get in return? You take advantage. You push. You treat me (and your mother, I thought) like crap. Well listen to me Kingsley, because I will not be treated this way anymore! Is that clear! I'm fed up! I've had it!"

I walked over to the door of the trailer and

 slammed it open. I was gratified at how it bounced and reverberated off the banister of the trailer stairs. In the 14 years that I've been teaching in my trailer, I've had some practice in throwing a tantrum or two. I like to use my props with as much flair as possible.

I turned to him and pointed outside. "Now either do the two hours of detention that you owe us without any more of your crap or just get the hell out of this classroom and never come back!"

What on earth was I saying? Oh dear, I'd gone too far. I had sent myself and Kingsley over the edge. My boss would kill me! He hates it when I play the brinksmanship game. What on earth made me go this far?

As I knew he would, Kingsley quietly responded with, "Sounds good," picked up his ghetto blaster, skateboard, and left. I had given him an out. Damn, but at that moment I really never wanted to see his ramrod-stiff body again. I watched him as he skateboarded like an animated broom across the parking lot.

Of course, the reason why my rage was so accessible that day was because on Monday, the day before, I had been shocked to discover myself feeling warm affection for Kingsley. As I felt the fluid purr of caring flow through me so that for once I could reach out and give his shoulders a hug without it being forced, no longer a cheap imitation of the real affect he craved, I felt hope. I'll be damned! I actually care about the son of a bitch. Perhaps he's over the hump. Maybe I really can help him now. From many years of working with these recalcitrant types, I had learned that when I reached the point of caring, soon afterwards they made progress.

Since November, I had noticed that on Mondays, after two delicious days of weekend vacation from Kingsley, he would try to reunite with me by teasing me in his own twisted way. Armed with his horrid portable radio, he made me tell him to turn it off, many times, each time grinning because I had taken the bait. Once when I wrote an assignment on the chalkboard, he came up and erased it, announcing that he wished to be helpful about keeping the room tidy. Another time while I ran a discussion, he refused to turn his body around the 90 degrees necessary so that we could see something besides the back of his head. "I would be willing to do so," he snipped, if the teachers would only ask nicely." In the middle of a field trip to a Superior Court, he went over to stand beneath a No Smoking sign and lit up. Finally during a class lecture, he came up to me and began to look for dandruff in my hair.

I interpreted these behaviors as... See Me! Notice Me! I am the special one here! I am back with you in this awful place and I want all of your time and attention! His actions were never mean or an attempt to bully. In fact, one time I told him that it must be hard to share me with his classmates, he shouted at me, adolescence bubbling out, "If I can't have all of your attention, I don't want anything to do with you at all!"

So on Monday, I waited for him. As soon as he sat down at his desk, I went up behind him and started rooting around in his hair. He stiffened.

"What are you doing?" he snapped.

"I'm doing to you, what you do to me every Monday. You always let me know you're back in my life by doing your weird things to me and making me crazy. I'm looking for dandruff and next I'm going to interfere with every move you try to make." I snatched up a bent machine-gun shell casing he keeps standing upright on his desk, clearly a sign of his potency. He grabbed it away from me.

"I'm just trying your way of saying hello," I said, moving back to stand next to his chair. I put my hand on his shoulder.

His face relaxed. Then suddenly he beamed a broad grin. He put his left arm around my waist and gave me a spontaneous hug. His first, and I loved him for it.

Of course, the next day I wanted to kill him.

That however, was the name of the game with Kingsley. I was continually being swung between extremes. That these extremes had become more polarized, was both a sign of improvement and of possible danger.

For over a decade I had observed that my most

95

difficult students have definite patterns of black and white thinking. There are only two bins for every event or person; I am either good or I am bad. I am either merged with them in gooey good fellowship or I am the identified enemy who needs to be obliterated. There are no grey areas, no in-between states. As their teacher I find myself being swung from pillar to post at their slightest whim. My goal is to get them to understand that I, as well as their parents, am sometimes good and sometimes bad, and that I live in the grey zone where all healthy people live.

An example of this occurred when I taught summer school with another teacher, Diana, a tall, statuesque, bronzed beauty. Our two classes became one class for 6 very long weeks. During the entire time, I was the identified bad guy while Diana, every young man's dream, was the good guy. Diana and I discussed this during our supervision with Julia, the staff psychologist. Julia suggested we wear labels, 'Good Guy' and 'Bad Guy' and act appropriately according to our label. After morning break, we would switch our labels and behaviors. The Good Guy would be the soothing mother, and the Bad Guy would be the disciplinarian.

We started out with Diana as the Good Guy and I played my usual role, the voice of authority. After break we switched tags. All right! I thought, I get to be the Good Guy. Alas, within seconds it was not to be.

Nat, my cursing surfer and one of her old students from the previous semester, came up to both of us and began to fuss only at me about his math paper. I behaved patiently, kindly. Diana reprimanded him forcefully. The small, wiry lad continued to bitch at me.

"Wait a minute," Diana said, "aren't you paying attention to our badges? Carolyn is the Good Guy now. I'm the one who's telling you to go back and correct your math errors. You should be yelling at me."

Nat leaned forward and peered myopically at our badges and squawked, "Hey, that's not right!" Then he reached out with his skinny little hands and unpinned my badge and handed it to Diana.

"Here," he said, "put this on. You're the Good Guy, not her. And don't go changing them around anymore!"

So I spent the rest of summer damned to be dowdy in comparison to sleek Diana, and the Bad Guy as well. Sigh!

But back to Kingsley. How on earth was I going to fix my unprofessional gaffe and get Kingsley back on my terms, not his? It was time to get help from the director of the school, Paul.

REYNARD'S MIRROR

February, 1986

Chapter Four

Getting Kingsley Back

Mostly the other students wanted nothing to do with Kingsley. He was always out of step, clumsily spoiling the mutual play that went on in the classroom. For example, one afternoon Sissy told us in despair of her flight from home the night before, of how she was locked out of the house, and forced to find refuge in a smelly concrete public toilet down at the beach. Kingsley interrupted, probably to stop this painful topic which was scaring him, and wondered if we knew that the price of gold had gone up.

So most of the time, people went about holding him off at arm's length. For him to give me a spontaneous hug and for me to discover feelings of affection meant that a big change had taken place in both of us.

However, I should have remembered that Kingsley cannot allow good things to continue unabated. I should have been prepared for his Tuesday regression but I wasn't. The betrayal surprised me and I went too far. I worried over whether or not I would be able to maneuver him back into class.

Right after I rashly banished Kingsley from my classroom I went to confess my crime to my boss[2]. Our

---

[2] In the California public school system a teacher would not have the authority to remove a student from her class permanently. At Mountainview, which was a private school, both administration and the parents could terminate a student's participation in the program when either party wished. Also, the administration was very

school was woefully short on students and cash since Reagan and his recent tax cuts had begun to inflict damage on the California school system. Public schools could barely afford to pay us to work with their difficult students. And because this was a private school, there were no protections for the teachers...no contracts, no union, no safeguards at all. It had already been decided that 1/3 of the staff would be cut. I knew Paul, my boss, would be upset with me, and I was concerned that he might toy with moving my name closer to the ranks of the unemployed. On the other hand, it is damned difficult to find people who can work well with these students. I was worried, but not too worried.

Paul is a tall friendly, bear of a man with an impish genius for working with kids. When I walked into his office, I found him sitting nose to nose with a chuckling eight year-old boy. Paul was grinning and seemed to be holding some imaginary object against his chest with his left hand while his right fist circled over the object. "Stirring the pot. Stirring the pot. That's what we do to mom and teacher isn't it? Just keep the pot boiling." Paul was mirroring the boy's instinctive behavior he uses on the maternal figures in his life. Paul had made the boy's style humorous and observable. It would help the boy understand himself. Paul uses visual humor to make a point with these verbally limited students.

I remember one student who threatened us with going home and beating up his mother unless we let him go home immediately. With his mother's permission, Paul kept him at school until the student gave up on his abusive blackmail plan...all night!

One of my favorite devices he uses is a lie-ometer, a paper plate cut in half. On one-half of the paper plate he

---

supportive of the teaching staff, so that a such decision by a teacher, while extremely rare, was allowed.

has divided it into pie wedges with the words True, Partly True, White Lies and Black Lies, He has an arrow which he twirls back and forth on the face of the plate, depending upon the truthfulness of the student. Another of his devices is a spray can of bathroom deodorant, which he pulls out and sprays around the room when it's clear that the student's stories have become especially stinky. I have watched Paul's sense of humor for years. He taught me how to laugh with my students. In fact, I was about to receive the same treatment myself.

Paul sat in the chair in front of his desk, arms folded, head down, while I guiltily told my story. He sighed, said something vaguely sympathetic and left the room to get a cup of coffee. I waited. He returned, sipped his coffee, and I watched anxiously while he drew dollar signs on paper airplanes and sailed them out the door. Feeling better he then turned to help me with my strategy.

I called the family, Kingsley's psychiatrist, and Kingsley's school district to explain that I did want Kingsley back, but on my terms for once. I told them Kingsley had to understand that he could push too far, that he could get people who are important to him to throw him away. They were doubtful of such methods but they would back me up by telling Kingsley he must return and handle the situation. Kingsley's psychiatrist piously suggested that I consider using a behavior modification management system of points and rewards instead of emotional hysteria to handle Kingsley. I thanked him for his advice and told him that it must be nice, working with Kingsley for one hour a week.

By throwing Kingsley out, I was gambling on the strength of our new bond. So far he had refused to do much more than engage in power plays with me. Instinctively I knew that by forcing him to face the potential loss of our relationship, he would have to identify its importance and learn how to give as well as take. It would be a big step for him.

When Kingsley came back two days later, I sighed with relief. He went to talk to Paul, describing in great detail my many inadequacies as a teacher who was not doing her job right, which was to take good care of him. Paul listened sympathetically, nodding his head with each complaint. Then he told Kingsley that even though he could understand how difficult a teacher I was, he would nevertheless have to clear things up with me before he could be readmitted into my class.

"I can handle her," he said with pubescent confidence. "We can get things settled during our regular counseling session we have at lunch today."

Paul muttered skepticism and Kingsley trotted off, optimistically certain that things would go his way. Paul raced out of his office and found me eating my peanut butter and jelly sandwich in the teachers' lounge and briefed me on Kingsley's intentions.

Paul recommended that I appear to be reluctant to take him back, putting the burden on Kingsley to solve the situation. In the meantime, out in my classroom, Kingsley walked in as if nothing unusual had ever taken place. Brooke looked up from the papers she was grading and disinterestedly told him that he could not be in the classroom until he had straightened things out with me. I walked in and pretended surprise at seeing him, "What are you doing here? You're not in this class anymore." Then I ignored him, leaving the room to take care of phone calls.

Kingsley went back to the office and told Paul, "You're right. She won't talk to me."

I was notified to come to the office while my class was having P.E. in the gym. Paul waited for me outside his office and waved me to one side, out of Kingsley's view. For Kingsley's benefit, I loudly refused to go in and talk to him. "I don't have anything more to say to him, Paul."

Improvisation being Paul's favorite thing to do, he loudly ordered me into the office. I grudgingly said I would come in, but not until I had taken care of a few things first. Paul whispered conspiratorially, "Take your time. Let him stew awhile."

I went to get Brooke to join us in the meeting. She looked at the smile on my face and cautioned me to shape up. "Now Carolyn, you look much too happy. Don't go in there and be nice to him. This is the first time we've ever had the upper hand with him. Don't give it away. Remember, be mad!" I struggled to wipe the grin from my face.

When Brooke and I entered Paul's small windowless square office, Kingsley was sitting, head bowed and absorbed in his pocket calculator. I sat in a black padded vinyl chair opposite Kingsley while Brooke chose the black padded vinyl couch facing Paul's desk. Paul took up his familiar position leaning against his desk facing Kingsley, head down, arms folded over his chest. Silence. It was my turn to be ignored. I let my eyes wander over Paul's brick walls covered with odds and ends of children's art work which somehow miraculously stayed taped to the brick surfaces. Then I looked over at Kingsley whose head was still bowed in either feigned or oblivious concentration over his calculator. I remembered how much he has trained me to hate his battery-powered gadgets. He uses them on me with such delight.

"I have a class returning from P.E. soon. Let's get this show on the road," I grumbled.

Kingsley looked up and saw that Brooke was present in the room. Surprisingly, he became irate. He claimed I was ganging up on him because I was afraid to handle him by myself. Brooke's presence gave me an unfair advantage. "You're too chicken to face me alone. You need her to save your..."

I cut through his impending rudeness and snapped, "You're in no position to be setting any terms, Kingsley." I looked over at Paul and told him. "I'm here against my will. I'm not going to put up with much of this." Paul nodded his head soberly in acknowledgement.

Of course, by now I had made several mistakes. Even though Paul had recommended that I make Kingsley wait, I should have come in sooner and alone. I had forgotten that as far as Kingsley was concerned, I was the one he had a relationship with. Brooke was an intruder. I knew my hopes for resolution were not to be achieved. I felt guilty already for my part in producing this fiasco, but at this point I could not back down. I had to set limits on his behavior.

Kingsley launched into his complaints about me. He was the mistreated one. I was going to have to change. There was no way he would let me win this battle. He wouldn't put up with this any longer! He clinched his fist and pounded on the arm of his chair, his face puffy with bluster.

Good grief, I thought, he's giving my own ultimatums back to me. We were still engaged in a power play. Once again, the role he was scripting for me to play was to be calm and coax him into reasonable behavior. I suddenly understood what it was like to be Kingsley's mother. I was sure that if I played my part, we would just continue to recycle his expectation that all the important female figures in his life must cater to his infantile needs.

I interrupted him and looked at Paul, "I don't know why I should have to listen to this. As far as I'm concerned, he's out. If you want to put him in another classroom, that's your business, but I'm fed up with his arrogance."

Kingsley jammed his calculator into its cover and said, "Fine! I'll go to continuation school.[3] That way I can

---

[3] A continuation school in the California public school system in the 1980's was an alternative public educational program. Students having difficulty with a regular high school might do better in a smaller, more informal setting. Attendance and academic requirements were more flexible. On the down side, many

go directly to college without having to worry about transitioning from here."

Paul asked him a question with concern in his voice, "But Kingsley, continuation school begins at eight o'clock. You're having trouble getting here by nine. Will you be able to manage that?"

"Of course. No problem. Once I get out of a school that plays with my head, I'll be in much better shape." The calculator was back out of its case. Kingsley was punching in numbers and telling us of his rosier future away from us.

I was getting tired of looking at the top of his head. "Well evidently you have it all planned out. What is it that you want from us, our blessing? Or are you hoping I'll coax you back? Don't hold your breath because that's not going to happen."

He jammed the calculator back into its cover again. "Fine! I'll just go then. I don't need you." Indignantly, he stood up and strode out of the office in a huff.

Oh dear, I had done it again. Anxiously, I looked over at Paul but he was grinning. He said, "That's good. He'll have the weekend to think about it and we can try again on Monday. I think it's better this way." Surprised, I looked at him and thought, "What a wonderful man! Even though the pay is crap, I'll work for him forever."

By now P.E. had ended. Brooke and Diana had both our classes in my trailer watching a film. Later Diana reported to us that in the flickering light of a re-creation of Genghis Khan leading his Mongol Horde across the Russian steppes, everyone in the class was watching the even more absorbing drama of Kingsley as he carefully and methodically collected all of the paraphernalia he had

---

continuation school students were at high risk of dropping out and drug use.

papered on the wall, and gathered his personal objects from his desk to put in his backpack. He did not forget his bent machine-gun shell. Each item was packed and repacked with meticulous care. All of his classmates were quietly fascinated by this process and its implications.

Diana and Brooke did not need me while they were running the film so I took a break in the front lobby with Julia, our school psychologist. Shelly, our Scuba-diving receptionist was absent and Julia was helping out between counseling sessions. I went behind the front counter where she was answering phones and sat down next to her. I wanted to tell her my troubles with Kingsley. Julia counsels Kingsley and knows him well. She looked at me with her open, fair face and her flyaway red-gold hair. She extended a welcoming arm, bearing several brightly colored sculptured bracelets from her last trip to Peru and encouraged me to tell her what had happened. I could always count on Julia's unfailing sympathy. I began to tell her about how I had made the situation worse by not being more available to Kingsley as soon as he showed up today.

Suddenly a livid Kingsley stood before us, interrupting me once again. "Excuse me," he intruded. He looked intently at Julia, heatedly ignoring my presence, and forged ahead. "I'm leaving now. I want to thank _**you**_ for all that you've taught me and for being a good teacher." Then he turned on his heel with military precision and marched out the front door. I watched that stiff, erect figure walking down the front steps, ghetto blaster in one hand; skateboard in the other, with his backpack filled with classroom mementoes and felt a mixture of relief and guilt.

Julia, ever the indomitable one, shouted cheerily and waved at his back, "See you on Monday!"

Naturally, Kingsley had to hold out until Tuesday. This time he wasn't angry. He wanted back in and he was ready to negotiate. By then, I too, was ready to get things settled. Confusing as it was to me, I wanted that stolid, oppositional lost soul back with me. It only took us 15 minutes to resolve the whole mess.

We met once again in Paul's office without Brooke's unsettling influence. We settled down in our customary chairs and right away, Kingsley began by apologizing to me.

"It's like you have a pet dog that really loves you and all at once for no good reason, you start kicking the dog. That's just not right." Pain passed over his face at the thought of the emotional kicks he had given me."

I shot a hostile glance at Paul. His head was down, barely swallowing sniggers of amusement at Kingsley's comparing me to a devoted pet dog. I managed to keep my mouth shut.

Kingsley, oblivious, solemnly plodded on. "With some teachers, they deserve to be taken advantage of, because that's what they do to students, but Carolyn never does that. She has always treated me right and it's wrong for me to behave like I do to her."

Warily, I chimed into this happy reunion. "I want you to know, Kingsley, that I did not mean to kick you out of class and I felt very badly about it. Before I knew it I had gone too far."

"Nevertheless, I still think it was important that I threw you out of my class. If we look back over the year and a half that I've worked with you, what have you done to me almost daily? You show me that I can't control you. In fact, that's one of the things you enjoy the most, showing me that I don't have any power over you."

He grinned at me, nodding his head.

"Last Tuesday," I continued, "I showed you that you can't control me either. I deserted you. I walked out on you. You forced me to make a choice between keeping you in class or keeping my sanity. You are not the only student out there who needs my attention. I can't allow you to upset me so much that I can't be a good teacher for the rest of the students."

He stared at me with expectant eyes. Such cooperation! Such compliance! I felt suspicious, but blundered on. "This last round was different. On Monday, I felt a lot of affection for you, more than I ever had before. On Tuesday, I wanted to be rid of you forever. I wonder if this is what it's like at home? Do you go from feeling warmth for your mom to feeling that you could hurt her?

His eyes opened wide and he nodded again in agreement. "Yeah, it's like there are these two poles and I get pulled from one to the other." Sounds suspiciously like something his therapist told him, I thought. Hopefully he can learn from rote memorization.

"I'm feeling a lot more affection and a lot more rage towards you, Kingsley, and I suspect you feel the same. Because these feelings are stronger, I am very afraid that you and I can be pushed to the point where you could become abusive towards me. If that ever happens, Kingsley, I will have nothing more to do with you. There will be no second chances. I want you to understand that clearly.

He reassured me that he would never hit me. "You have no worries whatsoever," he said confidently. "We've been building up to a blow-up for a long time. It had to come sooner or later. Now that it's over things will be better."

I found his insistence on my equal responsibility for this mutual build-up to be irksome, but I shoved it aside to finish my sermon. How I hate giving these preachy little lessons in life.

"You and I have to learn to live with each other in the middle ground, Kingsley. We cannot be swung from pole to pole. This is very important for you because if you can do it with me, then it may carry over to the rest of your life. We've both got to fight to stay in the middle and not the extremes."

Kingsley readily agreed. "I know you're right and I really will try to behave better in class."

Paul stood up, leaned over and shook Kingsley's hand, "Welcome back."

Kingsley and I stood up. I gave him a hug.

Well, Kingsley and I are getting along just fine now. It is still a question in my mind as to whether this was obedience or breakthrough. Time will tell. He certainly has been trying to change with a determination that I have never seen in him before.

Rey, I want to be sure that you understand when I describe one of my 'life's little lessons' speeches that I am never convinced I am saying the right thing. Usually it is more that I must say something, anything. The student says his words. I say mine. We probably both rehearse our parts later on, chuckling at our cleverness. The point is not so much what we say but that we manage to develop a relationship that is different, not a replication of the same old pattern. The end result of all this commotion with Kingsley was an increased awareness and respect for each other and perhaps a tenuous mutual pact to maintain a more stable relationship. It was not so much the words I said that made the difference. I could have spoken in tongues during our second meeting and the result would have been the same...well almost.

These kids do not work at the level of words and symbols. They function in the visual, the concrete, and the visceral. Like a wolf marking my territory on tundra shrubs, I snarled at him that he had gone too far. I had a right to be treated decently in my classroom. I could have calmly talked to Kingsley about the same issue till doomsday without making a dent in his oppositionality.

I also want you to know that I would definitely not recommend such behavior to another teacher or therapist. There are no recipes for working with these students. I think that in this case, throwing Kingsley out of my class worked. If I had done it two weeks earlier, it could have ended in disaster. If I tried it with another student, I might have been beaten up. The major reason why I succeeded was because Kingsley and I had found affection for each other first. He had learned about my capacity to care for him in spite of his miserable behavior, so he had the strength to withstand my anger.

When I shared this event in supervision with Mitchell, he suggested in his psychoanalytical way that Kingsley had been replaying his family history with me. In therapy, the client either places the therapist in the role of the aggressor or that of the victim. Kingsley was placing me in the infant position. Mitchell said that in my anger I might have spoken words that Kingsley could never utter, probably to his mostly absent father, "Treat me with respect or get out of my life." How could a dependent teenager say such a thing? How similar our tirades were, mine in the classroom and later, his in the office. We both had yelled that we would not be abused any longer.

Finally Mitchell warned me about our tendency at Mountainview to play out improvisational conspiracies against the student. Mitchell has always been bothered and intrigued by this manipulative side of our struggles with these kids. He said that whenever we lapse into tricks, we need to raise a red flag and play closer attention to the dynamics which are operating, especially if it 'works'. As I just asked, was it obedience or breakthrough?

However, I have to confess that I do delight in those fleeting moments when a bunch of us gang up on a kid who has rendered all the adults in his life impotent. Besides offering the teacher a few moments of blessed respite, these sessions do remind the infantile tyrant that he can be contained.

Again Rey, thank you for your unflappable confidence in me and your willingness to read my stories. Are you sure you wouldn't like to emigrate. We'd sure like to have you over here, if only for the delightful accent.

Carolyn

REYNARD'S MIRROR

March, 1986

Chapter Five

A Pillow for Shaun and a Jelly Donut for Me

Dear Rey,

Shaun has become a serious problem. I'll tell you about that later, but first, I want to give you a little background on why I am in such a funk today. And Shaun is making it all worse.

Last month, a four day holiday arrived so Zane and I decided to take our four dogs out to the desert for a camp-out. Cold weather had definitely set in out there. The rattlers would still be safely bedded down in whatever hidey-hole they tuck themselves into for the winter. When they are active during the summer, just before sunset, they crawl out to toast themselves groggily on the still warm ground. They are especially fond of asphalt highways and dirt roadbeds as the heat of the day dissipates into the clear night sky overhead. The weather was cold enough so that I wouldn't have to worry about one of the dogs stumbling over one at dusk.

Rain was predicted but rain rarely reaches that part of the desert where we would be camping. Zane and I, both being geographers, were confident that even though it might rain or snow in the nearby mountains, very little of it would reach us. At the very worst, we would be above the level of flash floods.

Camping with four large dogs in a VW bus

requires tolerance and a certain amount of wiliness. We all
manage to sleep inside the confines of the bus. Flash, the
largest and the aging patriarch, gets the front passenger
seat. The rest, Honey and her two overgrown pups, are in
the back with us. I settle in first, being sure to make
absolutely certain that every part of my body is covered
with blankets. Once the rest join in, there are no second
chances. Next come the dogs. Zane usually sits by the
campfire for a while and makes sure it's out for the night.
The dogs and I love our bit of time to stretch out in
luxury. When Zane joins us, the dogs are pushed and
pulled into their assigned spot for the night and there we
are, cemented into place until dawn, and that's when
being wily comes into play.

When dawn arrives, the dogs begin their vigil,
sitting vulture-like over us, transmitting little canine
thought waves into our brains... *wake up, wake up, wake
up.* If I want to enjoy the maximum amount of sleeping-
in I must never give any indication that I am awake.
There must be some kind of doggie pack code against the
indiscretion of waking up a pack leader, but if that pack
leader shows any sign of wakefulness, all bets are off. If I
am cautious enough I can sometimes grab another hour or
two after dawn. Only one eye at a time can be opened.
Any more than that will attract attention. Once they spot
the tiniest hint of life, the whines and complaints begin.
Cold noses are poked in our faces followed by impatient
whuffles. Paws scrape at our bodies.

The morning of our first day of camping, in the
reliably dry Mojave, I awoke to a muffled silence. I
opened one cautious eye and peeked at the window to
gauge the time of day. When the shock of snow encrusted
window panes finally penetrated, I sat bolt upright
yelping, "Zane! Look! Snow!" The dogs, elated at such
marvelous activity, began gamboling in delight all over our
bodies. In self-defense, I struggled against those frantic
hairy bodies, reached for the double door handle and

released the catch.

Dogs exploded from the bus and shock registered on all four fuzzy faces as they tumbled out into their first snowfall, three inches of it. It wedged icily between their toes, collected on their noses, and interfered with tantalizing jackrabbit scents. It could be eaten though and was soon found to be quite as nice as deer carcasses for wallowing in. It added a certain zest, a new flavor to a place already identified as eminently satisfying. Hysterically happy, they raced off down the ravine. I followed them as Zane began to organize the bus to make our escape.

I, too, felt delight at the feathery flakes drifting down about me. The desert had become unrecognizable. What had been a very familiar world of ochre, rust, and jade had become an alien world etched in black and white. It was beautiful! Joshua trees took on new, more dramatic shapes. Their bunches of spear-like spiky leaves which jab the unwary, had become puff balls of snow. The common rabbit brush, famous for inducing hay fever with its yellow blossoms, had become an intricate sculpture of tiny leaves, each one laden with perfectly symmetrical pellets of crystal white snow. The little jumping cholla (pronounced choya), an uncouth cactus which detaches bits of itself to embed in trouser legs or doggy paws and noses, had become small innocuous snowy humps on the blanketed desert floor, still waiting patiently to spread its body parts around.

By the time we got back to the bus, Zane had everything ready to go. The snow was now about half a foot deep. Still, we were confident. The bus had handled snow much deeper than this in Idaho. We were incredulous when after a few hundred yards, the bus lost traction and slid off the track. Evidently wet snow on dirt was much slicker than Idaho snow on asphalt. When there was any kind of a slope at all, it was just too much for the poor old bus.

We were camped about four miles from the main dirt road and there was another 10 miles of graded dirt road after that to get back to town. We had nothing but little hills and valleys between us and the main road to town. Zane got out the shovel. He and I took turns shoveling or using our boots to scrape out tracks ahead of each front tire. We began shoveling and scraping about eight in the morning.

By noon, we were about two miles from the graded dirt road. My down jacket was soaked and my mittenless freezing hands were wedged under my arm pits as my numbed feet robotically scuffed out the remaining endless miles of track in front of the bus. My mind registered only one thought, how much I hated snow. The window of the bus was steamed up by the four dogs. They wanted out and I wanted in, but we didn't want them outside when the bus took its next skid. They were safer inside. I was just beginning to think about giving up and camping out in the snow when two trucks complete with huge oversized tires and four-wheel drive poured over the rim of the valley and roared down the slope toward us.

Rescue! I shouted to myself. Thank God! An outdoorsy male climbed down from his cab garbed in a crisp olive and green camouflaged suit and strode over to us. I looked at his costume and his truck, which very nearly required a step ladder to get in and out of, and felt a teensy qualm. Ah well, he's probably one of the Marines from the base nearby. Even though he looks like he's dressed up to play G.I. Joe, he'll surely know about things like towing and pushing.

I was ignored as he walked past me to talk to my male. This guy was evidently the leader because even though other people arrived from the two trucks, he did all the talking.

"What's the matter, didn't you come prepared for this?" he scoffed. (It snows in this part of the desert about once every ten years.) I looked over at the rest of the party, two other matching G.I. Joes, and two women, dressed in furry pastel colored coats, mittens and hats. The two women waited discreetly in the background, huddled together.

After a while, it became clear to me that these three males weren't going to offer anything more than sarcasm. Finally, I put down my shovel and coaxed them into helping us push the bus out of its latest ditch. Occasionally, if we could get enough speed going, Zane could skim the bus over the surface of the snow for yards not feet. The three men and I put our shoulders to the task, leaning against the back of the bus while the dogs peered at us through the steamed up rear window. Zane revved up the engine, released the clutch and wet sand and mud spewed up from the rear wheels. The bus found hard rock, took off, then skidded perversely off the track with only ten feet of gain.

Looking down at his brand-new, but now muddied camouflage suit, the leader quickly decided they couldn't help us. Then they drove off about a hundred yards, so as not to be too discomfited by the sight of our labors, and frolicked in the snow with the squealing girls. On their way out, they paused by our new location, fifty feet further on, and shouted out that he was sure if we drove in his tracks, we'd have no trouble getting out.

As much as I despised the man, he was right. We were able to get out by using his oversized tire tracks and within two hours we made it to a donut stand in town. We walked into its steamy warmth and I leaned my forehead against the glass counter. Glazed donuts, jelly donuts, chocolate donuts and cinnamon rolls reposed languidly inches from my nose. The odor of hot coffee filled the air. Two salesgirls chatted happily in the back. I was starved. I was sopping wet. They laughed and gabbled on. I waited. I felt weak. Eye contact did not appear to be in their repertoire. No one waited on us. Hot coffee was just out of my reach.

I could stand it no longer. I pounded on the glass counter. I yelled out to the gossiping girls, "HEY! I'm dying out here! I want some coffee, NOW!

I shall never forget the bliss of that raspberry jelly donut and that hot cup of coffee. I lost five pounds that day.

I had wanted a little adventure in going out to the desert, something to help me forget the stress of my work, and especially Shaun who has become a major problem. Instead of a gentle getaway, the desert almost got me. For a while that afternoon, I could not feel my feet. They were just anonymous blocks that I stumped about on. I looked up into grey skies at the no longer delightful snowflakes pelting into my face and soaking my clothes, I almost gave up. The thought of laying aside my shovel and climbing into the bus with my warm toasty dogs and taking a cozy nap sang a siren song all day long.

Unbeknownst to me, I think my subconscious digested that day in a very negative way. For the next week I was in a terrible mood. Every day I came home from work and crawled into my nice warm bed. I craved warmth. I read, slept, crocheted and watched really stupid TV. I gained back five pounds.

I think being trapped in the snow and having to expend so much energy to extricate myself, reflected only too clearly the trap of continuing to work at Mountainview. I am powerless in my poverty, my students abuse me and the leader of our Camelot, Paul, is showing hints of irritation towards me. I have to admit that my risk-taking and my lifelong habit of chronic tardiness does not bode well for me. I now have to sign in each morning along with my boys.

Of course, we have no union, with a contract and a transparent pay scale. I've always had the suspicion that one of the teachers with fewer degrees than I have, but much chummier with the boss was raking in a more substantial salary. Without transparency that suspicion would continue to rankle my envious soul.

Enough of my miseries. I thought I would tell you about how Shaun is developing. I've been delivered another tall handsome youth who has been his mother's best friend and her youngest babe. Shaun has mastered being seductively manipulative. He watches Brooke and me speculatively, with his dark eyes and wonderfully crooked smile. Last week, for example, he wanted Brooke to give him a blackberry tea bag, naturally out of her own private supply. To gain his ends, he hunkered over, holding his hands together as if they were paws and began to nuzzle against her arm, producing a rumbling purr in his throat. This was certainly a technique used on mom and of course, the appealing kitten got his teabag.

One of the most important lessons I've learned from Mitchell, and you, is that these kids will replay old histories with me. Inevitably, I find myself in one of two situations, the role of the aggressor, such as a parent, or the role of the victim, usually the child. I've become callused when a student who has been physically or emotionally abused wants to push me around. In fact, I probably have too much tolerance for such behavior. I strap on my armor and prepare my mind and body for another assault, but when the attack takes the form of a hug, I am totally unprepared and confused. The process is very subtle. It's what makes working with these kids so insane. I find myself reacting strangely. I begin to wonder about myself. Who am I? Why am I being so cruel, or confused, or hostile? In the case of Shaun, I find myself feeling unaccountably like a victim in the role of a shy teenager or an overworked mother.

Let me give you some examples of the kinds of things he has done to me. Shaun has been in my class for nearly a month now. So far, I too have received the same pussycat treatment, and once when I had him sitting at my desk I found that no matter how often I moved my knee, his knee always ended up resting against mine. He is a canny lad, more responsive and intelligent than most of the adults I know. He is always one step ahead of me, instantly sizing me up and knowing what I will say or do next. Or, he can behave like an overgrown passive infant, laying down on the couch and becoming incapable of functioning. It is extremely unnerving, being treated with gallant masculinity one minute, then having to beg and cajole him to produce work the next.

Once, at the end of the school day, he ran out on detention and I tracked him down out in front of the main building where he was waiting for his mother to help him escape. School buses lined the curb, teachers were making sure their charges got on the right bus, and students caught up in the joy of freedom were pounding down the front steps. I spotted him, moved in between him and the parking lot, looked up at him and asked, "What is it that I am expecting from you right now?"

He spread his arms wide, pushed his chest up to my face, raised his arms to the skies and shouted, "My body!" Open-mouthed parents, teachers and dozens of students turned to look at us.

Notice how public the situation was. He made me feel overwhelmed and embarrassed. I was a shocked child.

Another event happened when I had managed to get him to sit at his desk instead of lying on the couch. Sitting, instead of lying down, seemed to be the sum total of my success because he was not producing. He plopped his head down on his papers and his eyes closed. Non-production being the bane of a teacher's existence, I went over to his desk and began to fuss at him to get started. After listening to me carp at him for a while, he suddenly sat up, turned towards me, put his arms around my waist and very nearly buried his face in my ample bosom. With lightning fast reaction, I pulled back and smacked him on the top of his head. The rest of the class goggled at this novel strategy for getting the teacher. Shaun was greatly admired for his daring.

The moment seemed at first to be a sexual maneuver to get the upper hand, but a tendril of guilt lurked in this explanation. Perhaps instead, this was the small beleaguered child, reaching for my cushiony comfort to bury his face in and find relief.

My guess is that if Shaun must produce for me, his classroom mother, he becomes depressed. Shaun has been his mother's partner and baby all wrapped up in one package. Producing means growing up and becoming more like father. So he avoids growth and protects his role as playmate and baby by seeking a place to nap. The battle to get him to sit at his desk is a major one. Only the couch, the pillows, or even the floor will do. Shaun is constantly in search of a pillow to nap on.

My problem is how do I cope with him? How do I keep from replaying his relationship with his mother? How can I avoid this trap without abandoning him? Like his real mother, his classroom mother must be completely devoted to him. When I cannot replay this relationship with Shaun, he falls into despair, sleeping on anything bearing a nodding resemblance to a pillow, or he becomes seductive, or worst case, oppositional. Above all, the goal is not to become responsible about growing up.

Like rage, sex is also present in any adolescent classroom. While therapists are given help through supervision, teachers are not and are expected to be immune. Because our role expectations for the classroom say that these emotional excesses should not exist, we pretend they are not there and we are shocked when they surface.

When a tall, attractive and certainly experienced young man engulfs me in a bear hug, I am astonished that for a split second, I feel giddy, rather than structured and in charge. And even though I recover my proper role as quickly as possible, I know I have a hard battle in front of me, one that is much, much different from the one I wage with Dawson.

I will definitely bring this up in supervision with Julia and Adriane. Too bad you're not here to give me advice.

Well, I think I will go and watch some really stupid TV and forget about work for a while. And maybe have a snack.

Carolyn

April 1986

Chapter Six

Lessons My Students Have Taught Me

Dear Rey,

Well, it's been three months since I last heard from you. Why I keep writing, I don't know. Perhaps I need a vague transatlantic father figure in order to keep writing my stories. My intuition tells me that you are not tired of these letters and that someday in the dim distant future, you will write back. Of course, you are scheduled to visit the psychoanalytic institute in June, so perhaps I will get some closure then about whether or not I should continue writing to you.

I thought that I'd like to share with you some of the little lessons that teaching special ed. provides on a daily basis. Every day there's something new to be learned if I can find the energy to pay attention to it.

Perhaps the most frequent lesson my students teach me is how to live with intrusion. Last week Dawson surpassed himself in reminding me once again that I must be more alert, less trusting and I should take greater safeguards with my possessions and boundaries. Behind my back the little bastard spit in my orange juice, gloated while I drank it, and then drew the class' attention to his feat by asking me how I enjoyed my juice. Oblivious teacher that I am, I didn't figure out what was going on until later in the day.

After lunch, I vaguely remembered Kingsley and Sonny making cryptic hints about Dawson and my orange juice. I began to cross-examine Dawson's classmates more rigorously. I did not want to believe what he had done to me, yet to pass it off would invite more intrusions from Dawson and his cronies.

I questioned him about it. I scanned his heavy-metaled person. His pale blue eyes smiled at me with sanctimonious patience through a tangle of dishwater blonde hair. Believe me, if I'd had to put money on the truthfulness of his answers, I'd have sworn that I was unfairly maligning him. I suddenly understood why Dawson's dad always believed him and not me.

"Carolyn," he said, "I'd do a lot of things, but do you really think I'd do that to you? I did take a straw from my coke and drain a little of that into your drink..."

"You did what? How dare you..." He ignored my sputters of outrage and smoothly continued.

"Yes, I'll admit to that, but there's no way I'd spit in your drink. How long have I been in your class? Do you really think I'm that kind of jerk?"

He looked me straight in the eye. His body, his gestures, his relaxed manner, all seemed so confident in the strength of our relationship to survive this blow. He would be patient with me in spite of my lapse into cruel accusations. I narrowed my eyes and glared at his open transparent face.

I wanted to believe him. It would be so much easier if I could trust his words, those earnest blue eyes, but I knew he was an expert at lying. He had to be, living with his extremely controlling father. Furthermore, I had gathered questionable testimony from three other sources, who admittedly would enjoy setting Dawson up. I weighed his honesty against the other three. He lost. I told him he was lying. In fact, I began to rant and rave. He confessed.

Since this was certainly not the first such intrusion of personal boundaries in our classroom, I made the class sit through a heartrending lecture on trust, betrayal, boundaries and 'just what kind of a classroom do you want to have anyhow'.

"Is this the kind of classroom you want? Every time you leave, you have to carry all of your important belongings and food with you because you can't trust your classmates. I have to lock the door and make you stay outside because you can't control your own behavior in this room without a teacher. What you do shapes the atmosphere in which we all live. Right now you are creating an unpleasant environment where no one feels that his possessions, or for that matter, his body is really safe. It's up to you. You will have to live with the kind of society you create, starting right here in this class."

You can see that I toppled off the deep end in my fervor, turning this event into a threat to the 'American Way of Life'. Nevertheless, the above topic is one of my regular themes which I drag out to wave before these students repeatedly. I think it is important to remind them when they commit another one of their nasty little acts, just what effect it has upon each of us singly, and as a group.

Yet, even though I gave Dawson detention for his prank, I had not done enough. I felt violated and my desire for revenge was not satisfied. I needed more. That evening during supervision with Mitchell, I told him what Dawson had done to me.

The next day I went to class and notified Dawson and his cronies I had been so upset about what he had done to me that I shared my distress with my supervisor. I told them that the psychoanalyst had given me an interpretation of Dawson's act.

"So Dawson," I asked, standing face to face with him in the middle of the classroom, "would you like to know what the psychological interpretation was of your spitting in my orange juice?"

I had captured the rest of the class' attention. They crowded around the two of us, squared off in the center of the narrow trailer. My partner, Brooke, said gleefully, "Oh boy, Dawson! A *psychological* interpretation!"

The class was chortling over this turn of events, happy to see the classroom bully put on the spot. Dawson, however, was not one to turn away from a challenge. He stepped closer to me, nose to nose.

"Yeah, so what is it?"

I paused. I made him wait. Just a little while longer, then…"Impregnation."

"What!" He leaped away from my middle-aged self as if I had become leprous. The class was delighted with his embarrassment. As his mental machinations ground slowly to find a way to defend his honor, he swaggered and huffed with clinched fists just outside of arms' reach. Finally, he launched into a highly offensive description of how unlikely a candidate I would be for his attentions. I interrupted him mid-insult.

"Well Dawson, now that I have been privileged to share your juices, you and I should be much…"

He ran over and spit in Brooke's glass.

This last week has been exhausting. Brooke and I hardly took any time off for lunch breaks the entire week and I would estimate that one of us was in the office with a misbehaving teenager at least 50% of the time. Every evening I come home, watch about an hour of TV and fall asleep by 8:00. Today is Saturday and I have spent the whole day napping and reading British cozy mysteries. I need at least a full day to rest up from the previous week.

I suppose I read tea and crumpet mysteries to

escape to another place and time. They allow me to leave my own unruly, dusty, unkempt world for one where there are thatch-covered cottages amid peaceful villages with well-mannered murderers. Besides, goodness always triumphs over evil, which I certainly don't experience much of in my line of work.

Brooke and I have much in common with detectives, you know. We are special ed's own Miss Marples. Well, that's not accurate; Brooke is a much better detective. I suppose I have to admit that instead of Miss Marple, I am really the clueless police inspector. As I go about naively wanting to believe in the innocence of my babes, Brooke senses and understands their dark revengeful natures and their greedy manipulations. While I earnestly try to get them to pay attention to a lesson on how to write a research paper, Brooke's bloodhound nose has caught the odor of pot and has zeroed in on the three who are sitting there grinning at me in glassy-eyed contentment. Or during break, while I am on the phone trying to track down yet another mysteriously unavailable school district official, Brooke has quietly seated herself at the adolescent's private rock out at their hangout. Still as a mouse, she overhears one student arranging with another, future plots and petty crimes. When in class, their voices lower and whispering occurs, Brooke's focus of attention instantly switches from grading papers to eavesdropping. I continue frantically searching for the next task, blithely unaware of conspiracies.

Last week, given a paltry 11 students, we managed to catch 4 illegal smokers, Nat escaping off-campus (probably for a quick puff on the odd joint), and the confiscation of one pair of brass knuckles, a six-inch knife, and a set of handcuffs. We also identified who had spread a mixture of gum and cigarette butts all over a teacher's car. Finally, I caught Sonny, my own little terrorist, beating up a kid half his age and size. When confronted, he declared he was suicidal and would blow his brains out with his stepfather's gun that night. We located his stepfather and had him remove the gun from the home.

As soon as we discover one crime, another is immediately presented to us. It is all the two of us can do to keep up with just eleven students (we have gained another student, Kent). It is exhausting to maintain the vigilance to catch them, yet if we don't, they begin to feel out of control, and that is really frightening to them. Over and over, I keep coming back to the theme of containment. I am sure that one of the reasons why these kids do not survive in large impersonal schools is because they cannot be contained well enough.

I struggle with these children every day. They can make me feel instantly incompetent, unfit for the job of teaching. They overwhelm me with emotions that I did not know I was even capable of feeling. The only recourse I have is to focus on the lost child underneath all that crap. Here is an example of an invitation to battle that Sissy offered me yesterday.

She turned her big brown eyes up to me and threatened me. "I'll call you a bitch and a cunt and I'll make you miserable for the rest of the day if I don't get to sit on the couch and do my math."

"That's all right. I'll still like you."

"Bitch."

"Cutey pie."

"Cunt."

"Cupcake."

"Cow."

"Sugarplum."

She burst into smiles and laughter. "Oh shut up. Leave me alone. I've got to do my math." She sat at her desk and worked, completely satisfied with life.

On another day, Nat, was stretched out on his belly on the couch, screaming red-faced at me. "You hate me. You're out to get me. You never believe me. It's always my fault. You always believe Sissy. You like her better than me. You always take her side."

I walked over to him, leaned over, patted his hand like a mother calming a little boy and cooed at him. "It'll be all right, Nat. I promise you. Everything will be all right."

He yanked his hand away from mine as if I had burned him. He tucked his head into the cushions on the couch, hiding his smile. I heard a muffled, "Go away. Don't touch me." But he is calm now.

The class watches, fascinated. They all feel mutual relief when I have the strength to resist hating them. It increases the chances of safety and affection for them all. The multi-headed organism breathes a sigh and progresses ever onward to the next crisis.

Brooke and I notice that we grasp at the smallest, teensiest act of charity they exhibit towards us. Brooke remembers fondly when Dawson finally offered her a cheese cracker from his lunch without snatching it from her at the last moment. The entire class watched as she gingerly inserted her forefinger and thumb into the ratty plastic baggy held before her, and she was thrilled when at last they closed over that orange flakey surface and the cracker was not yanked from her fingers complete with jeers at her gullibility for believing that he would share anything with her.

For myself, I was flooded with warm, sunlit feelings when our new student, Kent, smiled at me.

Kent hates me. He also hates Brooke, our school, and he especially hates math and P.E. He is a small lad for 17, a silent fuming pressure cooker of a boy. He is tan and wiry with beautiful dark eyes. Like a young colt, he is skittish and always just out of reach.

One day soon after he had arrived, we were having a research period for their papers on the Native

Americans. Dawson happened to ask if we were going to have a longer PE today. Knowing Kent's contempt for PE, I walked over to him and patted his hostile shoulders, saying, "Yep, I've arranged a longer PE today just for Kent."

As the study period progressed, Kent probed the possibilities of avoiding the horror of PE. "I can't go to PE if I don't do my notes, right?"

I looked over at him rocking precariously back and forth on the rear legs of his chair in front of his blank notepaper and said nothing in reply.

"You won't let me go to PE if I talk too much, will you?"

Again, I pretended I did not hear him.

"You won't let me go if I refuse to talk, huh?"

I turned to him and said, "Listen, I'll make you a deal. You promise me that you'll take one paragraph of notes and I'll protect you from having to go to PE. How's that?" His chair banged flat onto the floor and he looked as though he might pick up a pencil and actually take some notes. Hah, I thought to myself, at last I've maneuvered him into a place where I'll get some work out of him.

The coach showed up to collect the kids who would be going to the park to play baseball, and Kent shoved his chair back from his desk and his unmarred notepaper and said, "Well I guess I'll be going to PE."

As he walked towards the door, I told the coach, "I offered Kent a chance to get out of PE. I told him that if he'd give me just one paragraph of notes, I'd keep him back. It looks like taking notes for me is far worse than having to put up with your PE."

Kent looked back at me and grinned. I could not believe it! All that this silently enraged cherubic-faced lad had given me so far was frowns, averted eyes and one-word answers. Perhaps there is hope!

More than PE, Kent hates math. In an effort to

reduce this torture of his sensibilities, I gave him a two-week moratorium on math. The day came, however, when it was time to plunge back into the study of arithmetic. Kent is very bright and I thought I could ease him in gently by starting with calculator math; that way he could just push buttons and presto...the answer. But I made a mistake. I tried to teach him something that was challenging, using the bracket function in a simple equation. I sat down next to him and went through the explanation using simple concrete examples and demonstrating the difference between using brackets and not using them. Slowly, I became increasingly aware of his rigid indifference. He would not look at the paper, the calculator, or worst of all, me. He just sat tilted back on his chair, eyes staring up at the wall, radiating heated boredom.

"Kent, when I'm explaining something to you, I would like you to look at the assignment.

He glanced in its direction. "I know how to do that."

"Fine, then show me." Giving him the benefit of the doubt, I got up and left him alone. I thought perhaps he would be able to work better without a hovering critic.

I returned to check his paper. Every problem was wrong. I sat down and began again. His eyes returned to the wall. My anger surprised me as it surged to the surface. I know how bright he is and how much I could enjoy working with him if only he would let me. He was depriving me of himself as he was deprived by his mother. She had refused to take care of him. He had been abused through neglect and now I was being neglected. My knowledge of his sad childhood, however, did not protect me from my rising fury.

"Look," I said, "you're really making me mad. I'm trying to teach you something and you sit here allowing me to do my song and dance for you while you decide whether or not you're going to bother looking at it.

I'm not going to repeat myself three or four times because you find it just too bothersome to pay attention the first time. These four problems must be done correctly before you leave school today." I left him looking red-faced and pouty, yet absorbed in his wall, rocking precariously back and forth on the hind legs of his chair.

The end of the day arrived and he returned his last four problems to me at the very last second just as his classmates were getting their final check before dismissal. He slapped his paper down in front of me and rushed for the door. By now I had the four answers memorized, so I checked them. They were all wrong. I caught him unlocking his bike at the steps to the trailer and told him to return to the classroom. His baby face turned beet red.

"Why?" he challenged through clinched lips.

"I told you that all four problems had to be done correctly today. They are all wrong."

He came back in and sat on his desk, back to the wall, arms folded petulantly across his chest.

"I'll be glad to help you if you do not understand what to do, but you'll have to look at what I'm showing you."

He sat silently, visibly fuming. After twenty minutes of continued immobility I said, "Look get to it. I've been off duty for the last half hour. You are screwing around with my free time." It was my day for tea, muffins and supervision at the coffee shop. Playing the waiting game with this master of stubbornness was really making me angry.

Evidently in his mind this was a dismissal because he hopped off his desk, walked out the door, got on his bicycle and left. My blood pressure soared.   Tossing aside the comfort of tea and sympathy, I went into the office and unloaded on Paul. He sat there and let me vent, saying nothing. Finally, I figured out all by myself that angry as I was, I felt that if I pushed too far, Kent would refuse to come to school at all. On the other hand, his inability to express his feelings, his silent refusals to cooperate and his walking out had to be confronted.

As I vented my feelings to Paul, it became increasingly apparent that Kent's inability to ever tell anyone about how he really felt was very important, far more important than math or maintaining teacher control. Kent exuded distrust, an unwillingness to expose his true self, and a tightly packed core of rage. I decided that if math made him mad, perhaps it was a very useful tool. I would offer myself up for the expression of anger he so desperately needed to voice.

When he returned the next day I took him out to my private office, the steps of my trailer. I sat down. He stood. I asked him to have a seat on the stairs. Aloof, he looked off into the distance. I pestered and annoyed him enough so that he finally sat down one step above me.

So, why did you come back today, Kent?" craning my neck to look up at him.

I was ignored.

"I know that you could have refused to return today and gotten your way. What was it that made you come, especially when I know how much you hate emotional scenes? Considering that you and I had a fight yesterday, I can't imagine that you wanted to face me and the possibility of being fussed at."

Brooding silence and faraway eyes.

"I have to give you credit. Nobody brings you to school. You could have ditched, but you came."

It was like wandering in the dark. He gave no hint of how I was doing. I continued to grope about blindly.

"Now I know that you really don't want to study math. You show me by ignoring me when I try to teach it to you. But I've decided that you and I will have regular scenes over whether or not you will do your math and that these battles are very important. In fact, I think that the most important thing that you and I may do here is fight over math. I want you to know that I'm not upset about yesterday or any future fights we might have. In fact you can count on a math battle every day. I shall look forward to it.

He stared out across the playing field, apparently absorbed with some inner thoughts of greater importance. A sigh suggested impatience with me.

I plodded on. "Do you know what happened when you and I had that fight yesterday? Do you know how you made me feel? You do understand that it is my job, my role in the classroom to be your teacher. I have a lot invested in being a good teacher, and in doing my job well. You were not letting me do my job. You were ignoring me. I began to feel incompetent, that I wasn't of any use, and even odder, I began to feel almost as if I had disappeared. So I had to let you know that I do exist and that I am a teacher with skill and authority. You forced me to be angry."

He looked away from me. I kept going. "Something very important happens when one person makes another person angry. It means that you and I have managed to get in close enough to hurt or upset each other. In a way, it can be viewed as a kind of closeness. You pushed me into a corner far enough so that I had to come out fighting. I did the same thing to you so you got on your bike and left. We could even look at this as an improvement in our relationship. Anger is certainly much better than feeling ignored."

I thought I saw his eyes tearing up with moisture, but he looked away again so I could not see his face.

"Well anyway, I wanted you to know that I was impressed when I saw that you had returned today and I also wanted you to know that I think it's fine if we fight over math."

I took him back into the classroom and handed him the same four problems to him. I sat down at the desk next to him and explained the use of the brackets key on the calculator again. I watched him as he worked the problems. The little bastard refused to use the brackets key! He showed me that he understood the process, but he did it all without the brackets key.

"Why, Kent, won't you do it my way?" I pounded my fists on the desk where I was sitting next to him. "Why won't you ever do anything the way I want it done?"

I looked over at Dawson who was enjoying Kent's rebelliousness and said to him, "You think you're tough Dawson, with all of your yelling and threats, but Kent here has brought more teachers to their knees than you'll ever be able to beat down. Do you know how he does it? By silently ignoring them and refusing to cooperate. That makes a teacher really crazy."

Kent was grinning.

I turned to my aide for solace. "Brooke, help me out. He won't do it my way."

"Well," she said, "is he getting the right answers?"

"I don't know. Let me check." Not having the answers memorized today, I pulled out the answer book and checked the answer to the first problem. "Yes," I said, in a voice filled with resignation.

"Then leave him alone."

"Oh, all right, but I hate it when they won't let me have my way."

I got up and left Kent, who looked smugly gratified. If I had not been on my toes later that day, I would have missed his glancing mutter when he poked his paper on my desk and pointed to one problem as he dashed for the door. I looked at Brooke sitting next to me. "What did he say?"

"He said he did number four your way."

Well, let's see, what have my students taught me recently. Dawson taught me to defend my boundaries against intrusion. No perhaps I'd better rephrase that. Dawson taught me that I must <u>expect</u> intrusions. These kids cannot leave personal boundaries unmolested. Secondly, I learned that I can avoid their provocative entrapments by focusing on the child inside. And my third lesson was taught to me by Kent. He reminded me that it is not production or answers which are important, but the process, or the engagement in battle. It is the struggle which is most significant to these children.

Where do I find the strength to cope with these abuses? I must search for the child in them. I must continuously spell out what is happening in the relationship between us. I must describe how we affect each other. I must contain their monstrousness by showing them our common humanity. And most important of all, I must show them I can survive them and they won't be thrown away again. All of this I have learned from Mitchell and you...psychoanalysts!

I organize it all and hold myself together by writing to you. Are you sure you wouldn't like to write back? I could use a letter. Certainly my original intent of not asking you for replies has changed. That one and only letter was addictive. I need another shot, another hit of yourself. Your last letter was in January, years ago.

I am a fool to try to befriend an analyst. You all have such an odd code of behavior. I bet you guys are never able to stop those vicious rotating clockwork gears...probing, evaluating, analyzing, but above all, remaining blandly, maddeningly, NEUTRAL!

Carolyn

May 1986

Chapter Seven

Failing Shaun

Dear Rey,

I have failed Shaun. You remember him, don't you? He was the charming experienced young man, who wanted to be less of a student and more of a courtier. I was supposed to replay his enmeshment with his mother, keeping him as my special one and making no demands on him to grow up.

I knew that I could not play that role with him, so instead of being the devoted maternal figure, I parceled him out. Julia, our therapist, was supposed to look after his emotional needs. I hoped that the other women in his life would take care of his other requirements. I was going to safely lie low and merely be his teacher. You know, just do my job.

However, it looks as if doing my job with Shaun required more emotional investment than I was able to provide. It was a big mistake to keep my distance from Shaun. When I would not replay the devoted maternal role he had scripted for me, he became oppositional - passively, by laying down and sleeping wherever he put his body, and actively, by becoming a critical bitchy pack leader who successfully blocked the learning process in the classroom.

A couple of weeks ago, Shaun told me that his

father asked him if he was well enough to return to public school. Evidently, dad wanted a quick fix with a minimum of cost. Shaun had only been with us for a few months. I was sure he told me this with the hope that I could stop his father from removing him from our school. He knew they were telling him it was time to leave. He had no hope of staying, so why try to improve?

I tried to do something about it by making an appointment with the parents to have a meeting. The alleged purpose was to make a progress report on Shaun. The real purpose was to make clear my conviction that Shaun would not survive on a large campus where he would be lost in anonymity. They didn't show up.

I continued to teach in an atmosphere of Shaun's passivity and oppositionality. While I had hoped that he and Dawson would counterbalance each other, instead they had developed into a team, spreading contagious apathy throughout the class.

Brooke and I discussed the problem with Julia during supervision. In a desperate last-ditch effort we decided to try an experiment. We were going to let Dawson and Shaun act as teachers for the morning session while we would join the class as students. We had visions of sprawling on the couch, refusing to move to our desks, dawdling our way through our journal entries, and just generally having a good time with role reversal. I hoped that by having them play the authoritarian role, they would gain some insight about how they kept defeating the learning process.

I should have known that asking Shaun to perform as teacher was too threatening. I was asking him to do what he feared most, grow up and assume responsibility. In other words, I was asking him to play the role of father at a time when once again, father was betraying him. The morning of the experiment, right in the middle of it all, he walked out.

There were rumors that Shaun had a girlfriend,

his boss' wife. Besides school and his after-school job, he was probably also worn out from coping with that tricky situation. I'm sure his romance contributed enormously to his impatience with school. He wasn't getting enough sleep and he simply could not stay awake. His ravenous need for nurturance was being satisfied. He had little use for what either his mother or I wanted him to do. What was left on his agenda was acting out his oppositionality and separation from mother...useful for him, but hard on classroom discipline. When I began to ask the class to evaluate the costs of using their education as a battleground to prove their autonomy, he walked out; probably more because he knew it was what his parents wanted than because of my experiment.

On the day he left, he walked ten miles to get home, much to his mother's distress. As soon as he left the campus, I called to notify her of his absence and questioned her about what time he was coming home and getting to sleep. He was producing very little in the classroom because he was so tired, I said. "Could he be getting in a little late on school nights?" The parents' response was to engage Shaun in a ferocious argument, throw him out of the house, and withdraw him from school.

One of the administrators showed up in my trailer to reprimand me. Without trying to find anything out about my side of the situation, he launched into an indictment of my experiment. "I cannot justify such expenditures of time in the classroom to school district officials and parents," he announced stuffily, sounding just like the district bureaucrats I abhorred. I have to admit that on one level, he was right. I was feeling very guilty about the advisability of the experiment. I also wondered if Shaun's father hadn't been chewing on his professional dignity. This was very unlike the administration here, to get sucked into the parents' pathology.

I drew a deep breath and my rapier wit to defend myself. I listened to his indignant fussing for a bit, then I interrupted him and pointed out that the parents had been complaining about the high cost of tuition for a while now and they were probably looking for an excuse to get out of any more payments. I asked him why he thought Shaun's parents did not show up for the conference I had requested so that we could discuss the situation before it became a crisis. Then I reminded him that this was exactly...I repeated the word exactly...the way Shaun had been withdrawn from the hospital program before he came to us. That staff had no warning either, no chance to stop the parents from their rash decision, nor to say goodbye to Shaun. I looked at my superior and asked, "Doesn't this look like a set-up to you? Dad wanted a quick inexpensive fix. He was never going to commit to long-term treatment. This way dad can blame Shaun and us, put him into public school and wash his hands of his son's problems. He's done everything he could possibly do. There's a reason why Shaun can't produce in school."

I wondered at the time whether or not the ground was shifting under my feet at this school. We had prided ourselves on being experimental and open-ended, but here I was being chastised for something I had explored in supervision before I tried it out in the classroom. Still, I felt very guilty about what I had done.

Surprisingly, the next day Shaun showed up. He had spent the night sleeping in the storeroom where he worked. He was very angry with his parents. He would not return to them. He would not even let me arrange a conference with them. Nor would he allow a conference with Paul alone. He tried to claim that he had come back just for his silver blue sunglasses, but I did not believe him. He had walked ten miles back to say goodbye to us. He did collect his sunglasses, but he left behind a handmade coffee mug he had made himself and his backpack. He was leaving a portion of himself for our safekeeping.

Rather than letting him walk another ten miles back, I drove him to his job. On the way I was struck with great sadness that my cowardice had prevented me from doing more for him. I had known what I needed to do, get more involved. I had run from the demands I was sure he would make on me. I felt a great loss.

When we arrived at his work, an embarrassed silence settled over both of us. He reached for the door handle. "Wait," I said, "before you go, I want you to know that I feel awful about this. I think a big part of the fault for your having to leave is mine. I should have gotten to know you better. We should have had lots of talks. I am really sorry and I'm sure I am partly responsible for your leaving."

His eyes teared up, he looked away from me. Then he jumped out of the car and was gone.

There is no way to avoid pain in this kind of work. To help them get better we must care about them. We must repair or at least reveal some invisible injury in the relationship between them and their parents. But we are not their parents and they will leave us behind. Another loss. Another death.

Dispiritedly,

Carolyn

141

REYNARD'S MIRROR

June 1986

Chapter Eight

A Kindergarten Day with Kent

Dear Rey,

I am typing this letter down at school. I can use the school's electric typewriter at school after closing. It is evening and I am at Mountainview taking my chances with the neighborhood. It is dark outside and creepy inside.

To overcome the jitters this place produces in me at night, I have brought Flash with me, my old black lab of 14 years. He loves the chance to return to school. For about 5 years I used to bring him here every day. He was the school dog, our mascot. All the kids knew his name and would stop to pet him as he trotted along at my side.

He worked very hard during those years. He was most effective at pulling self-absorbed, scaredy-cat kids out of their shells. I would hire students to dog-sit after school. In order to do their job and receive their pay they had to learn to run and yell, and to exert themselves to make contact with another living being, or Flash would just ignore them. He simply stood and gazed vacantly off into the distance with his mouth full of the tennis ball my student was supposed to be throwing. An ignorant dog, yet he was the master of reinforcement schedules, refusing to play until the dog sitter had achieved the proper level of performance.

Before too long these kids learned how to scream

143

and holler, racing around the field after a dog who would not be caught until he was exhausted. They learned how to snatch balls out of benign, yet savage appearing jaws. This, they were certain, was an act of considerable courage although Flash could never have bitten a human being. Afterwards, leaning on each other in the shade of a huge eucalyptus tree they would sit panting together happily. Later, as I corrected papers I could hear Flash groaning with pleasure as he received the final dog sitting chore, his daily brushing.

He perks up every time I bring him down here. Once powerful hindquarters reassert themselves and prance around the premises. Outside, his grey muzzle checks out the scents of invaders into his domain and his own are superimposed. Now that he has completed his reconnaissance, he rests on the floor behind me, hopefully large and black enough to be intimidating to any intruders. Little do they know that he is completely deaf and partially blind.

This place seems especially hollow today. The chairs from Friday's evening lecture are still sitting silently white in their rows. Remainders of food and drink that celebrated your presence amongst us spill out of the trash cans. It all serves to remind me that yesterday you were here and now you will be absent for over a year. I have no great faith that I will survive that long. Tomorrow is much too unreliable; a year is definitely beyond my ken. I think therefore, that you might describe my state of mind as one of bereavement.

I had grown upset with you. One reply in nearly 5 months of devoted missives on my part, yet yesterday you took me aside in your rushed and harried day to encourage me to write and become a therapist. I think you made it abundantly clear that your intent is not to abandon me.

I felt tremendous relief when you asked for a few

moments of my time before your lecture. I was wonderfully embarrassed to have a short talk with you. We sat in my classroom and I wondered how to sit, where to put my hands, how to manage to look comfortable while my face was burning red. Only ten minutes to visit with you and I had a thousand things to ask, including your life history.

What I remember best about my interview occurred just as you were about to leave. As I turned away to search for my purse in the rapidly dimming light of the day, I heard you, sitting behind me, say, "You are capable of doing analysis, you know. You do it to me in your letters."

Turning back, I had the distinct impression that your bearded face thrust forward at me out of the gloom and that there was a hint of ire in your tone. My mind scrabbled around trying to make sense of this…approval, presumptuousness on my part, limit-setting, permission? I finally gaspingly decided that somewhere my impressions of you had some validity, but which ones? Tantalizing but with no closure. Fortunately, I am an expert at dealing with no closure.

You complained to me during our 10 minutes that it frustrates you to be introduced to a student like Kent, and not have his story finished. I have decided that I will complete the story of Kent for you. He will leave us in a few days. He will be going back to public school in the fall.

I must warn you that like myself, you will have to live with lack of closure, at least as far as reading these stories are concerned. I become very involved with my students and they leave when the school year ends, regardless of how they are doing at the time. Many return the following year and some come back to see me so that sometimes I am able to get a sense of how their lives are progressing. To teach special ed is to learn to live with unfinished stories and broken relationships.

Here is the continuing saga of Kent. It is one of my favorite stories.

A few days after the calculator battle, we received Kent's file in the mail from his former public school. It was a very thick one and it even had records that went back to when Kent was six years old. It is the custom that students never see their files, but I decided to share Kent's with him.

I took him to the detention room and attempted to set the file between us on a conference table so we could look at it together. Kent snatched it up. He would have control of this. I might peer over his shoulder if I liked, but he would be the one to hold onto these bits of information about himself.

Throughout his secondary school years the comments were all distressingly similar. "Never does more that the absolute minimum. He is never defiant, but is working far below his potential."

I was fascinated by the report of a 4th grade teacher. Kent should have been about 8 or 9 years old at the time. He had been referred by his teacher for special ed., and the form required an explanation of why she thought Kent needed extra support.

"Why are you referring this student?"

"All he does is sit and stare at his paper...all day long! I simply cannot get this boy to do any work!

"How are you handling the situation? What accommodations are you making?"

"He sneaks constantly. I have to watch him all the time. Nothing I say has any effect."

This was a teacher with whom I felt great sympathy. Look what little Kent was doing to her! I understood her frustration very well. Little Kent was doing the same things to me.

"Describe the student's areas of strength."

"In the 20 years I've been a teacher, I've never met a student who was so determined to accomplish so little work, day in and day out."

"Describe what is motivating to this student."

"The only motivation I can attribute to this child is that of opposing me and enjoying the satisfaction of driving me crazy!"

I shook my head in wonder and said, "Kent, you must have been something! You really had your teacher frothing at the mouth. You were a powerful little kid. I'm impressed!" Kent grinned and chuckled. We were both having a very good time.

Next we found a questionnaire with replies done in a very young scrawl by 6 year old Kent.

"Tell me how you feel about school. What do you like best?"

"et pla go hom"

"What do you not like about school?"

"werc"

"Tell me about your teacher."

"she don lik me i am stuped"

"Tell me when you are happiest"

"wen i am with tedybur"

I was hooked when I saw he was happiest with teddy bear. In that moment I found the child in the adolescent sitting next to me. I knew instantaneously that I would find the patience to work with him. I felt sorrow for the child who was not happiest when he was with mother, but when he was with an object. I was glad that it was a soft, cuddly object...a hopeful sign.

I knew that before Kent was adopted, he had been neglected or abused. I seemed to remember stories of his being locked in closets. I pictured him in the dark, hugging his fuzzy bundle for comfort. Whether or not any of this was true, I had found the small child beneath his 17 year-old bristly insolence. I was reminded again that a child who has been abused is often the most successful at making a teacher want to hit him, or throw him away, or hate him. Whether I was accurate or not, I had found a toehold. I felt hope. Once I find empathy, it is almost impossible to return to hate.

When we finished, I told him, "Well I want you to know that looking at this file has made me feel a lot better. I thought you were mad at me because you were forced into my class against your will, but I can see that you've always been like this. You're not mad at me, you're just mad! You've been like this since you were a very little child."

Wallowing in relief, I continued, "This is going to take a lot of pressure off me. How on earth can I possibly change habits you've had all your life? I won't be so hard on you or myself in the future. Furthermore..."

He cut me off. I knew I was saying the wrong things and I wouldn't get too far with the sermon on the tip of my tongue, but you know how it is, when you're labeled 'a teacher'. You feel obliged to introduce 'right way to live' commercials at every opportunity.

"Can I have this file?"

I looked at his eager face, his dark eyes filled with anticipation, a very rare expression to see directed at me by this lad. It was dazzling, almost disorienting. I told him when he was 18 he could probably have it, but I couldn't give it to him now. I had the oddest feeling that this moment of closeness was because he thought I had broken the rules when I let him see his file. Perhaps he was thinking that since we had conspired to commit one crime already, we could continue committing others together.

During supervision with Mitchell that evening, when I mentioned my suspicions to him, he suggested that shared sneaking might be an important connection with Kent. "Perhaps union or closeness coexists in his mind with being partners in crime."

Paying attention to Mitchell's advice I began to keep an even closer eye on Kent. Notice how he has me behaving just like his fourth grade teacher? He would sneak or cheat (such as stealing an answer book from my desk) and look up to find me watching him. I would smile and say, "Yes, you're right. I am watching you. I love to watch you sneak."

Then he would grin at me, a brilliant, happy smile which told me that Mitchell had been right. Here at last was one teacher who could appreciate him properly.

Soon after we shared his file together, he showed me more of the small child he used to be. Kent took me on a fascinating trip to his kindergarten days. For two days he relived his restless, anxious childhood in our high school classroom. Fortunately, you and Mitchell have taught me not to be so rigid about acting like a teacher; otherwise I would have missed this.

Brooke happened to bring in a huge book of kindergarten level activities and puzzles that she was planning to give to our classroom of 5 to 7 year olds. Kent spotted it on our desk and scooped it up like candy.

In order for you to properly appreciate what a departure Kent's subsequent behavior was, you must understand that every scrap of production we eke out of his grudging mind and body is thrown in the trash. He will even search our desk to find any incriminating assignments we might be hiding from him. Each assignment he retrieves is neatly folded up and thrown away, slipped into his wallet to be discarded out of our reach, or torn up first and thrown away. (I can imagine how long that file would have lasted if he had gotten his hands on it.)

We asked him one day why he folded some assignments and tore others up.

"Things can be unfolded and used against you, but they can't be put back together.

We complained, "But that was an A paper you tore up!"

"Those are the worst kind. They hold it over your head and expect you to live up to it."

So Kent begged to do kiddy puzzles and refused to do classwork. The result...detention during break. Yet I kept feeling uncomfortable about being a proper teacher and demanding high school work from him. Somehow I was missing an opportunity and I knew it. I talked it over with Brooke and we agreed that Kent should have his time with the kiddy book.

I collected crayons, pencils and the book and went to the detention room where Kent was sitting on the floor in the dark. He had turned out the light so he wouldn't be seen. "Look," I said, turning on the lights, "you were good about taking your detention time, so here, enjoy yourself."

"All right!" he cried, sitting up eagerly to snatch it all from my hands.

I extended his time in the detention room and came back for him thirty minutes later. He was stretched out flat on the floor, completely absorbed. He begged to stay in the detention room so he could color in peace and quiet. I managed to get him back to class where I mercilessly told him to lay on the couch and work on the puzzle book, or else. For once he was a willing worker. The other students watched him, confused but not willing to hassle him. They too, seemed to understand that this was important. They left him alone.

Later, I noticed Kent stealthily slipping a pair of

scissors off my desk. I watched while he cut the margins off two of his colorings and propped the pictures up against the wall on display at his desk. After lunch, I found that he had hung the same two pictures over each door of the trailer. I was stunned! This was the boy who hardly lets me check his work because it is too risky, too exposing. Yet here he was hanging his precisely colored pictures on the wall for all of us to see. Kent allowed us to look at them for the rest of the afternoon. Then they disappeared.

Kent had definitely given me a hint about the direction he needed to explore. He wanted to return to his childhood. It was not a time for me to insist upon being his teacher and make him produce. We were doing a different kind of learning and for the most part, Kent was being the teacher.

During the afternoon's PE slot, this was hammered home to me even more forcefully. Kent had refused to be on the baseball team. The coach was having team practice for a big game the next day. I allowed Kent to stay in the room with me and continue with his kiddy book. Nat was also in the room because he had sprained his ankle the previous Friday and the coach wanted him to stay off of it until the day of the game. Nat had plans of napping, but I told him it would be fractions instead. In an effort to make this cryptic topic more concrete, I collected several boxes of brightly colored pie-shaped wooden blocks cut up into different fractional sizes. Kent, still lying on the couch, contentedly connecting dots said, "Oh blocks! I like to play with blocks."

Once again, I could not believe what this 17 year-old was telling me. "Really? Would you let me review fractions with you if I used blocks?"

Happy with life, he said, "Yeah, sure." He grinned at me over his puzzle.

"OK. As soon as I finish with Nat, you get a turn. You certainly are in a kindergarten mood today."

"Yep, and after I finish with blocks I want to finger-paint, have nap time and then have a story read to me."

Brooke and I looked at each other in shock. He was serious. That was the incredible thing about it. We gave him a kindergarten day.

Instead of finger-painting, we borrowed some plastic clay from the primary classroom. Nat, Brooke, Kent and I spent a satisfying half-hour playing with the clay. I made a wonderful little pig, about 3 inches tall, with a ball-shaped body and a marble sized head, two perky floppy ears, four stubby legs, a snout and a curly tail. I sat it on the desk in front of me. I smiled at it. It grinned back at

me, pleasing and pink. Brooke and Nat admired it. Kent looked over at me, and saw my happiness with my little pig, then he reached over and smashed it flat.

I laughed out loud. Of course, I thought, what was I thinking? This was Kent's kindergarten day, not mine. How unempathic of me, to enjoy myself. Once Kent had regained control of the situation, he played with blocks, took a nap and Brooke read a story to him.

I could not put these two images of Kent together: the Kent who refuses to go on field trips with us lest he be seen and his reputation ruined forever, and the Kent who so openly showed us those cherished moments of his childhood, abandoning all concern over his manly façade. I was determined to explore further, or at least as far as my teacherly constraints and Kent's controlling nature would allow me to go. Remember, I was already in trouble for Shaun.

The next day was the big baseball game. I knew I would have some free time to continue with Kent because my entire class with the exception of Kent, Sissy, Deborah, and Sonny would be playing on the team. The coach wanted his players to come early for prep time. That would give me time to continue with Kent. Once the game started, however, it would be my sacred duty to go and admire my boys' prowess, memorizing particular feats of courage and endurance to recite back to them. Any teacher worth her salt knows this is one of her official duties.

Keeping Kent's pleasure about coloring in mind, Brooke and I decided to offer a coloring contest to those remaining in the room. If they wanted to participate, they could choose a page from Brooke's kiddy book to color. The prize was to be awarded by Shelly, the receptionist, whose beauty exempts her from accusations of bias. However, in spite of injuring all those other diligent colorers, we cheated. We manipulated the contest and told Shelly which one to pick. We knew that Kent had to win that prize.

We collected the finished drawings before afternoon break and delivered them to Shelly. During break she chose the correct winner and sent them back to us with Sonny. We did not ask Sonny for the results. As soon as Kent dashed in from break, the first thing he said was, "Who won?"

Brooke and I looked up, perfect models of curiosity as Sonny, our shocking punker, enviously grumbled, "Whoever did the teddy bear won."

Kent beamed and muttered to himself, "I knew I would." I felt a slight twinge of guilt for the others who had been the victims of a rigged contest, but I shrugged it away for a brighter cause. I posted them on the wall. Kent left his up for the remainder of the day.

Last Friday, Kent said something smart-alecky to me. It was some statement about my general incompetence. He has developed a habit of running an ongoing stream of rapier mimicry of me being teacher. That day, to the class' delight he scored a particularly penetrating stroke, so I walked over to him, leaned down and tapped my forefinger threateningly on his desk. I said, "I am giving you fair warning, young man. If you keep this up, I may not be able to overcome a growing urge to give you a hug."

Since it is nearly the end of the semester, I am surprised at my remorse for losing this class. We seem to have grown accepting and fond of each other. I find myself wanting to write more and more about them. I guess I want to capture them on paper before they slip away from me for good, especially Kent. I shall miss that pouty face which can suddenly turn radiantly happy, then disappear into another thundery glower before I can respond.

Kent is leaving. Dawson and the rest will be back in the fall but soon this particular class will disappear for good. New students will be introduced next year and the flavor of this group will be gone, that unlikely concoction of each one's special brand of despair, rage and frustration which when gently cooled can turn into unexpected delight.

Kingsley is still behaving, and Dawson has become very much the masterful young man. He even shows secret moments of thoughtfulness for the adults on campus. He thinks he has gotten away with it, but the teachers share these tidbits during lunch in the teachers' lounge. There is no escape on this campus. It is like living in a goldfish bowl, every act is under inspection.

Dawson still continues to show affection through abuse however. A few times during the last three weeks he has demonstrated his fondness for me by grabbing my coffee cup and pretending to spit in it, making me recall his crime of earlier this year. Each time this occurs he looks up at me expectantly and I respond with, "Why Dawson, you still care."

Well, I want to thank you again for the time you took with me when you visited. You are trapped in the unhappy position of being the victim of my idealizations, which is partly your fault. If you wrote back more often, I would see the real imperfect you. Wouldn't you prefer that?

Carolyn

August, 1986

Chapter Nine

Kent's Goodbye

Dear Rey,

I'm in love…with a 600 lb. sea lion named Clyde. He kissed me yesterday and captured my soul.

Since I am wallowing in the languor of summer vacation, I went to one of those marine parks. As I strolled through the park, avoiding crowds as much as was humanly possible, I chanced to look into an empty amphitheater between performances and found a young lady dressed in a fetching maid's costume who was putting Clyde through his paces.

I sat among the empty benches, cheering and shouting my admiration at his skill. Part of Clyde's finale is for the maid to bring him out to the front row to meet the audience. When he was in position, his pretty trainer turned to me and asked, "Do you want to meet Clyde?"

"Do I ever!" A millisecond later I was rubbing Clyde's magnificently corpulent damp neck and talking baby talk to him. Evidently this was just fine with him for as I leaned over and crooned to him about what a handsome fellow he was, he looked me firmly in the eye and poked his muzzle at me. Why, I wondered, is he poking his nose at me? Those large brown watery orbs waited expectantly, even impatiently for me. For what? What was I supposed to do?

Of course! He's trying to offer me a kiss! (That's

part of his act.) I put my right cheek (which shall never be washed again) closer to his saber-toothed, meat eating jaws and was nearly knocked off my feet as he smacked his muzzle up to my cheek and held his bristly whiskers and cold wet nose there for a joyously transporting few moments. It took me a full day to come back to earth. Even now as I remember those moist hopeful eyes and his bristle-brush nose, I sigh at the loss.

I have just finished teaching summer school. Because the older adolescents avoid summer school like the plague, I was stuck with a classroom full of 12 and 13 year-old boys. Horrible! I don't even have the energy or the interest to tell you about that ordeal, but I am determined to finish Kent's story so that you may have some closure.

We are leaving tomorrow for Idaho. I should be packing my aged VW bus instead of sitting here and writing to you. The dogs have sensed that a trip is about to happen. All four, even old Flash, are pacing around the house, whimpering in anticipation. Their anxiety reminds me of Kent.

As the year progressed, Kent became more playful and somewhat cooperative, often offering criticism or instructions to me about a better way to run the class.

"What a good idea," I would tell him. "I'm so glad that I have you here to keep me organized. He either chuckled brightly or looked at me blankly, depending on whether he thought I was making fun of him or not.

As we approached the last few weeks of school and the end of his time with us, I tried to get him to come to a final meeting with Paul, his father, Brooke and myself. He refused. I threatened him with holding back his final official transcript, which lists the classes and grades he had earned, until we had the meeting.

"Look, all I'm going to do is say nice things about

you. I refuse to let you leave here without listening to them."

He would not come to the meeting and he became increasingly agitated about his transcript. After he had furtively searched my desk and the classroom for the transcript, he gave up and confronted me. "If I'm going to get the classes I want in public high school, I've got to get my transcript. You're going to fuck up my last year by holding out on me."

He was right. I offered him a bargain which was less threatening. "If you sit here after school in the classroom for about 10 minutes and listen to what Brooke and I have to say to you, we'll call it even. Is that a deal?"

He grudgingly agreed. He climbed into the pillow cubbyhole between the flowered couch and the bookcase, covered himself with pillows and grabbed a book to hide his face. Thus armed, he thumbed disinterestedly through a photo book of World War II battles, then without lifting his eyes from the pages he announced, "OK, go ahead, but make this short. I'm not putting up with much of this."

I told him he'd done well this year. "We promised you that if you came to school and did your work, including math, we would ask your father to send you back to public school. I know it took enormous patience for you to come to this place every day. I would have liked it better if you had taken on harder work because you are very intelligent, but you did the work that the other kids did and your grades were good. You even let me teach you a thing or two and I know how much you hate to have the teacher work with you."

"I want you to know Kent that I am really going to miss you." Oh dear. I'm getting teary. I do feel awful about losing him. I really don't think he's ready for public school. He just noticed that I'm sounding a little emotional. He glanced up at me, checking me out with his big brown eyes. Now he's buried his face in the book

159

again.

"I'll miss that angelic face down at the end of the room (sniffle), looking so innocent while he mimics me as I nag at the class. He makes me watch him constantly to see what he's up to (wipe a tear away) and he usually gets away with it. Who's going to sneak a tape recorder into my classroom to get evidence against me? Who's going to search my desk, hunting for answer books and stealing his papers so he can destroy them? Who's going to disconnect the electrical system in the trailer to keep me from turning on the fluorescent lights you hate so much? Just think how boring it will be without you!"

Brooke joined in. "We hope you'll come back and visit us, Kent. We know you've told us that you wouldn't be caught dead back here, but we hope you will stay in touch. It's going to be tough over there at public school. Keep us in mind if we can help."

"That's it, Kent. We've finished. If you come with me, I'll get your transcript." He burst out of his cubbyhole with an explosion of pillows and dashed out the door. I took him to the teachers' lounge where I had hidden his transcript in my mailbox since I couldn't keep it in my classroom. I gave it to him and cut a hunk out of a teacher's chocolate birthday cake and gave that to him as well. Otherwise, he'd have sneaked back in and gotten some anyway. He was always so hungry for such a little fellow.

I'll have to complete this later. I've got to finish packing and get some sleep. We're getting up at five in the morning to leave for Idaho.

Boise National Forest, Idaho

I have just lit a rather pathetic campfire, with only one match! However, since the wood is mostly bark, the

160

fire will be reduced to ashes in no time. We are camped on a gravel bar by the Middle Fork of the Boise River. I shall gamble that my husband will return from his trout fishing before the fire expires and he can save the day. Otherwise I will be writing to you by candlelight.

Right now we are camped outside of Atlanta, a small town at the end of 70 miles of dirt road resting with its back up against the Sawtooth Wilderness Area. Atlanta is a gem among old mining towns. Containing 50 souls and 4 bars, the citizens only enjoy electrical power from 9 to 12 in the morning and 6 to 11 at night. If one wants such luxuries as gasoline and air for tires, forethought is required since pumps do not work without electricity. The third saloon we investigated also contained a small market. Since it was three in the afternoon, non-electrical hours, it was a small, *dark* market. We have been out in the boonies for nearly two weeks and to us that murky room took on the proportions of a big city supermarket. It was a bonanza! We peered through the gloom and found treasures like cookies! And potato chips! What bliss! There were even canned cocktails of bourbon and coke, another example of the priorities of American ingenuity and wilderness wherewithal.

Ah! Here comes the husband now. Yes, we have trout tonight. This makes four days in a row. Zane can be a real provider and pathfinder when he wants to be. I didn't even have to ask and he's getting out the axe and lopping off hunks of wood from a log washed up on the bar. It is turning out to be a sweet-smelling cedar. I think I'll go get a canned bourbon and coke.

We've finished our fresh trout for dinner and it
has gotten quite dark. The dogs have all just voluntarily
climbed into the bus. They do not like dark woods,
campfires and hard, cold gravel to lie on. They like soft
upholstery in VW buses. Maybe they have a point. I
think I'll join them. I can use the overhead light to finish
writing. I'm determined to finish Kent's story tonight.

As soon as Brooke and I told Kent we were going
to miss him, he became impossible. After a few days of his
sour disposition, I confronted him. It was my usual 'so-
how-are-you-going-to-end-your-time-with-us' talk. I told
him that I was sure that being mean and uncooperative
would make it easier for him to leave us. If he could get us
mad at him it would be less painful to say goodbye. Then
I asked him if he really wanted to end like this. He
scowled at me and said he didn't know what I was talking
about.

A few hours later I found the lyrics to a song,
"Prisoner" by Iron Maiden, lying on my desk. It was
written very tidily with my calligraphy pen which he'd
taken from my desk.

The lyrics told of how the prisoner was breaking
free of his bonds. It mentioned spitting in his keeper's eye,
and even exacting vengeance and death if the keeper tried
to hold onto him. The prisoner is free to run, fight and
breathe; to do whatever he wants. Nobody had better get
in his way.

Well I certainly wouldn't have too much trouble
understanding the message intended here. At least, he
succeeded in expressing his anger to me before he left. I
viewed it as a kind of present. I looked over at him sitting
at his desk.

I asked him out to my office on the trailer steps.

162

We went through the usual seating ritual. He stood. I pestered him until he sat down one step above me. Craning my neck to look over my shoulder at him I began, "I think that when you wrote these lyrics out for me you were telling me how you feel. It tells me what you would like to say, but can't."

He frowned at me, poised, ready for flight if I went too far.

"This song tells me a lot about how much you want to escape this place. I'm glad you shared it with me. I didn't understand how very angry you are and how much you had to overcome to force yourself to go to school every day. Thanks for letting me know how you've been feeling."

No response. Silence. Then, "All right. Fine." and he escaped down the steps and out of my clutches.

Thursday was to be my last day to see Kent. He basically ignored me the whole day. At the end of the day I went out to the adolescent hangout. There were about four kids standing around and Kent was sitting on his bike.

Feeling out of place on their turf, I sort of lamely hung around on the periphery, not wanting to get too close. I was ignored by all. Finally, I edged closer to Kent and said, "You've been giving me the cold shoulder all day."

He beamed at me, gratified that I had noticed and said, "What do you mean?"

"Well you and I haven't been able to be pleasant to each other at all today, and this is your last day."

He looked away. I thought he would not answer me. Then he said, "What were the first words that you spoke to me today?" The other teenagers noticed this exchange and began to pay attention.

Good grief, a test no less. Damned if I could remember. Then it dawned on me. My first words were mostly a screech. I believe they were, "Damn it Kent! Don't you dare!" as he rammed his bicycle into the front of my VW bus, his tire bouncing off my brand new metallic powder blue paint job.

I dutifully repeated them to Kent. He mimicked my screech and we all laughed.

"Well what did you expect, Kent. What else would I say? You set that one up."

Kent lost interest in me and began staring off into the distance. This was not the most auspicious place to try for resolution, surrounded by his peers, but I was running out of time. In a valiant attempt to make Kent's last day end on an upbeat note, I persevered. "Well, I sure wish we could finish your last day more positively, but if this is the way you want it..." I didn't complete the sentence. I just let it dangle as he continued to ignore me. I left.

I returned to my room and discovered that he had torn up any pictures I had of him as well as his file which contained his objectives and tests for the year. He had cleared out all traces of his presence. Even at the very end, he still deprived me of himself. He left me nothing to remember him by. Well, I still win. I have these letters to remember him.

There. I've finished Kent's story at last. Are you feeling closure? No I thought not. What will become of him?

What did I gain from my time with Kent? He taught me a lot about the small child waiting inside these sullen adolescents. He may have smiled at me a dozen times...quick, secret, glimpses of his brightness. Then of course, there were the lovingly colored pictures, especially the prize-winning teddy bear, the rage of a set of lyrics, and the destruction of my papers and mementos. And that's it. All I have left are a few glimmers of a child who was happiest with teddy bear.

That's why it's so important for me to be kissed

by 600 lb. Clyde and to have my time in Idaho with Zane and my dogs. I need my holidays, desperately!

Carolyn

September, 1986

Chapter Ten

Roles, Rage and Dawson

Dear Rey,

  I can't tell you how awful the thought of going back to work is. It is Labor Day weekend, the last few moments of summer freedom before the grind starts again. I have been dragging myself to Mountainview for the past few days, trying to get my classroom in some semblance of order. I am never ready. I should be down there today, but I refuse. Teaching is the sort of job that can expand into every waking moment. I must set some limits or the job will engulf me.

  On top of it all, Paul has sent out a set of rules to the staff. Well, I think it's for the whole staff. It may be just for me. I returned from hiking through green mossy woods and swimming in cold velvety rivers to find a packet of regulations awaiting me. Most concerning among the new rules are that my field trips are to be severely curtailed, and my supervision will no longer be focused on the students' psychological issues, but on my academic accountability. This, from a school which prided itself on being rule-free and experimental. As I read them, I could feel the harness settling over my shoulders, my keepers brusquely tugging and pulling at any straps that might be too loose, tightening until I could feel them chafing my skin. I have been betrayed. In the name of economic need and professional appearance, my

167

employer is hitching me to a plow. Where I had been promised I could run free, I am now a plow horse.

Tell me, why should I continue to work here? I stayed because I believed in our benevolent dictator, in the support of my colleagues, and the freedom to explore. After 15 years I am still earning the equivalence of a first year teacher's wages in the public school system with no pension and limited medical benefits. I have no savings. I spend the totality of each month's wages on bills and expenses. The roof on my house still leaks and the carpet at the front door has a huge hole from 30 years' wear and tear. If now, I must behave like those poor bureaucratically hounded public school teachers without any of the union benefits they have, why stay?

Anyway, we have a new teacher. I was asked to advise her and explain how I work with these kids. Confusing, don't you think? Evidently I must be reined in, yet I was asked to counsel a new teacher. I was amazed at how much I had to tell her. I didn't realize I had learned so much, yet I still feel so ignorant.

One of the subjects that kept resurfacing was how to cope with anger and hostility. Since you are one of the few people who really appreciate hatred, I wrote some of my anger stories up for you.

One of the most difficult aspects of the teaching profession is taking on its role and expectations. When I was a youth at the university, I decided that I preferred the action of working with kids, rather than being a cartographer. Working with pen and ink was an art heading fast for oblivion as computer technology developed. I especially wanted to work with the kids who had trouble learning. Like the aforementioned therapists who wanted to love their clients to health, I too, thought that caring and good intentions could make a difference in children's lives.

However, my student teaching soon taught me

that being a teacher was much like becoming a company man, public relations being vitally important. I had to be careful of my appearance. My room must always look shipshape. My bulletin boards had to be creative, reflecting my student's proud accomplishments. My lesson plans (regardless of how useless they were) had to be ready a week ahead of time. My students should all be well under control at my quiet, firm, disciplined hand. My students' test scores should prove my accountability.

Being a person who can juggle many demands, I persisted with missionary zeal for the salvation of the uneducated, but soon came the unhappy realization that my students didn't want to cooperate with my good intentions. In fact, they often preferred to view me as the enemy. My role as a teacher had put me in the front line trenches, students taking pot shots at me from the front, while bureaucracy with the heavy armament was lobbing cannonballs into my bunker from the rear.

Another obstacle I had to grasp in order to teach special ed was just how incredibly ignorant my students are. A _very_ common mistake is to assume they have managed to acquire basic information. I was continually shocked when I discovered that I was teaching over their heads. They may not know the simplest things which we are certain they must know. For example, teenagers may not know the cardinal directions. They don't know the difference between a continent and a country. Europe and Asia could appear anywhere on the globe. They may not be able to tell you the months of the year in sequence. They might not even be able to tell time without a digital clock. The Revolutionary War, World War I or II cannot be used as temporal anchoring points. Columbus discovered America in 1869. They can calculate a simple arithmetic problem set up for them on a worksheet, but give them a real life problem such as, "Pearl Harbor was attacked in 1941. How long ago was that?", and they do not know how to set up the problem for solution. They cannot choose when to add, subtract, multiply or divide. They cannot spell the days of the week or basic numerals. They cannot memorize. They cannot concentrate. They cannot read at grade level. They hate learning. They have given up.

Why? There are hard-working, dedicated teachers out there, people who became teachers to help them.

When these students are asked to take on learning, they are being asked much more than we realize. Of course there are biological or developmental reasons that explain why some students have problems learning, but there are also emotional ones. These children have not achieved the capacity to focus and attend to anything other than their own immediate needs. All of their energies are wrapped up in a continuous search to allay anxiety, depression, insanity or rage. Dawson, whose role in life is to victimize others, watches hawk-like for someone to injure, then vents his rage upon the hapless teacher for stopping him. Kingsley, dissolving into anonymous oblivion, seizes any opportunity to turn oppositional. Sissy, sits busily orienting the world to its proper focus, herself. "Why should I have to learn anything about something that happened hundreds of years ago? It has nothing to do with me. Can we pop popcorn? I'm starving. My stomach hurts."

So a teacher of these kinds of adolescents who attempts to really teach, that is, to help them learn how to memorize, to concentrate, to master an area of knowledge, is venturing out into a no-man's land that is terrifying to the student and unmapped for the teacher. Students will be threatened by demands which take their attention away from their search for tension reduction. Eel-like their thoughts slide past the memorization of the multiplication tables to return to the depressing dark holes of their worries and anxieties. They fidget, they play, they seek stimulation. Anything is better than being in touch with those bad feelings.

An interesting change occurs when there is a shift from working with the whole class, to working one-on-one. Then the student is usually eager to learn, even willing to concentrate. They try their best. What makes the difference? Simply that teacher is right there next to them. Hopefully, they are safe in the shelter of the surrogate mother. Their worries are set aside. Their minds can be put to learning, for mom's sake.

Experiments have been done where mothers take their toddlers into a strange room full of toys.[4] Those children who feel safely connected with their mothers are able to wander and explore away from mother's knee. Anxious children, who cannot count on a consistent maternal response, do not wander far or explore much. When I ask my students to explore and concentrate on external data, I am asking them to leave their mother's knee, to venture out into the unknown, and to begin the first step towards growing up.

As I sit here in the peace and quiet of my home with Elizabethan lute music murmuring in the background, I find myself having trouble thinking about anger in the classroom. From this safe vantage point as I recall those moments of lost self-control when a student produced an angry outburst, it was because I did not really see or understand the student.

On the other hand, when I have had the outburst it was for the same reason, my not being offered the proper deference due a teacher by her student. Remembering those times when I have been driven to fury, it was as if I was trying to penetrate some complacent wall that was

---

[4] Ainsworth, M. D. S., Blehar, M. C., Waters, E., & Wall, S. (1978). Patterns of attachment: A psychological study of the strange situation, Hillsdale, N.J.: Erlbaum.

railroading my own identity into obscurity. In one of my letters I wrote to you about Kingsley, when he had pushed me to the point of rage. My anger with him was a statement of assertion. It had a coalescing impact. It was strengthening. It allowed me to overcome my fear.

My students savor their anger; it is so much better than the fear they feel. They tenaciously hold on to it because it validates their existence and arms them with the reality of their egocentrism. Watching an adolescent poised on a cliff's edge of violent self-indulgence, I want to reach out, give him a poke and watch him topple over and fall into a tantrum. Instead of the eternal strain of having to accommodate to his tyrannically infantile stance, I could finally be rid of him forever by causing him to act out. Let me give you an example of what it is like to teach Dawson anything.

Dawson resists any kind of production and uses this resistance to embattle the authority figures around him. I interpret this as the infant's squalling demand to stay little. Like an infant in a playpen, he wants to be catered to; he wants to have his way. He is not ready to grow up.

When Dawson gets a break or a lunchtime interruption, he never manages to get back on time. He regards the notion as foolish, that he should be expected to use the restroom on his break time. Once in the classroom, he plops down on the couch where it is our job to get him moved over to his desk. Then we must find the materials for him which he has lost since yesterday, or provide him with new ones. Finally, after a great amount of harassment from Brooke or me, some illegible scrawls are purged out of his reluctant mind and body that have a bare nodding relationship with 'learning'. I feel just like a mother whose infant son will not produce on the pot. He is determined to mess in his diapers and make mommy do all the work of waiting on him...and naturally, I feel rage.

If we can accept the proposition that one of the major purposes of anger is to reduce fear by asserting one's identity, then the student will have less reason to act out if the teacher can let him know what he is feeling. When confronting a student, I _try_ to insert running commentary about his point of view as well as how he is feeling about me. I often describe his point of view as a conflict. First, I _try_ to remember to set forth the side of him that wants to be good, and then I portray the side of him that wants to be self-indulgent. To let him know that I understand how he is feeling lessens his need to hit me in order to make me see him. It also increases his capacity to hear what I am saying since he does not need to be quite so preoccupied with preparing his own defense. Finally, these kids are basically non-verbal, and they really are not equipped to express their conflict verbally.

It is much more difficult though, to get the student to understand a teacher's reality. They are poorly

equipped for emotional reciprocity. The teacher will never measure up to their expectations. These students are experts in making her feel like she has no value whatsoever. Everything she tries to teach is boring. She is inadequate because she cannot make them whole and happy. She always likes somebody else better. She is unreasonable and unfair.

If she is to survive in special education, she must come to terms with this definition of herself. She, like her students' parents, like the student himself, is inadequate. They force the teacher to fight the same battle they face, that they have no value. They are worthless trash which should be thrown away. They will test the teacher unmercifully to prove that this is true. And, Darwinishly speaking, if the teacher can't overcome this harsh test, she should get out of special ed.

To live with anger and hatred and survive, the teacher must recognize her role as the explainer. In the same sense that a mother must explain to an irritable child that he is cranky because he missed his afternoon nap, these students need the same care. They do not always understand the connection between the overwhelming emotions that make them feel as if they might blow apart, and their source.

All of my students participate in group therapy, and most have individual therapy. Since I am presently in a Master's program in Psychology and a requirement of that program is that I participate in group therapy with supervision, I help Julia out with one of her groups. This particular group includes Dawson and happily, Deborah, who is a particularly bright spot in a very dim group. She is mature, thoughtful and kind, and she is determined to make the most of her education and improve her life. She lives alone with her mother, who she basically takes care of. She came to us because she had suicidal episodes, but she appears to be beyond that now. I consider having her in my classroom to be a huge boon.

I had been working with Julia and her groups for a few years now, and so far they have all been very peaceful. Today would be different. There were about five kids in the group, and besides Dawson and Deborah, we also had Jeffrey, a pudgy, rich student from Diana's class. He was verbally sarcastic but mostly he played the role of an infantile victim.

In group, Dawson often tells us about how much he hates his father. He shares his dreams in which he fantasizes about slipping into his father's bedroom in the middle of the night and slitting his throat. As I told you before, one of the reasons for his rage is that father restricts his movements in everything while at the same time delivering the message that a real man is wild and reckless. Thus, hate-filled Dawson flings his body around on Dad's motorcycle, taking great risks and more often than not, injuring himself. This time he broke his left arm and came to school in a cast.

So Dawson carries a seething mass of hostility around with him and he brings it, pre-packaged, to our group counseling sessions. Jeffrey brings his predilection for being a victim. Dawson and Jeffrey are a perfect pair, two infants cooperating with each other in mutual injury and victimization, but up until today they had kept their physical encounters outside of group therapy.

We were all shocked, when out of the blue, Jeffrey offered up his body for trauma by stretching out on the floor and insulting Dawson. In spite of his cast, Dawson leaped up joyfully to play his part. Deborah, who was sitting next to Dawson, and knowing what kind of damage that cast could do to Jeffrey, reached out and grabbed Dawson's good arm.

Evidently, this was painful, because Dawson cried out. He turned around, doubled up his right fist and hit her with all his might in the middle of her back as she turned to avoid the blow. I jumped up and screamed at the top of my lungs for him to back off. He did. Deborah stared unbelievingly at him, her eyes filled with tears. I watched him become suffused with barely containable fury. He turned to the table behind his chair that was covered with craft supplies. He was looking for something, probably scissors, knowing his desire to attack his father with a knife.

"I know what you're looking for and you'd better not find it," I yelled.

He picked up a small broken plastic tube with a jagged edge and rubbed his finger over it, testing its sharpness.

"You'd better not try using that either," I demanded. What the hell I was going to do to stop him, I hadn't the faintest idea. It was a choice between putting my body between Dawson and Deborah, or my ability to yell loud and make quick grabs, not much of an arsenal for a kid as big as Dawson. Julia made a quick phone call to Nick to come and help us.

All of my orders, threats and demands made no impression on him. He stood there breathing heavily, irises shrunken to pin-points, staring right through me as though I didn't exist. I only had an effect when I told him I knew just how he was feeling.

"You're holding onto this anger, Dawson. You know damn good and well that Deborah did not mean to hurt you. She only wanted to keep you from hurting Jeffrey, our professional victim. Deborah is someone you are very fond of and has been a good friend to you. Yet you persist in choosing to believe that she purposefully hurt you. You are enjoying this rage and you have no intention of letting it go. You are holding onto it, relishing every moment of it."

"I'm certain this is how you feel when your father tries to control your life...when he tells you that you can't go to the beach, or a concert, or camping. I can see you sitting in your room feeling just like this, thinking of all the horrible things you'd like to do to him."

"You want to stay angry so that you can do to someone else what you want to do to him. You would love to go out of control, to go berserk. You'd love to kick and hit Deborah, but in your mind, you would be attacking your father.

He continued to stand there waiting for Deborah to give him the slightest excuse to hurt her. Now, however, his eyes were rimmed with tears and his focus seemed to have shifted very slightly from Deborah to something inside himself. I stopped talking and eventually he sat down.

Again, who knows if I was right, but evidently something I said explained his anger to him and allowed him to calm down.

More important than explaining the student to himself is the relief that an explanation provides for the teacher. If, for example, Dawson has done something particularly horrible to one of the weaker students on campus, my first reaction is to feel disgust with him. I may find unconscious ways to strike back at him.

Instead of acting out my own self-indulgent anger, I must realize anew that Dawson is not an equal who I face in the dusty streets for a shoot-out at high noon, but a tinhorn kid, quick on the draw perhaps, but one in need of understanding, rather than a duel to the death. So, I must try to grasp what makes him be mean to others. When I think I understand, I will not find him disgusting any longer, something to be crushed and eliminated, but another vulnerable person. To provide him with an explanation for his behavior is to tell him that he does not overwhelm me and that I can contain even the ugliest side of him. To provide myself with an explanation is to give me the space and patience to keep working with him and his hideousness. Let me give you an example of this.

During a single lunch period Dawson and Nat managed to be hurtful to two students on campus who are both a little retarded and a little crazy as well. Timmy, a 13 year-old boy going on five, had gone out to the adolescents' hangout to share his treasure with his heroes. He had achieved 100% on a math paper that a slow-witted first grader would consider child's play. In spite of his simpleton grin which he wears perpetually to force a reflexive smile from everyone he encounters, Timmy's pride and joy was yanked out of his hands and burned to ash.

After that, the co-conspirators enticed our grandmotherly play therapist out of her session with 15 year-old Joyce, who lives in her own reality and regularly shouts her love for Dawson across the campus. Nat, the con artist of the two, kept the play therapist outside her room by telling her of his imaginary young cousin who needs to come to her for therapy. Meanwhile, Dawson climbed up on a chair outside of a window in the play therapy room and exposed his butt to Joyce. She fled from the room.

Kingsley came and told me what had happened to Timmy and Joyce, but refused to name the culprits. By careful sleuthing, Brooke and I acted as if we knew more about what happened than we actually did and were able to piece together who did what. Naturally, Dawson had been the primary villain in both these acts.

After being grilled and interrogated by Paul for these pranks, I was privileged to have Dawson for detention after school. I tried to get him to finish some class assignments. Claiming a tummy ache, he was lying on the orange couch, an apparent sanctuary from schoolwork as far as he was concerned. He whined that he was too sick to get up and work. I started to re-engage in my eternal battle of getting Dawson to produce, then decided, what the hell, let's try the paradoxical approach.

"Well, since you are sick Dawson, I think you're right about lying on the couch. You shouldn't get up. Just rest and relax. In fact, I want you to lie there for your entire detention time. You're certainly in no shape to be doing work. Just stay where you are until your father comes to pick you up."

"No," he said, "as soon as I sit for a while I'll be able to get something done."

"Now Dawson, I want you to just stay where you are. I don't want you to do something you'll regret later. Just stretch out on the couch."

Raising his voice and enunciating each word carefully for his bone-headed teacher he said, "Listen, if

I'm well enough to go to the taco stand at lunch, walk all the way over there and all the way back (about half a block). Then I can certainly do a little work."

He had taken the words out of my mouth, but I didn't want to appear too eager. Grudgingly I said, "Well, I don't like it much, but if you're so determined..."

His mind-boggling willingness to work made me feel forgiving towards him, so we began to talk. He wanted to know why, in the heat of the moment when I had caught him, I had told him that he was cruel to females and the weak.

"Dawson, I know that you and Nat were only trying to get Timmy and Joyce to stop coming out to your hangout and bothering you, but I think you can find a better way to handle it than by being mean to them."

"So what am I supposed to do? Timmy comes out with this simple-shit paper and says, 'Duh, look at my paper! Will you sign it for me?' I suppose I should say, 'Nice work, son' and sign it, then pat him on the head, right?"

"I understand what you're saying Dawson. There's something about Timmy that makes people crazy. You're not alone in that feeling, you know." He certainly makes me crazy, I said to myself. I dread the day when he's put into my classroom. Day by day he moves relentlessly towards becoming my student with his imperviously simpering smile. Each demanding grin is like water torture, every plop battering my forehead.

Dawson interrupted my self-torture. "He comes out and exposes all his soft parts and I'm supposed to do something about it. He makes me sick!"

"You're right. There's something about Timmy that makes you feel as if you're going to have to take care of him. It's almost as if you're being manipulated in some way." (Notice that this is <u>exactly</u> what Dawson does to me, manipulate me into taking care of him.)

"Right!" he cried in relief. He sat up straight on the

couch and looked me in the eye. We were certainly having a meeting of the minds.

I continued, "Both Timmy and Joyce have that same quality. As for Joyce, you do understand that she can't always understand the difference between fantasy and reality?"

"What do you mean?"

"Well, sometimes she can't separate the way she wants things to be from the way things really are. So for example, we know that Joyce has been following you around and announcing to everyone that she loves you. When you performed your mooning exhibition, you thought it would scare her so much that she wouldn't bother you anymore."

"For Joyce however, my guess is that she had two reactions. One would be fear. We know she ran out of the room right afterwards, but the other reaction might be stimulation. That is, by showing your butt to Joyce, you declared that you are willing to share the most intimate parts of your body with her."

Dawson was shocked. For the first time in my experience with him, he turned red. He squirmed on the cushions of the couch. He writhed in embarrassment. I loved it! Once again my base desires for revenge had surfaced. I had no real clue what Joyce's reaction really was, but for a few delicious moments, I actually had him squirming. What a heavenly feeling. Power!

When Dawson expressed his disgust with Timmy for exposing his soft parts, I began to give myself an explanation for his reasons to injure and keep his distance from Timmy. I had a split-second image of Dawson as a small child who was still coming to terms with his own soft parts...his weaknesses, his ambivalence about growing up, and his own desire to have his head patted for doing a good job. Timmy and Joyce's adoration frightened him. To destroy them was to destroy his own weaknesses.

When I sensed these possible explanations for Dawson's miserable behavior, my anger drained away. While Dawson needed to understand why he behaved so cruelly, I probably needed it more. As soon as I thought I could understand his motives, I knew I could keep on working with him. And that, rather than the accuracy of my interpretations, was probably the most important thing I could do for him.

Because of our role expectations, such as 'good teachers don't feel hatred', we remain unaware of such feelings in ourselves. When it does surface, it overwhelms us, making us do things we will regret. One of the ways that hatred announces its presence is through our dreams.

Dawson and I had dreams of killing each other on the same night. These dreams occurred after I notified him that he would be losing credits this year due to poor attendance and production. He screamed at me that I was trying to keep him in this school for the rest of his life. I accepted his rage and did not react to it, letting him pour it all over me. Besides, I was enjoying myself. My wish for revenge had surfaced once again with this kid. To all appearances though, I was impervious to the ferocity of his attack. However, that night I dreamed that Dawson wanted to kill me.

It was late at night and I was in a dark cellar. I looked out of a small rectangular open window set high in the wall, but recessed just below the level of the lawn outside. I knew Dawson was outside trying to gain entry and that he had a knife. I was certain he was deadly serious. Still, it was not in me to kill him to protect myself, even though I too was armed with a knife. Suddenly, I saw his bare feet as he stepped down onto the open window sill ledge. To keep him from entering, I slashed at his ankles with my knife. I hoped those injuries would make him run away. He would not stop. He slid into the cellar oblivious of his bleeding ankles.

As we looked at each other there seemed to be no real malice between us, yet I knew that he would murder me. He lifted his knife to strike down at me. With amazing agility, unrealized in my waking life, I slipped to one side and inserted my knife, which had now become a stiletto, into his skull at an upward angle just above the spine. It slipped in and out of his brain quite easily. (An unfortunate image, I know.) He stopped his attack, turned to me and said, "Now that wasn't a nice thing to do." I nodded in mute agreement and he fell heavily against me. Then the two of us, him somewhat enfeebled but still able to walk, began to search for a hospital to make him well again.

For some reason, the next day I told him about my dream. He loved it. He made me repeat it to the rest of the class. Then he told us all about what he had dreamt the same night.

"Well I had this sawed-off twelve gauge shotgun and I was trying to kill someone, or some people. I'm not sure just who it was that I was trying to kill. They were standing right in front of me and I'd let go with both barrels." He took his imaginary shotgun and aimed it straight at me. He cocked the shotgun and like a small child, and he made convincing explosive noises to accompany his story.

"The shot would head straight for them and just as it got to them it would separate and go around on both sides of their bodies. I kept shooting and shooting but I couldn't ever hit them."

The image in his dream reflected how I had felt the day before when he had been showering me with abuse. I asked him if he thought perhaps I might have been one of the people he was trying to kill since I had given him such bad news the day before. His eyes widened in recognition of some internal image and he said, "Yeah! Maybe it was you!"

These dreams give ample credence to the notion that rage is part of the classroom experience. To try to deny it is to have it get out of control. We know students feel anger towards their teachers, but we also need to be aware that hatred has a palpable existence in the heart of every teacher and she needs to understand that side of her own personality in order to be equipped to handle it.

And so, to summarize...one of the most powerful sources of hatred in the classroom comes out of a teacher's own role expectations. As a teacher we are supposed to get our students to be obedient and to produce. When they refuse, this threatens our sense of competence and even our ability to earn a living. This causes us to resort to extremes. We become frightened at our loss of control. We look for panaceas, for recipes to handle very idiosyncratic people. Rules and reinforcement schedules are set up. We harden up in our dichotomous thinking. Situations are right or wrong, or black and white. The teacher and the student are not able to interact with each other as individuals, but as opponents in the battle for the student's submission to the role expectations of the teacher and her employers.

If a special ed. adolescent is going to learn from me, we must discover the mutuality of our roles with each other. He must teach me his answers. We must face our hatred and affection for each other. We must laugh at ourselves and enjoy each other. Perhaps, having been consistently perceived as a unique individual of value rather than an object to program with bits of data, the student can begin to feel consolidated enough to venture away from his classroom mother's knee to explore the world, hopefully more confident in his capacity to cope with the unknown.

Well, I have spent most of my last day of freedom writing to you. How can I make it through another year? I can't do it! There has to be an easier way to earn a living...perhaps being a therapist. The lure of only spending just one hour with only one adolescent basket case at a time is very powerful. You tell me I could be a good therapist. I'm already in a masters' program. It's the end of summer and I don't want to go back into that primeval pool filled with Pliocene sharks. My hide is too tender! Furthermore, I'm no longer sure if the sharks are my students or my employer. I do miss my old playful Paul.

Carolyn

October, 1986

Chapter Eleven

Night Visitor

Dear Rey,

This pen won't work. I have lost my favorite calligraphy pen, a bright red one. I have a new one and it scratches and skips. It pulls at the surface of these official

forms like fingernails on a blackboard. My frustration mounts as I drag my wretched pen across yet another special ed form. My year's goals and objectives for each student are dreadfully overdue. Each school district requires them for every student they've enrolled in our school. I am in trouble once again. I have received an ultimatum from Paul. I am terrible at writing these things. I write them out and forget about them until it is time to declare whether or not I've met the goals. Then I get really creative. I am the last one in the school to get them done.

Each new objective I write is more mind-numbing than the last. Since this is Charlie's set of goals and objectives, and depression and suicide are his major issues, I am daring to objectify his emotional problems. Goals and objectives are written mostly to make sure the student is making academic gains. Emotional goals are rarely written. They are too hard to quantify, even though they are central to the student's problems.

> <u>Annual Goal:</u> To reduce depression and increase appropriate assertive behavior.

> <u>Objective:</u> Given a conflict situation or a classroom discussion where Charlie has strong feelings, he will directly communicate his opinions to the parties involved in an appropriate manner 50% of the time.

Presently, when his feelings are hurt, Charlie runs and hides behind my trailer or under my desk to sulk, especially when he has had a fight with his grandmother. On the other hand when I set limits in class and he thinks I'm being unfair, he blasts me out of my chair screaming that I'm being too heavy-handed and unjust. This goal, a pathetic effort to quantify a complex psychological problem so I can be held accountable is nonsense of course, but it's the best educational jargon I can come up with. The bureaucrats will scoff at it and turn instead to his problems with mathematics, but at least I have something down on paper.

Nope, what I have to do with Charlie is a lot more complicated than these simpleminded objectives. He will have to teach me about himself by dragging me into his misery. I will have to grow fond of him in spite of his dreary disagreeableness. I will have to limit him, say no to him, and fight with him. We will have to laugh. We will have to play. We will grow together and at the end he might even become a bit parental towards me as he gains enough confidence to see my frailties and accept them.

I have grave doubts that I can do any of this with Charlie. He is very secretive about his feelings. Any time I try to engage with him, he shoves me away. He has closed up tight like a little armadillo and no one seems to be able to pry him open.

He brags about his prowess and experience and tries to convince the other students about how cool he is. He wears heavy black boots, chains, and his hair is cut in the latest punk style. The class gives him the benefit of the doubt and allows him whatever coloration he chooses to wear, probably because they recognize the brittleness beneath the veneer. I just don't know what to do with this kid who is so dependent on his grandmother for any sense of well-being, yet tries to act like a hard core delinquent.

It is dark outside. The neighborhood, no longer safe, promises rape or injury. My trailer is lit up like a goldfish bowl set separately from the protection of the main building. I am a sitting duck out here. Worry nudges me as my mind wrestles feebly for another way to objectify what I am going to do for miserable Charlie. Oh, how I hate the people who make me write this stuff to allegedly measure Charlie's and my performance.

Tap, tap, tap on the window in the door behind me.

I am gripped by momentary terror.

I turn and grapple with the male mustached face grinning at me through the window and my brain instantaneously computes facial templates in a hopeful search for friend, not foe.

Brett! Delight pours through me. My six foot, 23 year-old! One of my most favorite students has come to visit me. God, what a treat he was! It all rushes in on me again as I look at his healthy beaming face.

He has a little four year-old cutie pie with him, a little girl named Jennie who is the daughter of his 34 year-old girlfriend. She clearly adores her new 'daddy'. He and

Jennie sit down on the couch across from my desk. The sky-blue shirt he is wearing matches his eyes perfectly. He looks as if he's just come from the beach. While we talk, Jennie crawls in his lap, tugging at him, trying to distract him from me, the interloper. In spite of Jennie, he still favors me with that old attentive, responsive look. This lad was always able to see right through me and he was quicker and more intuitive than I was. He was mature way beyond his years.

Once when I took the class out for a treat, we all went to see 'Star Wars', the second episode. I sat next to Brett, and throughout the film, he would lean over and tell me which literary allusion had just appeared in the film. When the hero climbed into the belly of a beast of transport during a blizzard, Brett whispered "To Build a Fire". When C3PO was disassembled and one of the characters picked up his head and contemplated it, Brett leaned over and said, "Alas poor Yorick, I knew him well." But worst of all, when I shared these comments with my colleagues, they didn't know what Brett was talking about. In many ways Brett was more of a colleague to me than my own peers were.

We talked for about half an hour and he brought me up to date about his life. He no longer hates his parents. He even likes them now. He has a job and is leading a productive life. Of course, he still has this unfortunate tendency to become attached to women who are 10 to 15 years older than he is.

Brett grows restless trying to keep both Jennie and myself entertained. We have run out of news. I know he will leave soon, so to show him that he is still remembered, I point to the wall above my desk where his photographs reside amidst my collections of students who have moved on. Then I point to his sports awards that are hanging on the wall at the other end of the trailer. Brett jumps up and tows Jennie down to his prizes.

"See these?" He points them out to her. "Brett

won these for being the very best student in the class…in the whole school. I used to go to school here. This was my classroom. Carolyn was my teacher. She was my mentor. She saved my life."

He comes back and hugs me goodbye, walks to the door, then returns and hugs me again. "I miss you so much. I'll come visit again soon." Right, I think, don't hold your breath for that one. I'd estimate the next appearance will be in two or three years if he doesn't get distracted.[5]

He takes little Jennie's hand. She and I look adoringly at him. He helps her toddle down the stairs and they walk off hand in hand into the darkness. I lock the rickety trailer door again and turn back to the meaninglessness of overdue objectives, each one emptier than the last.

> Annual Goal: To increase Charlie's mathematics grade level by one year.
>
> Objective: Given daily assignment sheets in identified areas of need (fractions, decimals, percent) Charlie will demonstrate that he can perform the four basic operations on them (add, subtract, multiply and divide). He will accomplish these tasks on schedule with an accuracy level of 80% or better.

I stop and look up at the pictures of Brett hanging on the wall over my desk. Most of these pictures are of the camping trips Brooke and I have taken with the class over the years. There is Brett and Brooke sitting on a

---

[5] The next time I spoke to Brett was on the phone 20 years later. He continues to be on good terms with his parents, he owns his own small business and he has put Jennie through college. She is attending grad school.

boulder in the mountains laughing down at me as I try to catch up with them. Brett with his truck stuck in the sand out in the Mojave Desert and finally, Brett receiving his diploma from Paul. It wasn't goals and objectives that saved Brett's life; in fact, they didn't help in the least. What helped Brett was demanding and taxing emotional involvement on Brooke's and my part.

I pick up my ink pen and scratch in the final objective for the night. I don't care if I do get into trouble. I'm going home.

> Annual Goal: To reduce Carolyn's gagging by 50% below present levels every time she has to fill out one of these damned special ed forms.

> Objective: Given another batch of worthless paperwork demanded by a constipated, behavioristic, paternalistic bureaucracy, she will remember Brett and repeat to herself, 'Any amount of crap they give me is worth it. Brett was definitely worth it.'

Goodnight,

Carolyn

November, 1986

Chapter Twelve

Boundaries and a Barbecue

Dear Rey,

I am presently sitting cross-legged on my bed with a new typewriter in front of me. It is Thanksgiving vacation and I can take some time to write to you. I've indulged in spending a huge cut of my pathetic salary to rent a lovely little electric typewriter. She's virgin white with a 20 character memory for self-corrections; the best I can afford. She invites me to come and play and to see if I can really become a writer, like you seem to think. The packet of rules I received last September forbids my staying late at the school and using school equipment, so I had no other choice but to go out and rent my own.

This is my favorite place to write. I can spread dictionary, scissors and stapler all around me except when the animals want to join me. Tom, my big gray cat has assumed possession on top of the pillow behind my back. Two of my four dogs, have just mooched their way up onto the bed. Hoss has his head under my left arm. Flash has his back up to the typewriter and is insistently claiming more and more space, each time pushing the keyboard closer so that we are a tightly packed companionable group.

When I go through the week, wrestling with whatever my charges present to me, I often wonder what you would think about how I am handling a situation, and how you would interpret what a student is trying to tell me. I would relish your words of advice and comfort for the harried and stumbling moments when I am at a loss, and running on blind instinct. This letter is definitely about one of those times when I could have used your help.

Organization has been on my mind a lot lately. By organization I mean having a life which is structured with definite limits and rules. I went to see the play 'Mary Barnes' by David Edgar at a small theater. It is the story of an experiment in which R.D. Laing and his colleagues lived on the same premises with their schizophrenic patients. The main character, Mary, is a nurse who has waited tenaciously to move in so that she can finally have her nervous breakdown. I loved the play. It was a more naked and excretory version of what I face at work. I left feeling comforted that my more well-developed borderline adolescents were a cinch compared to living with schizophrenics.

At one point in the drama, the four professionals who were living in the same household with their patients began to argue heatedly over Mary's disintegrating effect upon everyone in the house. One therapist wanted limits set and rules established. He could not stand the disorganization and chaos any longer.

I understood his distress very well. I recognized his need to have a few unguarded moments of peace that the therapist believed structure would produce.

Years ago, I had a student, Phillip, a fair-haired kindly young man, who was having a psychotic break in my classroom. For Phillip, each day was a dizzying blast of stimuli which could not be sorted, organized or managed. My aide at that time became very angry because I could not make him contain himself and because the school administration would not encourage his parents to send him to a hospital. I had to organize Phillip's every moment. If I left the room at all, he became increasingly unstable.

Everyone felt threatened by his psychosis. When Phillip left the classroom to go to individual therapy with Julia, I had to give pep talks to the class to reassure them that Phillip's condition was not catching. Privately, I was not so sure of this because it did seem to put the less stable ones at risk. In fact, one of my girls told me she was just as crazy as Phillip, only I didn't have the sense to see it. Furthermore, she too, should be having the privileges of my personal time, point systems and rewards of baby food that Phillip was receiving. Like Mary Barnes she wanted to have her regression and enjoy the maternal care that went with it.

Phillip, I noticed, had his own set of rules which provided him with comfort. Silver dollars were his protective charm, as powerful as a crucifix. They were carried around to ward off attacks by the Devil and Hitler.

One day, Phillip disappeared from campus. We were all in an uproar, wondering what had become of him. He showed up about an hour later with two silver dollars which he presented to me. Since my presence was critical for his safety, he had walked across the street to a bank to purchase them for me. He wanted to be certain that I would be protected from evil.

Last week, a much improved Phillip came back to visit me and he checked to see if I was still carrying my charms. I had to confess that one of them had fallen out of my wallet, but to this day, I still carry the other one.

Rules, order, goals, objectives, organization, and of course, charms – they all yield the illusion of safety, whether psychotic or sane. And of course, a more professional school is what Paul is trying to achieve. I am afraid our experimental days are over. Like R.D. Laing's colleagues, he now wants structure, order and rules.

As I sit here with my aching back and cramped legs crossed in front of the typewriter and let my thoughts wander on, my students' monstrousness disturbs me. I have to admit that I feel some sympathy towards Paul who is trying to create a more orderly school. There are times when I too, need to set limits.

One of the younger students I have been working with in play therapy surprised me last week. Little Travis, with his undersized 10 year-old body looked up at me at the end of our session, fixed his serious brown eyes on mine and firmly told me that once he had done something so bad that if I knew about it, I would be changed. I would turn into something different.

While I doubt that Travis' secret would change me into a different person, I am certain that some of my students do have that potential, unless I hang onto my limits, my boundaries, and my magical charms.

These kids can take you on horrible journeys. They will ferret out your vulnerabilities, raise up ghastly images of yourself, threaten your sense of competence and expose you for what you are. To live with disturbed adolescents and to be able to love them is to take a harrowing pilgrimage to come to know yourself, and to have your nose rubbed in what you find.

Now I want to tell you about the bad trip two of my males took me on the last day before Thanksgiving vacation. They showed me their worst...vile, obscene, sexist cruelty towards a new female classmate who threatened their fragile sense of masculinity. I'm afraid I acted like some of the therapists in the play 'Mary Barnes'. I had to set limits to protect myself, and I wanted to abandon them for good.

This year my class is especially difficult to take out of the classroom. In spite of the fact that I am now limited to only one field trip a month, I try to use field trips to widen their miniscule view of the world. For example, when I could use field trips freely, I might take them to a steel foundry where they could see a blast furnace in action, a huge dairy where they could attempt to milk a cow, or a newspaper where they could watch miles and miles of news roll down an assembly line. The purpose was to get their minds thinking beyond what they could magically pick off a shelf, never imagining what went into the process. I also took them bowling, sailing, swimming and camping. I would involve them in the process, asking them to make a choice, and to make the phone calls and the arrangements themselves. In fact, one student became so adept at this that when we went to a local water bottling plant, they thought she was the teacher and I was a parent tagging along.

Special ed students lose jobs not because of their academic weaknesses, but because they do not know how to work as a team, or how to interact with others constructively. Field trips advance this capacity far beyond anything I could teach in a classroom with pencil and paper.

I have to admit that Paul is right. Taking emotionally disturbed kids out into the world is risky, but it is important and so far no disasters have occurred, although there have been some close calls.

The last day of school before Thanksgiving I managed to get them to agree to go over to Sissy's apartment to cook lunch together. Sissy and her parents had mutually agreed that they couldn't live together any longer. They felt that it would be far preferable for Sissy to live with her older sister, than to have her spending anymore nights in public toilets down at the beach whenever she walked out on them. They financed an apartment so she could live with her sister who was attending a local community college. It was my plan to show my reluctant students that it might be nice to grow up and have an apartment of their own someday. I wanted them to see Sissy's semi-independence.

Oh yes, I should also tell you we have a new student, Gillian. She has been promoted from a younger class into ours. She has just returned from being hospitalized for violent behavior.

The day started off very well. We had arrived at Sissy's apartment and everyone was settled in and working on preparing their lunch. I left Brooke in charge while I drove Sissy and Dawson over to the market to buy some tortilla chips.

Sissy is a bright, diminutive bundle of needy enthusiasm. As soon as she jumped in the car, her hand darted to the radio to change the station to the romanticized visions of future love that protect her from present day fears at having been abandoned into adult life. As a favorite song came on, she chattered about how much she loved that particular musical star.

"I just love Michael Jackson. I'd love to have a baby with him," she cooed. "He's so cute. Those eyes. I just love those eyes! My Billy looks just like him. I want you to meet him. He's just like Michael Jackson."

Dawson, who you well know is my personal torturer, was sitting in back, dressed in a black t-shirt with an anti-social hard rock motto on the front. I looked in the rear view mirror and Dawson rolled his eyes heavenward and grimaced in distaste at Sissy's excessive display. He exhibited great patience with Sissy's music, limiting himself to the simple complaint, "I hate that disco crap."

"Why's that, Dawson?" I asked, peering at him in the rear view mirror

"You can't get it out of your brain. Once you hear it, it just keeps recycling over and over again. It's like it takes over. Do you like that stuff, Carolyn?" he asked incredulously. I have been Dawson's only ally in the class for the cause of heavy metal. He was a lonely lad, surrounded by punk and disco aficionados. That I should enjoy music from the enemy camp was a most distressing thought to him.

"I have to be honest with you Dawson. I like Michael Jackson, too."

"Well, you're not my teacher anymore then."

"I'm sorry if I've disappointed you, Dawson."

A disgruntled "Harrumph," came from the back seat.

We went to the market and made our purchases. On our way back to Sissy's apartment commentary was offered regarding my inadequacy as a driver, the cheap quality of the car I drive, and recommendations on the kind of car that any respectable person ought to have, especially if I expected to haul them around in public. They were feeling very good.

When we returned, parked and began to wind our way through the concrete and asphalt maze of garages behind Sissy's apartment complex, I complained that they were walking too fast. Immediately a contest began, each one bragging about how they were the fastest walker of all their friends. Both began strutting their hardest down the driveways between the garages. Little Sissy had to break stride to keep up with long-legged Dawson. I shouted out that Dawson was the winner and complained again that they were way too far out in front of me now.

"Wait for me!"

Not slowing down a bit, Sissy turned around and shouted back, "Come on, you old fogey!"

Dawson, in his endearing way, chimed in with, "Yeah, hurry up, you old fart!" and sneered playfully at me. They were both feeling very affectionate towards me, as you can plainly see. About half a block away, Sissy and Dawson turned a corner and disappeared from sight.

"Oh no!" I wailed. "Now I'm lost! Where did they go? I'll never find Sissy's apartment now. I'll be lost and wander helplessly in here for days, trying to find my way back to my car!"

Of course, there was only one place where they could be, in back of the garages, but I feigned distress, then shock and relief when they jumped out at me. They laughed delightedly at having gotten me once again.

When we finally reached the lawn in the front of this huge apartment complex, Sissy became a tour guide. "Now this sidewalk is the one that I take when I come home from the beauty college and it's dark. That sidewalk over there is the one I use when I come home from our school. "This," she said with pride, "is my mail box. Of course, it is the ordinary run-of-the-mill sort of mailbox. We did hope to have something more modern, but it does the job and we can live with it. And this," she said, pointing to the grassy lawn we were walking on, "is the shortcut that I take when I don't want to stay on the sidewalk. I'm supposed to stay on the sidewalk, but after all, I'm paying for the upkeep of the grass and if I want to walk on it I should be able to do so."

"I'm glad you're giving us such a complete tour. I don't want to miss one single little detail about your first apartment," I said.

When we entered Sissy's sparsely furnished apartment I discovered that four of her friends had shown up and were perched stiffly and self-consciously on one end of a couch. This was an unusual development for a field trip, but not one that I would normally have problems with. However, remember this is a very white portion of upper class conservative California, and three out of the four visitors were African-American and looking exceedingly miffed. Evidently, Billy, with the Michael Jackson eyes, and his friends had come for a visit.

I had been running films on American social issues and confronting these kids at length about their racist attitudes. Theoretically they were willing to go along with my inclusive notions, but here they were facing a situation most of them had never really dealt with before. Those who had escaped this alarming state of affairs were out in the patio gathered in a knot and ostensibly barbecuing. The braver ones were sitting around in the living room looking as if three minotaurs had just dropped by for a chat and a sacrifice. Things had become a bit taut. I tried to break the ice by talking to them, but the aliens looked at me as if I were talking gibberish, making it obvious to even someone as obtuse as myself that they preferred talking among themselves.

I headed for the kitchen that had a large rectangular opening over its counter so I could keep an eye on the living room while helping with the cooking. During one of the few moments when I had the luxury of jamming a few chips into my mouth, mostly out of nervousness at the racial paranoia accumulating in the living room, I noticed some cross words pass between Gillian and Dawson. When she offered him some chips covered with melted cheese, he responded with, "Well are you sure I'm not too sleazy and diseased to touch one of your chips?"

I asked Dawson what that was all about and he said, "She fell apart when I accidentally picked up her glass and drank out of it. She's afraid I'm filled with germs and I'll infect her with my diseases."

Gillian is a compulsively fastidious girl. She is also a tall, athletically built girl. Her dark brown hair is cropped close to her head and she is extremely tidy about her dress and appearance. She has been hospitalized on more than one occasion for becoming too paranoid and violent to function outside.

She is very bright and concerned with the correct way of doing things to the point where she had already become maddening even though she had only been in our class for one week. For example, my simple act of just getting ice out of the freezer produced a stream of criticism from her over whether I used too much water to refill an ice tray, the degree of wetness that leftover cubes should have when they were put back into the freezer, and the inadequacies of storing cubes in their tray rather than another container. My response was mild although my teeth were clinched in exasperation. "I can see, Gillian, that living with me and my way of doing things is going to be a great strain on you." I suppressed the rest of the sentence.

Gillian was not new to our school, only our classroom. She and Nat, my surfing conman, were old enemies from previous classrooms. I was praying that a resurgence of old grievances would not occur, another example of my foolhardy optimism.

Finally, after an eternity, everyone had eaten and we cleaned up. It was beginning to be time to get back to school and I was fearful that one of my bigots would say something stupid, even though they appeared too frightened to even open their mouths. I offered to take anyone back to school who had to make bus connections. My partner Brooke would follow with the rest. Naturally, that resulted in the most fearful clamoring to go. I was to take Kingsley, Gillian, Dawson and Nat in my VW bus. That left Brooke with Sonny, Charlie and the very pleasant Deborah and Randy.

I collected the four of them and we said our goodbyes. Things had finally loosened up enough so that there was even some good-natured banter going on across color lines. Kingsley, I noticed, was being his most sociable and friendly self as he said goodbye to the visitors, making sure that he knew everyone's name before he left. He was a bit too formal, but I was proud of him for approaching rather than avoiding them. He was doing a better job at befriending them than I had. Dawson and Nat rushed out the front door as fast as they could. Gillian tagged along with me.

Nat strode along in front of us, the sun shining on his sun-streaked hair and his tanned body. I am fond of him; he can display a lot of integrity, but he also has a mean mouth. In fact, one of the reasons he is with us rather than in public school is that he is a bit too frank with his opinions for most teachers. I knew that he did not like Gillian and I was worried about what he might say.

As we approached my VW bus, I felt some anxiety. Would one of these males have to argue over who wouldn't sit next to Gillian? They didn't. Good. We had just passed the 'fighting for shotgun' hurdle as far as who got to sit in the front seat and who had to sit in back with Gillian.

However, things quickly went from ok to worse to horrible. Kingsley had claimed the front passenger seat and no one complained, probably because he had provided the barbecue for the lunch. The remaining three sat on the bench in the back. As we drove out of the parking lot, Dawson and Nat began to needle Kingsley. They suggested that Gillian would like to sit in his lap.

I was going to drop Kingsley off at his house on the way back to school. I was supposed to be bringing back the barbecue, but it had been too hot to put into my bus, so Kingsley and his mom were going to retrieve it after it cooled off.

Kingsley only lived five minutes away. In those five minutes I was transported from a state of pleasant satisfaction on this last day of school before Thanksgiving vacation to one of murderous rage at Nat and Dawson. They had already begun their opening salvo.

Nat said, "Yeah, Gillian would like to sit on Kingsley's lap. She'd like to get her hands down Kingsley's pants."

By now we were out in traffic and they knew damned well that it would be impossible for me to control them and drive at the same time.

I happened to have two containers of liquids on the floor behind the back seats. One was rubbing alcohol and the other was WD 40, a lubricant. I was carrying them around in case I needed to clean the connections in my distributor which had been giving me trouble. As usual, my bus was leaking oil.

Dawson picked up the alcohol and pretended to drink some of it. Then he offered it to Kingsley, suggesting that perhaps he needed to get drunk if he was going to get it on with Gillian.

"You'll need some of this. You won't be able to do it unless you're drunk."

I shouted at them to stop. I was ignored. I tried to concentrate on negotiating traffic on crowded streets. I looked for a place to pull over.

Nat joined in. Picking up the WD 40, he said, "And here's some lubrication, for when she gets too dry."

"Shut up!" I yelled. Again, I was ignored.

Gillian, however, did not seem too upset. She condescendingly told them that they were acting like children and that she would never have any interest in any male in this class.

Nat, perhaps stung by the ineffectiveness of his last taunt, upped the ante and shouted, "Oh no! You and your lesbo friend, Maggie, would rather go off to the back of the trailers and get it on with two pop bottles. That's what gets you excited, pop bottles and your lesbo girlfriend."

Dawson offered the WD40 again. "And don't forget this. You'll need it for the pop bottles."

Nat added, "Yeah, and you'll need the alcohol to rub into all those sores you've got in your pussy. You won't want the infection to spread."

I had been trying to head this off with something, anything that would save Gillian from the injury they were inflicting upon her. They began to get even more graphically brutal.

I screamed, "Shut up! Shut up! Shut Up!" at the top of my lungs. I almost slammed on my brakes, but had the sense to check the traffic flow behind me. My driving became erratic as I searched for a place to stop the car, these obscenities. I managed to remember which street to turn into for Kingsley's house. They began to start up again. I have no recollection of what they said, but in a voice filled with threat, I told them not to say one more word. They began to joke about me to each other.

"Ho Ho! It looks like we got the teacher mad," Nat said in a self-satisfied tone. I glanced in the rear-view mirror and found him grinning at me. Did he actually think that I would respond to that seductive little boy grin after what he had just done?

I pulled to a halt in front of Kingsley's house. Kingsley got out and hovered about on his front lawn keeping an eye on what was happening in the bus. Gillian got up and crawled past the gear shift to the front seat. I turned the engine off. I craned my body around to look at Nat and Dawson.

"I have never been so disgusted with any students in my life as I am with you two right now! I have never heard such vicious cruelty to a member of my class before. I will not put up with this kind of obscene behavior!"

Dawson began to tell me that it was all Gillian's fault. "If she hadn't gone off the deep end about me drinking her coke..."

"Bullshit!" I snapped.

Gillian opened up the door and got out. Oh dear, I thought, she's going to walk off and I'll have to get out and coax her back in the car. But instead, she opened the double doors of the bus where Dawson sat.

"Get out," she said quietly.

What now, I thought.

"Why should I?" Dawson snorted.

"Because I am going to beat you to a pulp," Gillian stated, quietly and firmly. Dawson was shocked. So was I. I was experiencing a flood of emotions. Gillian was doing to Dawson what I would have liked to do with all those countless mouthy bastards who have said cruel things to me when safely in the company of their fellow males. I was suddenly glad to have Gillian as an ally. A frightening vision flashed before my eyes – the females against the males on the lawn in front of one of my student's houses. I was enjoying Dawson's hollow pretense of machismo being challenged by a female who could probably do just what she claimed she could do. I was desperately trying to think of what to do next. I decided on a holding action. I shut up and let them play it out.

"Get out," she repeated, adding a cautionary, "I've beat up guys tougher than you."

There were two sides at war in me. One of them was chortling. Wonderful! I love it! Sock'em one for me too! The other side was worried about consequences for my unprofessional behavior. This would definitely put a ban on all future field trips. I should get this stopped right now. Nowhere was I worried about Dawson and his damaged male ego. In the back of my mind, I noticed that Nat wasn't offering to join in and help Dawson out. He was just sitting very quietly.

When Gillian got out of the bus, she had been holding a steak knife and fork which she brought for the barbecue with her usual tedious preplanning. She tossed them into the front seat. Another point for her, our side. She was so confident that she could afford to throw away weapons and make it easier for Dawson to take her on.

Dawson copped to the only face-saving course of action left to him. He laughed amusedly at Gillian's challenge and said, "I don't fight women."

I had just remembered that the last time Dawson was hospitalized and he lost control, it took seven people to hold him down. Maybe he was being noble, but I doubted it. What male wants to risk getting his ass kicked by a woman?

Gillian persisted. "What's the matter, are you chicken?" Her perfectly manicured forefinger made beckoning motions towards the lawn, the potential arena to inflict mayhem upon Dawson's body. I stifled another guffaw.

"I couldn't fight you!" Dawson was offended that

she would suggest such a thing to a male of his moral fiber. "I'd end up really hurting you. I'd break your bones and stuff them down your throat." He folded his arms across his midsection and gazed firmly forward into the distance.

"Yeah, you're really crazy to try and fight Dawson. He'd kill you." Nat had belatedly discovered the lyrics to his chorus, the lines for his part, but he still wasn't offering to actually help Dawson.

Gillian reaffirmed her stance. "I can take care of myself. I've been in plenty of fights and most of the guys were bigger than you. I even broke one's nose." Impatiently she added, "Are you getting out or not?"

Dawson scoffed, "Well they must have been real puds if they'd fight a girl."

Gillian waited for a while longer, then slammed shut the double doors of the bus and climbed back into the front seat. Internally I sighed with relief. Silence dropped into the bus. Then I heard a tap, tap, tap on the window by my head. I turned around to find Kingsley and his pale frightened mother standing in the street in her house robe. Her eyes were staring hugely at me.

I had forgotten about the barbecue grill. I had promised to explain to his mother why I couldn't return the grill so Kingsley wouldn't get into trouble. Suddenly, I was furious at all the piddling details, niceties and parental foibles that I have to keep juggling daily, all to be kept balanced while sitting on a keg of dynamite with a short fuse. This present one, for example, could not tolerate my attention being diverted for a second. Besides, I was very angry and Kingsley's mother was radiating her usual signals of offering herself up as a willing victim. She seemed ready to sacrifice herself by offering her throat, or anything to stave off this unpleasantness. I yanked open the window with my fangs bared and growled at Kingsley.

"I think Kingsley, that you and your mother can figure out and handle the problem of the barbecue without having to involve me. I think you can see that I am busy with something which requires my complete attention right now and is much more important. I am quite sure you can explain the problem without my help."

Mother nodded mutely. I slammed the window shut. I was irritated to notice that she was genuinely concerned and wanted to help even though all she could do was be helpless and even interfering with what I had to do. Nevertheless, in that instantaneous flash of a glance that passed between us, I knew I was being unfair. She was standing in the middle of the street in her house robe because she was worried about us, not because of a barbecue. Irked by one more thing to divide my attention, in this case, guilt, I turned back to my foul-mouthed adolescents.

"I believe I've made it clear to you both that I will not tolerate cruelty to anyone in my classroom. If I have to choose between putting up with behavior that you two have exhibited today and having the doubtful pleasure of your company, there is no choice."

Dawson immediately retreated to his 'sour grapes' stance, "Well I've had enough of that place anyway. I come to that school and all I get is hassle. It's just not worth it."

Nat agreed that he too, thought that dropping out was preferable to having to put up with school.

In a calm, reasonable, voice I agreed with them. "What you say may really be true for both of you. I think you two ought to put some careful consideration into whether or not you want to be in school."

Silence.

More silence.

Dawson, beginning to fidget, said, "Well if you're waiting for me to brown-nose her, it'll never happen. I won't ever apologize to her. I might as well get out and start walking."

"Oh? Are you trying to intimidate me Dawson?" He was threatening me with my professional accountability, a common ploy used by these types.

"Well, you'll have my father pretty mad at you if he has to come over here to get me."

"I doubt that Dawson. I'm certain he'll support anything I want to do with you in this situation." As you know Rey, his father and I have crossed swords on many occasions and this time I was pretty sure he would be on my side, but I didn't give a damn what the bastard thought. I was bluffing, but Dawson believed me.

Nat also began to fuss. "Well let's get this fucking car moving or I'm going to get out and walk."

Gillian joined in and snipped as well, "Yes, I would like to get to school also."

In that same reasonable voice, I offered, "Well I think all three of you ought to consider walking. I'm not moving this car anyplace until I'm certain that you can control yourselves and your mouths. I will not drive until I'm confident that it's safe to do so."

My head was on automatic and I was saying all the right teacherly things, but I didn't know why I continued to sit with these three in front of Kingsley's house. I knew that as soon as I got them back to campus I would lose what little control I had over the situation. Somehow, I wanted to fix it all, to solve this problem before I let them go for a four-day holiday without any resolution. They would stew about this and there was a good chance that when school started again I would suffer for not having finished this properly. I also knew that if I waited much longer, I would push them into another incident, so I muttered a silent prayer, turned the key in the ignition switch (thank heavens the car started) and headed back to school. I turned onto the freeway and checked the rearview mirror. I looked at the faces of the two boys sitting back there. Dawson showed no remorse at all. Nat even looked pleased with himself.

After a few miles of tense freeway silence Dawson asked Gillian, "Am I going to have to worry about you making a scene in the parking lot when we get back to school?"

"I don't fight anyone," Gillian replied archly, "unless they're ready."

That woke Nat up. "The hell you don't! You came after me with a hockey stick once! You almost killed me!" Now I knew the reason for Nat's politic reticence at backing Dawson up. Slowing down threateningly, I told them all to be quiet or I'd stop right there on the edge of the freeway. They stopped.

I began to tell them how I felt about this while I still had a few moments of control left. "All I've got to say is this is a damn crappy way to end a very nice day before you leave for four days. I think it's much easier for you two to behave horribly than it is for you to say goodbye decently." The exit for the school appeared and I pulled off the freeway.

"Oh yeah, we're broken up about not having to put up with this bullshit for four days," Dawson scoffed.

"You know what Dawson: I think you've found yourself a way out of having to cope with school. Now you have a reason to quit. Yep, I think this is going to be just what you need and it's too damn bad. You two don't seem to think very much of being in school, but I was feeling very good about both of you this week, especially you Dawson. I was really enjoying you for a change, and you had to turn into an absolute turd on the last hour of the last day!" By now I had really begun to feel my disappointment. I was close to tears and they knew it. We drove into the school parking lot. All three jumped out and escaped down their various paths.

I sat in the bus and wondered for the umpteenth time, what I had done wrong, and how I could have handled it better, or prevented it all and how on earth was I going to cope with recurrences of this behavior when they came back. I felt overwhelmingly sad and depressed. I had hoped so much that they could set aside their petty grievances and enjoy each other. That, of course, was my mistake. I should be more realistic about their capacities, but if I were any more realistic I'm not sure I could continue to function or be able to offer them anything, so depleting and enervating is the world they live in.

I had grown used to Nat's vicious mouth. His behavior was no shock to me so I was able to adjust myself in relation to him more easily. Dawson was different. I had been through so much with him, trying to get him to function at even a minimal level. I had even visited him twice a week when he was hospitalized during his last breakdown.

At school he required incredible self-control on my part. He functioned like a two-year old, clinging to my skirts and whimpering about how he couldn't do any work today. At the same time he made me act out the myth of his masculine superiority. I knew it for the frail façade it was, but like many women I know, I participated in the illusion for his sake. What was the logical consequence of that? It was a female he victimized when he was threatened with exposure, when he must cope with his anxiety about another race, and when he must face his own conflicted feelings about Gillian. I could not see Dawson anymore in my anger at him. All I could see was that the infant I had been allowing to consume so much of my energy and concern was a viper at my breast, a potential rapist, a racist or any of a number of masculinely prized atrocities.

Dawson had exposed an ultimate existential reality for me as a teacher. The choice that he made by verbally raping Gillian had aroused disgust in me. He had violated another female and he probably had the power to do to me what little 10 year-old Travis and his secret could not do. Travis was sure that if I knew his secret, I would turn into someone different. I think Dawson could change me into a different person; he could turn me into his own disintegrating and violent image.

So, as I sat pondering this dilemma in the parking lot of the school, my role as a teacher versus my existence as a female human being, I decided that I must set my limits. If he must be that cruel, I will throw him away. I do not really know if this decision is for the welfare of my whole class or a self-indulgent response to protect myself and keep my sanity intact.

Well Rey, if you were here I know I could count on you to tell me that I had been good and was trying my best. When the relief of that had sunk into my brain, you would be able to pluck me up from my rejecting stance and set me down where Dawson lives, no matter how miserable and awful that place might be. For the moment, I would understand how his fear and cruelty are perhaps the best he can manage. Maybe I could see him once again as an overwhelmed child who is trying his best.

But you are not around and I will have to muddle through this as best as I can, even though my mind balks at putting effort into such a distasteful task, that of feeling empathy for Dawson. It would be far easier to hate him and throw him away, or even to quit teaching than to feel love for this monster.

Overcoming disgust. That's the name of the game, isn't it? Do you suppose there is any relationship between lack of supportive supervision and teacher burn-out?

Carolyn

December, 1986

Chapter Thirteen

Sonny's Journal

Dear Rey,

I have just completed my walking quota for the day, seven miles. I am now writing in a taco stand, with my quesadilla and coke nearby. The people in the next booth are having a wonderful time laughing over memories of shooting jackrabbits in the head, body and other parts of those small helpless creatures. To eliminate their brutalities from my awareness I have just put a classical album into my tape player. The sadistic conversationalists are fascinating to an old fellow who is probably an indigent alcoholic or psychotic or both.

I have heard that there are many communities who deal with their inconvenient populations by arresting them and offering them a bus ticket to wherever they want to go. Guess where they want to go? That's right, sunny southern California. As a result, since Governor Reagan tossed all the mental health patients out on the streets, I have to wind my way through many a muttering aluminum helmeted person in this tourist paradise during my walking exercises.

At any rate, the fellow keeps getting up and pacing back and forth in front of my violent neighbors' table. With the acuity of the insane he knows that I am bothered by him and them. He watches me as well. Can concentration and Bach's Passacaglia in C Minor overcome these distractions? A little somber perhaps, but better than listening to my neighbors. Let's see.

I can never find the time to polish up my old stories. If I work on one of the old ones, the gems lying in my brain at this very moment dissolve away. I thought I might tell you more about Sonny today.

These cruel and crazy people have much in common with Sonny. He is, as you may recall, my shocking punk infant. He was abandoned by his real mother and was adopted when he was three years old. He is not getting along too well with his present adoptive family. It is his goal in life to shock. His district was more than happy to pay us to take him off their hands. He arrived dressed outrageously. In the classroom he would try to sing disgusting lyrics, make homosexual overtures to his peers, drive a safety pin through the loose skin in his neck out of boredom, write obscenities to me in his daily journal and bully small children on the playground.

If the above were all there was to Sonny, I would have rejected him. Sonny was a confusing package. In spite of his diligent efforts to shock me he aroused strong maternal affection in me. He never, under any circumstances, disobeyed me in the classroom. Favors were requested with a most beguiling little boy grin. One of his happiest days was spent at Brooke's house where, complete with black leather jacket, studs, chains, steel-toed boots and death's head tattoo, he sat at her kitchen table, sifting, mixing, baking and stuffing himself with Christmas cookies.

Both of these feelings that he elicited from me, affection and disgust, had to be acknowledged to him. These two discordant responses in me represented the conflict Sonny felt within himself. To only pay attention to the pleasant affect, my maternal feelings, would deny a very real part of himself and would force him to act out, as his therapist soon discovered.

His adoptive parents were sacrificing to send Sonny to a psychiatrist every week. He despised the woman.

"I hate her. I'm never going back. She makes me sick. She does it all wrong."

"What," I asked him, "is she doing to you that makes you hate her so much?"

"She treats me nice. She plays games with me. She brings in snacks and keeps telling me what a good kid I am."

"Oh," I said, "well it's clear to me what the problem is."

"What?"

"She likes you. She doesn't think you're disgusting. I bet she is even fond of you."

"Exactly! And I'm not putting up with it anymore!"

And to my distress, he didn't. No matter how much we threatened him, even with dismissal from school and separation from Brooke and me, two women who truly appreciated him for the slime that he really was, he would not return to his therapist. We had to find him another.

I have managed by liberal applications of detention to keep his obscenities contained mostly within his journal. Since he has been in my class for over a year we have filled two journals and there is quite a difference between the two. I have them in my backpack and I shall copy out some excerpts from them. For the most part, I shall edit or just indicate his curses. Generally his entries are from six to ten lines long. I will only give the first two or three lines. They are very repetitive. These are from his first journal.

He wrote:

> *"I hate I hate. I watch her masturbate. I would stick my stinky twinky inside her…"*

I wrote:

> *"Yech, Blech, You are Disgusting! Is that the right reaction? Which would you prefer? Should I: a) be concerned, b) be mad, or c) just ignore your obscenities."*

It is possible that these entries are lyrics to songs from the underground culture he is so involved in. Anyway, he circled "be mad". The next day he tried again to shock me. He knows that I hate racism so naturally, he offered:

> *"We're the sons of Hitler heil. We march with a smile. Niggers are losers that's life…"*

I wrote:

> *"You have found a way to really make me crazy, haven't you, you little SOB."*

He responded:

> *"Yes I guess I am a little sob arnt I. Well Carolyn lets see what else I can do."*
>
> *"Lies Lies Lies just sit down, shut up and spread your thys."*

After a few months of this sort of thing I tried a new tack.

> *"Dear Sonny,*
>
> *I can see that this is war. OK, you*

214

asked for it. I'm going to get mean now.

"Sonnykins is the sweetest, nicest boy I know. He makes me feel like holding him on my lap to sing lullabies to him. I feel like I should hold his hand when he crosses the street and I should mash up his food so he won't choke on it.

He is a dear little cutey pie and terribly lovable. He has the nicest kindest nature and I am extraordinarily fortunate to have snookums in my classroom.
So there! Take that!"

This strategy was derived from my knowledge of his history, that he was thrown away as an infant, and expelled as a teenager. By reliving both his lost infancy and his shocking monstrousness in his journal, perhaps he would find some resolution for himself.

When he read my entry, he looked up at me beaming. "What's this you wrote in my journal? I love it!" His written response was quite different though.

"You may think I'm just a sweet little boy but you wait. Snookums is going to win this war."

I love cunt. Its no fucking stunt...

Your eternal hated
Snookums"

I wrote:

"Well Snookums, I call you a little boy and you write back about how much you like to have sex. Surely I should be seeing that you are a man and not a little boy.

215

Is that what I won't see? No wonder you must keep telling me about your powerful masculinity.

He wrote:

"Well Carolyn Snookums has something else to say. I will I will continue to show you my powerful masculinity until I win the war. You may have won the battle but I will win the war.

p.s. Carolyn will burn in hell.

Don't despair Christmas will soon be here. Fuck Fuck off you fucking queer..."

I wrote:

"How will I know when you have won the war?"

His reply:

"Well Carolyn my DEAR DEAR teacher. The way you can tell who's won is who writes the best paragraph.
p.s. you just lost.
p.s. fuck 10
shit 10
cunt 10
hore 10
ass 10
prick 10
This is worth 60 points

I continued to attack by referring to his infancy. Here is another example:

"I bet you were a sloppy eater. Your momma would sit you in your high chair. She had a little baby's silver spoon and she fed you only the very best. You ate mashed spinach (to make you strong like Popeye) and mashed carrots (to make your eyes sharp) and mashed apples (to make you sweet)."

"You dribbled all over your chin. You threw your spoon on the floor over and over again. You made your mother pick it up a thousand times. You made her mad. You cackled with glee at the disappearing spoon and the power you had to make her bend over and pick it up for you. You were a lovable little tyrant!"

His reply:

"That was pretty Good Carolyn. I like the observation. Now it's my turn."

"Were the sons of Hitler hile. We march with a smile..."

Towards Christmas of 1985 I received my present early. He had hinted that something would happen about Christmas time. Here it is:

Hi Carolyn! How are you today? I love today. What are you doing Christmas?
"Yesterday was pretty cool except I had stomach cramps and that hurt like hell. Well when you are done reading this wonderful page of good progress you will see some more shit tomorrow so enjoy this page while you can.

217

Love, Snookums'

I replied:

> *"This is wonderful! You have shocked me! This is earthshaking. Thank you, thank you, thank you!!!*
>
> *Must you return to the yucky Sonny?"*

He answered:

> *"Yes I think it would be best if I did. ASS SHIT CUNT FUCK..."*

Immediately after Christmas he returned to the same horrible entries. There were only a few pages left in his first journal. I was getting very tired of it and I suspected he was too. I complained:

> *"Listen Sonny, what do you want from me in this journal? Just to read your obscenities and be shocked? To write about little Sonny and remind you of what a cute little baby you were? To try and appeal to your reasonable side? What? Frankly, your entries are making me crazy.*

His reply:

> *"I want war famin hate and to rape and sodimize my mother.*
> *I want to kill my father..."*

He did change though. After I wrote the above to him, his new journal of January 1985 began to read quite differently. It was almost as if he had made a conscious decision to change. Perhaps he did it to please me, although I hope not. It was also about this time that he started spending an hour in the afternoon playing with the kindergarteners. Remember how he used to bully small children? Now he has become a father figure to them. Every time he enters the kindergarten room, the little ones run to him and hug his legs. For whatever reason, while he did have occasional relapses in his journal, for the most part we actually communicated.

As I read them, I could understand why he resorted to obscenities. When he really began to talk about how he was feeling, they were very depressing entries, much more so than the vulgarities, which at least had strength and vigor. These entries were real and they showed me what his life was like. Here are some of them:

> *"Today is an alright day could be better could be worse. I don't know. I feel cold tired and grouchy. I feel some what angry. I want to get out of my muck. I'm sick of shit."*

> *"I hate today it sucks my big one. Today Timmy brought his stupid toy on the bus which causes trouble and bugs me. I never want to ride that bus again. Picture how I feel being in a school full of hipocrits, including that fag Dawson."*

> *"I hate today. Dirt bag Nat and Dawson think their the top studs of the class. This includes Sissy. A bitch as always. Well Ill make do with what iv got. Fuckem. Fuckem all.*

Depressing as these are, they still represented

progress. And recently, he has shown even more growth. I'll include one last set, written a few weeks ago, that gives a good indication of his greater capacity to be both positive and reciprocal in his relationship with me. He wrote:

> *"My sobriety is ok. I go to about two meetings a week* (Alcoholics Anonymous). *I'm going to one tonite with Mark. I hope you feel better during the day. You look uptight.*
>
> *Love Snookums"*

I wrote:

> *"I'm glad to hear you are attending AA regularly. Why do you think I might be uptight. You be the shrink."*

He wrote:

> *"You my dear have been screaming alot yesterday. Making accusations. Don't feel bad. We are all like that one day or another.*
> *I love you. You are my favorite teacher."*
>
> *"Love and 10 millions hate worth of shit."*

I wrote back:

> *"I feel much better now Dr. Snookums. Thank you. I appreciate your advice and support. What I don't understand is the '10 millions hate worth of shit'. Could you explain that?"*

220

His answer:

> *"The 10 millions worth of hate and*
> *shit is to cover the love, help and*
> *understanding you've given me all these*
> *years. And that adorable nickname. Well*
> *have a very good weekend.*
>
> *Love, Snookums"*

Most schools would not have allowed Sonny such freedom of expression, and I seriously doubt whether Mountainview will continue to do so. I think it's very important that I did, at least within the confines of his journal. I let him overwhelm me with his obscenities. I'm not at all sure what they meant - rage perhaps or an identification with power. More importantly, I did not abandon him because he was too shocking. His real mother had left him. Schools had thrown him away. I kept him *and* his disgusting behaviors. I managed to survive this horrible infant. That was the role I had been assigned to play out with him. I'm very fond of him, as I'm sure you've noticed.

Carolyn

REYNARD'S MIRROR

January, 1987

Chapter Fourteen

January, Camellias and Death

Dear Rey,

A ten-foot camellia bush grows just outside my front door. Every January deep rose blossoms appear and I remember picking those blooms to take to my mother in the hospital just before she died four years ago. And now my beloved Labrador, Flash, has died. I look at those delicate rose blossoms and I hate them.

I had Flash for nearly 16 years, almost as long as I lived with my mother, and now he is gone too. He deteriorated quickly, after a life of good health. It was not a bad death. We did not have to agonize more than two days over what to do about him. It was clear that he had to be 'put to sleep'. He could not walk and he was suffering from both liver and kidney failure.

Zane says that Flash had a better life than most people have. I found him when I lived in a redwood forest outside of Santa Cruz. He was about six months old, all waggily black tail and smiles. We said hello to each other and I invited him in for a visit. He spent the rest of the day snoozing on the couch while I sat on the floor next to him typing a long letter to a friend. For the remainder of the week, I left the door open for him to come and go as he pleased. He chose to stay. I made a half-hearted attempt to find the owners.

My husband asks me, "How many people make it

all the way from Alaska to Texas, swimming in creeks, oceans and lakes, hiking through deep forests, across deserts, tundra and chaparral? In Juneau, on a trail up to a glacier, when the porcupine got him right in the nose, did it slow him down?" It took three of us to restrain him. I was certain that Zane dislocated his jaw trying to hold him still enough to yank bloody quills out of his tender nose with pliers. Flash never even growled at us. Three days later he was sliding nose first down delicious snowy slopes as we paused while heading across Three Guardsmen Pass in the Yukon.

Just a while ago, he was out in the Mojave Desert with us. He was almost blind in one eye, totally deaf and his front left paw was so crippled with arthritis that he would sometimes trip over it and fall nose first into the gritty desert floor. Still he would not be left behind and so we walked slowly and not very far during his last years.

We decided to bury him out in the Mojave. I thought I was handling his death with stoic resolve because I had been expecting it for so long. I was proved wrong when we folded back the cardboard flaps, still cold from the vet's freezer and I saw that precious black body curled up just as if he was napping, and his terrible loss all rushed in on me like a collapsing vacuum.

"Oh, my poor baby," I sobbed. I reached out to touch that fur which had become second nature to me because it has been just within reach for nearly 16 years. His floppy velvety ear was frozen solid. I would never again sit on a mountain boulder while he leaned up against me, a perfect fit as I wrapped my arm around his powerful shoulders. One of the worst losses for me is the tactile one...the thickness of his fur, his soft fuzzy ears, the shape and flow of him as I used to sit and run my hand over his body, and that wagging tail that could knock me over.

Zane made a wooden coffin for him and we took him to the Mojave, his last trip. I was determined to bury him deep. We managed to get four feet down before we hit rock and hard pan. Then we lowered the coffin in and filled the grave with cold damp desert sand. We collected rocks and made a three foot-high cairn. It was good to be able to bury a loved one myself.

For the last week I have been coming to terms with Flash's absence. I find myself dividing snacks up into fourths when there are only three dogs left. I have been avoiding my writing room. It's lonely in there now. I was unaware of how much Flash's quiet presence, always padding just behind me, had protected me from feeling alone. For all of those 16 years I thought I had been coming to terms with the solitariness of existence, but Flash had always been there, a silent brown-eyed buffer against loneliness.

The other three dogs mostly left Flash and me to ourselves. They had become Zane's dogs. Lately, they've begun to spend more time with me. Right now, for example, Hoss, Flash's biggest pup...all 95 pounds of him...is curled up on the bed looking expectantly at me. He's a lap dog. Most of my time with him I am avoiding being squashed.

I'm very glad that we bred Flash at the human equivalent of 77 years of age. I like having another big furry creature who drags me down the street for his walk, chews on my ear when he's saying hello, grabs my hand with his prehensile claw to make me scratch his chest, and of course, as is the way with most males when they are feeling wonderfully expansive after a good meal and an invigorating romp, tries to hump my leg while I'm writing to you.

Carolyn

February, 1987

Chapter Fifteen

A Reprieve

Dear Rey,

I am feeling elated. Shaun came back for a visit today! If you remember, he was the one I lost because his parents prematurely yanked him out of school. I think they would have returned him to public school regardless, but I behaved cowardly towards him because I knew the emotional demands he would make of me. I made the mistake of keeping my distance.

On the day he returned, I had the class out on our once-a-month field trip, or rather I had part of the class out on a field trip. The others ditched, came too late, or forgot their permission slips so that I only took one-half of the insufferable little creeps to the Natural History Museum. Brooke was stuck staying behind with the reluctant ones. I told her to make their day as miserable as possible.

"Is that where the Blacks and Mexicans are? I was asked the day before the trip by Sonny, my obscene infant.

"Probably, but you'll be safe with me. Besides it'll do you good to meet somebody besides homogenized whites." He frowned skeptically at me.

He showed up for the field trip looking far worse than he usually does, complete with a black mascaraed eyes, a Mohawk haircut and studded clothes, steel-toed boots and a studded dog collar. I assume he'd dressed up and changed his hairdo to scare off the bad guys. He absolutely refused to go with us if we asked him to remove any of his accessories. I absolutely refused to let him use costuming to get out of the field trip. I took his complaining body as it was.

Returning from our trip at the end of the school day with Sonny intact, I drove into the parking lot to find Shaun sitting on the rock out at the adolescents' hangout. He was dressed in a black cowboy hat, an old comfy blue plaid flannel shirt tucked into faded jeans, and his silvery blue sunglasses. He looked like he had just come in off the range and was ready to set a spell on the cabin porch.

I jumped out of the bus, rushed over to him and said, "I'm so glad to see you. I thought I'd never see you again." I leaned down, put one arm around him and gave him a hug.

He aimed his silvery blue glasses at me. I was faced with my own raggedy reflection. "You didn't have to worry about me coming back," he reassured me.

"You know you still have a lot of stuff you left in the classroom."

"What'd I leave?"

"Your handmade mug, a backpack and a plastic container that once held your special guacamole dip." I found it about a month after he left. It took much fortitude to clean it up.

"Do you want to get them now, or do you want to leave them here so you have a reason to come back and see us again?"

"I'll leave 'em."

"Good."

He told me that he was failing in public school. He had already been dismissed from one program for being too confrontational of their methods. "I just told them that all I do around here is fill in the blanks and keep quiet."

228

He described falling asleep in third period class. "I remember that somebody tried to wake me up, but I just kept sleeping. Next somebody started shaking me. I was all dopey and I looked up and saw the principal looking down at me. It was now fourth period class. I laughed, and because I thought it was a dream, I put my head down again."

"No son," the principal said, "this is reality. You're going to have to wake up. To teach you a lesson about staying awake in class you'll have to spend the rest of the day in my office."

Insolently, Shaun covered his face with his hands and cried out. "Oh no! Not that, anything but that!"

Shaun seemed rather pleased with this story, and I was supposed to be enjoying his clever retort. I was not happy. I felt sympathy for the teacher who tried to wake him up and get him to produce. Shaun had been extraordinarily powerful at not producing and even encouraging his peers to follow his example. Everything he was doing at public school, he had done to me. Shaun was in a worse situation now because teachers in public school have far fewer therapeutic resources and a much larger population to manage. I seriously doubted that Shaun would graduate. I felt very sad for him.

I knew Shaun had come a long way from home so I offered to drive him back. As we walked out to my VW bus, he threw an arm around my shoulders and kept it there, chatting with me in easy familiarity. I had forgotten how he used to do that to me whenever we walked across campus together.

When we were getting close to his home, he asked me instead to drop him off at a nearby corner, ominously where a liquor store was located. He grabbed the door handle and was about to leap out when I grabbed his arm and said, "Wait. You do not get to leave just yet. I want to say a few things to you. I will try to make this as quick and painless as possible."

He looked down at his hands and said, "It doesn't have to be quick."

I told him again that I still felt terrible about his being pulled out of our school. "I think that if I had paid more attention to you, it might not have happened. I'm very worried about how you are doing in public school. I want you to know that if you need any tutoring, or if you'd just like to talk, then I would really like you to come and see me"

"Yeah," he said, "I'd like that."

"Would you like to just go ahead and set up a regular time to meet?" I hoped that if I could stabilize him enough, he could graduate from public school.

"Yes, I would."

Suddenly, we were interrupted by a homeless man who had lurched up to Shaun's side of the bus. He looked drunk. "I hate to bother you and your girlfriend, but I need fifteen cents for the bus. To prove his point, he stuck his open palm filled with coins into the bus, all the way up to his armpit. His hand wavered to and fro between Shaun and myself. "Do you have an extra fifteen cents?"

Shaun, quick to seize an opportunity, said, "Yes, but you'll have to do me a favor." He climbed out of the bus, promised to come and see me next week, then turned his charming smile on the man who blinked blearily up at him. They spoke for a minute, and the stranger broke into a broad gapped-toothed grin. The two walked off together toward the liquor store, Shaun offered a stabilizing hand to his tottery new friend.

Carolyn

April, 1987

Chapter Sixteen

Termination Blues

Dear Rey,

Well I haven't written to you for two months. I hope that you've noticed and are missing my letters. Sometimes I feel like giving up on you. I could easily push that gladness of writing you off to one side. I could set your salt-and-pepper bearded visage upon the shelf and turn your face to the wall. It is a depressing thought, but manageably so. I wonder what it would do to my writing.

I am not happy with the new regime. Rumor has it that administration is tired of dealing with adolescents and all the problems they bring. Just by being teenagers, they look untidy, uncooperative, and threatening.

On top of that, for the last few weeks when I've arrived at work on Mondays, I've felt lost and ineffectual. Everything seems vague. I can't quite get a picture of anything, or be decisive when I'm supposed to be. It's as if I'm peering through a grimy window. Everything is too bleary, too much trouble and too exhausting. I begin to wonder if there isn't a less futile way of earning a living. I look at my students and think, they really are a hopeless lot of losers. They haven't a chance of surviving decently.

Now Julia, my supervisor, is trying to tell me that this is all because of my birthday. Soon I shall be 48 years old. I certainly wouldn't deny that as the year rolls around

231

to the pivotal point in the cycle of my aging process, I have a few anxieties of which I'm not aware. Still, if I were going to place the blame for my vagueness or depression anywhere, it would have to be because of what I call 'termination blues'. That would be the upcoming loss of my students, the half-finished job I've been able to do with them, end-of-the-year testing, reviews of my accountability and evaluations, and finally, anticipated battles with public school districts over students and funding.

My disillusionment with my students is because as we get close to the end of the year, my students regress. Old problems re-emerge, perhaps to ease the pain of separation, the loss of the little family we have created here, or perhaps out of fear at taking the next step forward. As they express their despair through their oddments of oppositional, anti-social and non-productive behavior, even more effort is required on my part to help hold them together. I must be more containing, more alert, more structured and empathic. This has to be done even though I am disorganized at my own losses.

Secondly, this is the time of year when I must go to the school district meetings. I feel resentment towards the educational bureaucracy that strains my capacities and yanks me out of the classroom for meetings when I most need my energies to hold the kids and myself together until the end.

This year, four out of my nine students are going to graduate. Kingsley, Randy, Deborah and Gillian will be leaving us. Those remaining are Dawson, Nat, Charlie, Sissy and Sonny. If Kingsley's attendance doesn't improve, he may have to go to summer school. The ones who are leaving are anxious, abandoned and panicky. The ones who are staying behind are wondering if they will ever manage to graduate and escape this man-made purgatory.

To cheer things up and make the end of the year

special for them I thought I might take them all on a camping trip, if I can get approval from Paul. After all, most high schools have a senior trip. I was fairly sure I could make a good case for one last field trip with this class. It is an extremely foolhardy thing for me to do, because of the risk involved in taking such unstable adolescents junketing around California. The main reason why I continue in this mad endeavor is because whenever old students come back to see me and I ask them what was most important to them during their time with me, the answer is invariably, the camping trip. So this Monday, in spite of a certain nebulousness, I began a discussion on a potential camping trip.

We were in the middle of considering possible places to go when Dawson came in, an hour late. Now I know that Dawson is at his worst in the mornings, especially on a Monday morning when he is also tardy, but the next day was my birthday and my head was full of cobwebs. I was simply unprepared for his hostility. When Dawson entered, the class was in a good mood. By the time he got through with us we were all mired down in a pool of negativity.

I was describing Sequoia National Park in the Sierra Nevada as a possibility, although a cold one for early June. Dawson crankily asserted that Sequoia was no damn good and that Yosemite was the only possible Sierra camping site worth the bother.

I looked over at his sour face. "Sequoia is about four hours closer and is a perfectly good place. What does Yosemite have that would make it worth all that extra effort?"

"Shit, Sequoia is nothing. It's a pussy place to camp. Yosemite has great scenery, bitchin' waterfalls, mountains, trees. It's got it all over Sequoia."

"Sequoia has all that," I said mildly. Sequoia is about 150 miles closer and in the same mountain range. It has waterfalls, and many more of the huge famous *gigantea* redwood trees. True, it doesn't have spectacular Yosemite Valley under the sheer face of Half Dome, but driving these kids another three or four hours hardly justified the difference. I began to wonder if Dawson knew anything about Sequoia.

"Sequoia doesn't have the women and the parties!" he snapped back. There was a murmur of agreement at Dawson's perspective.

"Yeah, there ya' go!" Randy voted his support in his slow country drawl, nodding in approval. "That sounds more like it!"

I began to feel that I had better make some efforts to pierce my mental fog. Hints of insurrection were appearing amongst the ranks.

"That's even more reason to _not_ go there. I can't be taking you to places where you can indulge in your favorite pastimes. We've had this discussion more than once when we talk about field trips. I can't take you on a trip unless you agree to stay with the group, use no dope or alcohol, and no taking up with strange men or women. Those are the terms. I am responsible for you and the fact is, I can be sued for anything that happens to you.

Dawson, of course, leaped at the opportunity to take his morning blahs out on me. "You guys have got to have your power trip so you can order us around. Anytime you aren't getting your way, you use your establishment bullshit so you can keep us under control. If something happened to me, my parents wouldn't sue." (Hah! I thought. Dad would consider it the opportunity of a lifetime.) "If you acted cool everything would be fine, but no, you've got to do your authority number on us every chance you get!"

I was furiously angry with him and very nearly cancelled the trip right then and there out of a reaction to him. As I sat and let the shower of his accusations pour over me I asked myself, "Is this the same kid I described in my year-end evaluation as having reduced his black and white thinking? If so, I was clearly off my rocker, because here he is again, telling me that this is another event in his simplistic scoreboard of 'power hungry authoritarian vs. innocent adolescent victim'. I don't think the son of a bitch has improved one iota."

While Dawson continued to rant, I remembered our last monthly field trip. We had gone over to Gillian's house to cook lunch and watch a video. In spite of Gillian's anxiety towards her classmates and what they might do if she allowed them into her compulsively tidy home, she had risen to the occasion and invited us over. I was proud of her for taking such a big step.

The film we had chosen to watch was, 'Conan the Barbarian'. Dawson knew this film by heart. He loved to watch the weight-lifting hero's sword-wielding battles against the forces of evil with the devoted warrior maiden at his side, ready to die for him. When we climbed back into my VW, after having spent a very pleasant afternoon together, Dawson spoke up. "I feel like going to battle. I wish it was back in the old days. I'd love to have a sword to swing around and kill the enemy." Childlike he hacked away at an imaginary foe as we drove down the streets of a 20th century California metropolis.

"I can see that this would not be a good time for me to tell you that you have to stay after school today for not doing your homework," I joked.

"Hell no! I'd take up my sword, lop off your head, grab it up by the hair and roll it down the middle of the classroom. Then the students would be free of your hypnotic powers forever."

Dawson's present day wrath over how unreasonable I was being, giving up my free time to endure a four-day weekend with him, intruded into my reverie of the good old days when I had hypnotic powers. They were certainly missing today.

"If you teachers had your way, you'd turn this trip into one of those goddamned nature walks to make us learn stuff. You always want us to learn stuff! Can't you just loosen up for once and get down off your high horse!"

I looked at the rest of the students. Where before there had been anticipation and even eagerness about going camping, now there was anger, frustration and negativity. It has always amazed me how communicative negativity can be. All of us had been tarred by Dawson's sticky hopelessness, gumming up our wing feathers, keeping us earthbound and incapable of flight. I looked at them all and wondered where on earth I would find the energy to drag them out of this bleak depression.

They were all looking pretty pathetic by this time of year. Dawson, as we have just seen, was unbearable. Once again I toyed with getting rid of him, for the sake of the rest of us. Kingsley was so frightened of graduating that he was staying home 40% of the time, a replay of his behavior when he came to us. I began to wonder if he would not have another psychotic break rather than emerge from the cotton wool of his adolescent cocoon into adulthood. Deborah was in a frantic search for more important things to do rather than go through the final days of separation from a place that had changed her from a school-phobic, suicidal girl into an independent young woman. She was presently trying to schedule herself into as limited an amount of time as possible on campus with appointments for college and jobs. Charlie was ditching and snapping at me. Until recently, he had been doing very well, even receiving school-wide honors. Now, he was returning to the narrow grassy alley behind the trailer, sitting steeped in depression, knees drawn up to his chin. Sonny's obscenities had achieved new heights of self-expression. Horrifying images were being poked into my brain daily via his journal. Sissy bounced between rage and clinging. Anyone who attempted to spend time with her classroom mother, Brooke, was taking a chance with personal injury, so extreme was her jealousy. Randy had developed mysterious ailments and needed to stay at home to be nursed by a willing mom. Nat was becoming unmanageable, refusing to work and lying on the couch at school with another set of mysterious ailments, hoping I would do the nursing that would not occur at home. Only Gillian was improving and that was being done with such last-ditch determination that I feared for her when she bumped her toe on the first obstacle in the personally forged path of her iron-will.

They were searching for a victim to displace their distress upon. I might do, or perhaps Gillian who is always so superior and goody-goody, although to express anger at her was to risk your bodily well-being. Each student was toying with his own style of terminating, generally regression to old defensive styles of sickness, oppositionality and depression.

Rey, I want you to understand everything I have to juggle and manage at this time of year. First, I am faced with the niggling worry of the creeping machinery of time rolling over me with yet another year of aging. Second, I am conflicted about remaining at Mountainview. Should I get out of teaching and become a therapist, or should I find work in public school where I would have benefits, union protection and a decent salary? Third, I am expected by my monsters' hopeless faces to pull myself together and keep them from falling apart. And fourth, I must also cope with that leviathan of bureaucracy, the State Department of Education, or in these particular instances, its representatives, the local school districts.

When I have to deal with agents of the state, I undergo culture shock. I am transported to an alien land with bizarre norms and traditions. I am wrenched from my precarious yet familiar world where I have been assiduously working away at the priorities the kids have presented to me during the year. You know things like...theft, assault, potential mental breakdown, possible suicides, pregnancy scares, substance abuse...things like that. Then I am pushed into various conference rooms, surrounded by aliens who want to know if Dawson has constructed a paragraph with a topic sentence during the last year.

Yes, it is time for me to go to the Individualized Educational Plan (IEP) meetings. During these meetings, last year's objectives are checked to see if they have been met, then new ones are set up. Then the school district, the parents and the private school argue over whether or not funding should be provided for the student to go to an alternative setting other than public school. Basically our private school usually wins when it looks like it's going to be cheaper to send them to us rather than the hospital, which is the next most logical placement. In other words, we get funding when the student is close to requiring residential care which would cost many times more than our tuition.

I must bring to the meeting the results of whether or not I've fulfilled last year's goals. It's odd that no one ever seems to care whether or not I've met them, or even what they are. Nonetheless, I feel I haven't done a good job if I can't say that I've met them.

Most of the goals are in academic areas, while social-emotional goals are basically tokenism. For example, at last year's meeting for Dawson, even though I knew I was hoping for the miraculous, I offered the following objective:

> Given a conflict situation, Dawson will reduce the frequency of distortion of events into black and white thinking, such as authoritarian vs. victim terms. This frequency will be reduced 50% below present levels of performance.

Now, as I have just described, this is something that Dawson does chronically, but this large committee of people, only one of whom had actually met Dawson, couldn't accept this goal.

"How will you measure that?" I was asked by a grey-haired special ed. teacher who probably couldn't keep Dawson in her room for ten minutes.

"By watching his behavior and talking to him," I answered. She snorted dismissively.

Regardless of my feelings or experience with the actual Dawson, the goal was tortured into, "Dawson will assume greater responsibility for his behavior." Good grief, I thought. Responsibility yet! That'll be the day! I might as well teach him to walk on water. And what kind of responsibility were they talking about anyway? How much did they want me to get him to produce? Did tying his shoelaces and eating breakfast count? I couldn't resist a return sally at the prim special ed. teacher.

"How am I going to measure that?" I asked.

Both eyebrows arched imperiously and she snipped, "Well by his behavior, of course!" Silly me, I should have known the answer.

The most revealing moment of the meeting was exposed was when the earthquake drill happened. A piercing buzzer rang and all eight of us climbed under our long conference table. Underneath there, we were pocketed into four separate groups divided by wooden partitions set at right angles which served as table legs. We had to stay there until someone came to check and see if we had properly squirreled ourselves in our holes. To my left, I was squatting cheek by jowl with my favorite person in the whole world, Dawson's dad.

A wall of wood was on my right. I edged my way as close as I could to that barrier. The district psychologist was on the other side of my partition. Undaunted in her determination to stay on schedule, she continued to run the meeting, shouting out objectives for me to answer as to whether Dawson had met them or not. I peered through the gloom at my notes and yelled my results at the wooden wall. Of course, the rest of this august decision-making body were able to concentrate to the best of their abilities over the fate of Dawson as they listened to our disjointed questions and answers while squatting in their own dark little recesses.

Finally, we climbed back up into the bright fluorescent lighting and resumed our careful deliberations. Surprise! The district wanted nothing to do with Dawson, that sour package of depression and mental instability. They were quite happy to fund him for another exhausting year in my classroom. I was delighted.

On Tuesday, the anniversary of my birth 48 years ago, the little monsters prepared a wonderful surprise for me, with Brooke's supervision. While I was out bouncing from district to district wrestling with IEPs, she had been asking the class if they wanted to do anything for my birthday. She had offered them a cause to rally around at a time when they needed one. They came forth with their assigned tasks and chores for the day with responsibility and enthusiasm.

It's really not fair. Just as I managed to work up a nicely objectified disinterest in whether or not they survive in this life, they gang up on me and do something nice. Dawson, who tells me that cooking is women's work and he wouldn't be caught dead in a kitchen, baked me a huge plateful of chewy chocolate chip cookies. Appended to the cookies was a note which said, in marvelously tidy script, "On behaf of your birthday, I Dawson McGill promis to be on time for the rest of the week." He ditched the next day.

Kingsley, instead of lying in bed at home and toying with becoming psychotic, had managed to bring his obligatory birthday cake to school. His mother had been browbeaten into baking it for him. He also brought me a present, a plastic cup full of uninspiring grey rocks, scavenged himself at the beach, and therefore worthy as a gift.

Nat brought me a bottle of plum wine.

On Wednesday, the day following my birthday, he was very disappointed with me when I confessed that I did not get wasted on his wine. He could scarcely believe I could be so remiss on my birthday. We were alone having a visit, out at the adolescent hangout sitting on the boulders under the trees.

"Nope," I told him, "I'm going to make it last. This way I can give you a toast every night for weeks. I gave you one last night."

"Toast? What kind of toast?" he inquired warily.

Even today, I can't believe what I said to him. It was pure uncensored impulse. "Every night, as I drink my plum wine, I raise my wine glass and say, 'Here's to the little fucker. Long may he live.'"

He glowed with appreciation. I had said just the right thing. Remember, Nat is the one with the mean mouth. I was talking his language. It's important to be able to speak in their language. In the same way that I have to be able to speak educationalese at IEP meetings, I must also be able to hold my own with the barbaric trade language of the adolescent.

In those carefree halcyon days at the university when I was living hand to mouth working my way through an MA in Geography, I studied the role of the beachcomber in 18th century Polynesia, especially Tonga. He was a useful fellow, serving as a cultural translator, who stood between the worlds of, for example, the native Tongan, the Methodist missionary, and the British imperialist.

The beachcomber on Tonga was usually a European who escaped from a British ship and had 'gone native'. He had to be a practical man. He had to face the realities of existence for both the native culture in which he had insinuated himself, and the 'civilized' culture of his origin with its superior technology and weaponry. He had to know the limitations of his adopted culture and their view of the world or he might not survive. He also had to understand the idealistic zeal of the missionary, who tried to impose impossible standards upon a people who often viewed warfare and murder as a diverting entertainment and a method of improving one's status in life...actually not that different from the 18th century European's idea of social mobility.

I understand very well, how those beachcombers felt. Faced with idealism and the clean unsullied theories of the educator on one side and the brutal realities of the adolescent on the other, I must be able to speak to both in their own languages. Unfortunately, they both speak related forms of English. I feel the greatest strain in my credibility when the missionary educator comes to watch me teach the barbarian. Often they are appalled by the coarseness in my room. Is it not my function to civilize them? At the same time the primitive adolescent is watching me to see if I speak with forked tongue. Will I sell them out to the power structure?

Last week I went to an IEP meeting for Nat, my mean-mouthed surfing con man and the giver of plum wine. Since the school district was toying with whether they wanted to pull Nat back into their system and save the cost of sending him to Mountainview, my competition was at the meeting, the special ed teacher Nat would have at public school. In preparation for this meeting, Nat had observed her classroom. Both Nat and his father felt that she had been condescending and had given them the impression she didn't want his kind in her classroom. Nat had responded to her rudeness by telling her what she could do with her classroom in very graphic terms. As we have seen, obscenity is a verbal skill in which Nat excels.

At the meeting she told us that Nat had used foul language when other children were present. While she had a valid point, I wondered if the woman had ever heard adolescents talk to each other. Knowing that this woman existed on a different planet from Nat's world, I said, "That's part of Nat's package." meaning that if the district wanted him back to save money, they'd have to take his mouth as well.

"Well, it isn't appropriate in my classroom," she said disdainfully, "and furthermore..." bright red artificial fingernails tapped the table top, punctuating the strength of her feelings about this, "...it isn't appropriate behavior for any public school classroom." The unfinished portion of that sentence was...but we know very well the sorts of things you people allow at your school.

I was torn between rising to Nat's and my school's defense, and the impulse to laugh out loud, realizing that the woman had just chalked up another student on our ledger. I would not have to fight for Nat. This biddy would never allow him in her classroom.

Nat curses because he feels terrible about himself. Cursing gives him power. He is highly defensive and as prickly as they come. That public school teacher has a limited experience of the world and idealized expectations of classroom behavior. I agree with her. We should return to the days of my childhood when students sat quietly, behaved obediently and were eager to learn, only I sure don't know how to return to those days. My students are emotional wrecks. I am certainly not going to focus on eliminating cursing or reaching acceptable levels of test scores as my first priority. Besides, cursing is rarely the real issue for a teacher. In this case the real issue was power. Nat was not going to be submissive enough for her, and she had no way to cope with him other than disapproval and rejection. He threatened her with that most frightening aspect of teaching – loss of control in the classroom.

She and Nat do not speak the same language. Nat needs a beachcomber who can help him make the transition to civilized society where anger is handled differently, more insidiously. Oh yes, other than the disastrous barbecue, Nat has only cursed at me once or twice so far this year and I wouldn't be surprised if I didn't deserve it.

But I digress, back to my surprise birthday. There I sat in my trailer, with balloons taped to all available surfaces. The kids were sitting all around me, each offering me a scrap of paper with a personally written sentiment on it, perhaps a promise to do better. Finally, I received a card that said, "For your birthday, we, your class, have arranged with Paul to take you anyplace you want to go today. We love you." I chose to go to a wonderful garden nursery in the nearby hills and to have a hike in the 'gulley', a bit of wildness down in a nearby river bed.

I wish you could have seen how manfully my young males held up under the strain of going to a nursery to look at spring flowers. They took one quick double-time run through the place and found a corner in which to form their familiar knot. Kingsley, of course, was my shadow, never leaving my side for a minute.

They were very patient with me, waiting without their usual complaints of, "How much longer are we going to be, Carolyn?" and "Let's go! I'm going crazy waiting around here!" Instead, they waited quietly while I rummaged happily among the bulbs, smelled the roses, tracked down the foxglove and purchased petunias and dahlias.

Then we went to the gulley. Nat was in his element there. He knew this place like the back of his hand. I was no slouch down there either. For a while I had lived nearby and I used to take Flash for a run every day down in those acres of tall willows and pampas grass. There is a strip of sub-surface drainage which runs diagonally across the fields to the river. It becomes swampy during the rainy season. Growing atop this strip is a tangle of 20-30 ft. tall willows. It is possible to feel lost in there, but by walking straight east or west, the woods can be escaped within 30 or 40 yards. In those woods, Flash and I had found foxes, rabbits, skunks and makeshift hobo homes.

I had taken one of my younger counseling groups down there and was delighted as they plunged into the bushes as eagerly as Flash had. It seemed like a rite of passage as tense, defensive, angry boys turned into trackers, explorers and adventurers. They reveled in it. They came back panting and happily coated with mud and stickers. I was reminded that if these boys were living in a hunting society, they would be leaders of the tribe.

These kids are incredibly canny. They can read me like a book. They are much more aware of what is happening around them than I am. I remember once when I took the students to a local zoo and we discovered an otter pond. We were hanging over a fence watching one right beneath us. He was repeatedly doing backflips, neurotically pushing off a rock into the water, and rising to push off again and again. I remember Dawson saying, "You hear that?"

"What?" I could hear nothing but the background noises of the park.

"Listen, you can hear him suck in a breath of air, just before he pushes off again."

Sure enough, when I leaned forward and concentrated on the small otter, I could hear, "Zup", then a splash, resurface and then another "Zup" Noticing that small sound connected me forever to the little fellow. I can still see his little whiskery mouth opening and closing before the next dive.

These kids have a lot to teach us and they thrive away from the classroom. I wondered how my older students would react to my patch of swampy willows.

The class had brought snacks for lunch. As we

marched along, following in Nat's footsteps, potato chips and Dawson's chocolate chip cookies were handed up and down the line. Finally we found a place where there were some downed branches to sit on, the ground being too muddy. We shared onion dip, salsa, chips and passed liter bottles of warm soda around with warnings of no backwashing.

After this adolescent version of lunch was consumed, Nat suggested that we play Ditchem, a kind of hide and seek in teams. Naturally all the 'cool' ones were on one team while the teachers, the girls and of course, Kingsley were on the other team. Brooke started to complain about how the teams had been set up, but I stopped her. I wanted to see what would happen. Would these older boys react like the youngsters in my counseling group?

They did. They were nearly scared to death by a long snake. We could hear their howls through the bushes. Later, they boasted about how they could have caught it if they'd really wanted to. They were delighted with the thousands of tiny frogs that were everywhere, like a plague of grasshoppers. It was impossible to walk without stirring up hundreds of small green leaping bodies.

Our two teams crept around in the underbrush looking for each other. We were clumsy Indian scouts, inept frontiersmen, crackling, whispering and laughing,

but we finally caught the boys. Of course they claimed that they let us catch them, but we knew better.

Next, I took them to a murky pond I knew about, where we found a crawfish. It was courageous Nat who picked it up to wave in front of the squealing girls. The other boys tried to not look squeamish. Then Nat led us back out of the woods.

As we walked back to the cars, Dawson, in the tradition of Conan, the Barbarian Hero, was up front where strong men belong. I yelled at him, "Hey Dawson! Do you know what we did today?"

He stopped, turned around and frowned at me.

"We went on one of those damned nature hikes where teachers force their students to learn stuff."

He scowled at me and returned to his pathfinder role.

The following Friday, I gave them all thank you notes. Here is what I wrote to Dawson.

"Dear Dawson,

I want to tell you how much those cookies meant to me. On Monday, when you came in and gave me such a hard time, I felt very low and depressed. On Tuesday you brought me cookies and a promise, and I felt great. Did you know you were that powerful?

As much as I'd like to say I never want to see Dawson again, I don't because in spite of your miserable side, you have another side that is reasonable, generous and sensitive. It's that side of you I can't throw away, that keeps me hanging in there because I know that's the real Dawson – the Dawson who wants to keep a promise, but just can't, and who knows how good a plate of cookies will make me feel. You drive me crazy, but you can also be a sweetheart.

Carolyn"

Dawson's response to this was to wad up the note and throw it in my face, just as I was trying to get the class settled down for a lesson. Angrily, I told him, "Now how would you like to pick that up?"

"And how would you like to blow it out your nose?" he challenged back.

But before I could sputter out words of expulsion from the classroom, he got up with a grin and came over to me. He bent over and picked up the note. I thought, well, that's a miracle! He never does anything that might be construed as sucking up to authority.

Then he stood up and moved to where he was just inches from my face. He looked down at me with a sneer, leaned over and muttered so that only I could hear, "That was a pretty good thank you note."

This afternoon, I was having tea with a sort-of-friend of mine who is a beginning therapist and interning at our school. She had just received her PhD from one of those pay-your-way graduate schools and she had just tackled her first adolescent. Guess who? That's right, Dawson. She kept repeating, "They are weird! They are just weird!" She plunged her fingers through her long, auburn hair which had fallen once again over her right eye and tossed it back over her shoulder... for the umpteenth time.

I mistakenly assumed that she was interested in my point of view when it came to dealing with adolescents, especially Dawson. I tried to explain that the reason for this weirdness is because of the containment in one transformational body both adult and child behaviors. She tossed her red hair back, wrinkled her freckled nose and looked at me skeptically.

I persisted, "They wax and wane before your eyes from children bouncing through bushes to young men, challenging and playing with you. As they flow like quicksilver from one extreme to another, so does your own identity become a little blurred around the edges as you find yourself playing hide and seek on your 48th birthday or telling a young man he can be a sweetheart." (Hair toss.)

I also told her that in spite of all the wear and tear they inflict upon whoever is working with them, that simply by being in the state of adolescence they offer something special which other students don't. "They keep you in touch with the energy of life. For them, this is a time of flowering. They are charged with earnest intensity. Some of their sparkle spills over onto whoever has the sticktoitiveness to work with them. They can be quite rejuvenating for a 48 year-old." (Hair toss.)

My sort-of-friend, being a new PhD, was sure that she could sum it all up more pithily, that I didn't have it quite right, but somehow she just couldn't put her finger on where I was wrong. (Hair toss.) I shifted into listening to what she wanted to talk about (my proper role), finished tea and returned home to write all this down to you. You, my sort-of-guru, don't deserve such wonderful letters.

Carolyn

REYNARD'S MIRROR

May, 1987

Chapter Seventeen

Rey's Messenger

Dear Rey,

You have been very good to me so I have decided to write to you again, in spite of the fact that it's been nearly a year since I've heard from you.

I am in a coffee shop, seated right next to a wonderful aquarium. Shiny gold and silver fish are sucking up gravel, gumming on the tidbits for a while, then spitting them back out. I am gumming up cherry pie (with no pits to spit out) and sipping coffee in celebration of the wonderful day I had yesterday with the psychoanalyst you sent to visit us.

Thank you, thank you, thank you for sending Dr. Semmering to spend a day with us at our school. What a treat! What an honor! And the kids loved him! But before I report to you about what his day was like, I would first like to describe the high point of his visit for me.

After he had spent the day at school, Julia, our school psychologist, and I took him down to a small craft harbor on the coast. We had settled down in an outdoor café by the docking areas so that he, being an avid sailor, could watch the sailboats. He and Julia had wine and I had a Cappuccino Americaine, aptly named, since it consisted of a tablespoon of expresso buried under mounds of whipped cream and chocolate bits. We sat in the cool spring day, watching the progress of sailboats and mammoth cabin cruisers gliding by on sapphire blue water wrinkled by the breeze. Suddenly Semmering became very still. Clearly he was about to say something important. I looked worriedly at his graying hair and weathered face, pensively organizing what he was going to say. Julia and I perched expectantly on the edge of our chairs.

"I want to tell you..." Pause. Wait. He ruminated with furrowed brow over how best to phrase this. All right! I said to myself, he's going to say something nice about our school and his day with us!

Suddenly he looked up and fixed his sea blue eyes on mine. Oh dear. This is for me, not us.

"...how much Rey enjoys your letters."

A silent 'Whoopee!' coursed through my body. Finally, now I know that you are enjoying my letters! Grudgingly, I must give you credit. You may not write back, but you certainly have a classy way of finally letting a person know she is appreciated.

Perhaps because you chose him and told us that we would like him, we felt an almost instant rapport and affection for him. Before the three of us were finished with our day, we had all told our life histories to each other. Throughout the day I had to keep mentally kicking myself to remember that this charming gentleman was, in fact, a faculty member of one of the nation's most prominent ivy league universities and that underneath his deceptively open exterior there was a tough-as-nails, razor-sharp mind.

He came to visit my classroom for an hour. I had prepared my students with background on him and on psychoanalysis so they would have topics to discuss with him. We were to have a tea party. Can't you just see it? My barely tamed carnivores with teacups and cookies in their paws, asking polite questions of the visiting professor?

We all knew when he arrived on campus. Our classroom would be the last one he visited. My students were as hyperactive as jackrabbits bouncing and hopping off the walls of the trailer. I ran a discussion about proper behavior for an honored guest and made a few helpfully containing threats if they weren't well-mannered. Naturally, they began to act out the show they'd put on for him. They turned into raving lunatics. Dawson and Nat engaged in mutual mock strangulation. Sonny began to drool at the mouth, his body thrashing around in an imitation epileptic fit. His white t-shirt (White! Not funereal black!) sported a new button purchased especially for this occasion which declared, "I'm going crazy. Wanna come with me?"

Their voices joined in a chorus of primal screams. Later, Semmering told me that he could hear them when he was in the trailer next door. I had just calmed them down when I was called to the telephone which, of course, was across the campus in the main building. Brooke had already left the room with the girls to make the tea and to set the cookies out on plates. The distance to that phone call seemed as far away as a trek across the Sahara. I snarled a few more threats about how they'd better behave themselves while I was gone and sprinted for the phone.

I raced back to find the radio blaring and the entire bunch (except for Gillian, and Kingsley) linked arm-in-arm doing high kicks to the music. Charlie was dancing on my desk, his head bouncing off the trailer ceiling. "Out!" I screamed. "Go take a break and come back in 15 minutes ready to be gracious hosts, or else!" As one, they jammed their bodies through the trailer doors and went howling across the playground, stopping to peek into the next door trailer to catch a glimpse of Dr. Semmering.

Fifteen minutes later you would have thought we were sitting in a college seminar. They were the very image of polite, eager students. Semmering charmed us

253

all. Sonny and Kingsley, who must always lurk as far in the back of the room as is humanly possible, began to scooch forward. Finally we were a tightly packed little group hanging onto his every word.

The day before Charlie had been shouting his condemnation in words of no more than four letters for anyone who would become a shrink. Today he was transformed into a polite young man capable of only saying shucks and golly. I was a little disappointed at such commendable behavior because I wanted Semmering to see them as they really are.

Just before Semmering left he said, "I have a question. He pointed to the large poster of the gold mask of Tutankhamen hanging upside down on the wall and asked, "Why is King Tut upside down?"

I told him that I had recently been sick for three days. On the day I returned I found all the moveable furniture had been tidily and carefully turned upside down, including the picture of King Tut. "When I saw what they had done, I told them that I was fairly sure this was their way of telling me they had missed me and were glad to have me back."

Semmering laughed, "Well, certainly! They were telling you that the world is upside down when you are gone."

"Oh!" I said, "Of course. How nice!" I beamed at them all, my little darlings.

He left to talk to the administrators and the school psychologists, but he was not going to escape my class so easily. They were not finished with him. Sonny, with his brand-new button, tracked him down in the restroom. He slipped into a stall, and while Semmering was busy at the urinal, he heard a voice echoing over the partition, "Do you think punk rock music makes people go bad?"

Sitting by the bay over wine and cappuccino, he

began to discuss his observations of the kids. He thought that the students were both fearful of him and the possible intrusion he might cause as a psychoanalyst. He also thought they had a great wish to be known and understood.

He also commented on what a sense of group unity they had. I was suddenly struck with how often they had shown me that this was indeed the case. My enthusiasm overcame me and I began to babble. I was as bad as Sonny had been in the men's room.

Just yesterday, I told him, Charlie and I happened to return from lunch at the same time. We climbed up the steps to the trailer together. The door was thrust open from the inside by Sissy who threw her arms around Charlie, sighing, "Oh, hubby, thank heavens you're home!"

Perplexed, I squeezed my way around the happy couple to see what was happening inside. Brooke was grinning at me. Sissy notified me that I was the grandmother of Deborah, who was married to Randy. Brooke was Randy's grandmother. Deborah and Randy were the parents of Sissy who, as I had just discovered, was married to Charlie. Dawson was Charlie's perverted brother who kept making advances to Deborah, his brother's mother-in-law. Sonny was the family dog. Nobody wanted Kingsley in the family, but they finally generously offered him the post of Sissy and Charlie's son. He accepted. Nat was absent, probably down at the beach. Gillian wasn't playing. She was mulishly doing her homework.

They proceeded to play out family dynamics. I sat on my desk and watched the drama unfold. It was fascinating. The very best soap opera...alcoholism, infidelity, incest, affection, and fights. I kept my mouth shut and forgot about teaching.

All this I told to Dr. Semmering, and more. I was doing fine, prattling on about my little educational victories, but then, he turned the tables on me. Suddenly he asked me to tell him about my own personal life and I discovered the power of the listener.

Not surprisingly, with this kindly father figure attentively consuming my every word, I found myself talking about my own father who died unexpectedly when I was only 22. He was a man who was always away on business, so that even though he and I were great friends, he spent very little time at home. I've told many people about him but they rarely made me feel like crying over such a long-ago tragedy. In this man's presence, my tale loomed with significance. I watched myself through his eyes as I re-experienced losing my father.

He said very little as I talked. Mostly he listened, but I knew this was a man who could see past my brittle words to the shuddering impact that death had made upon a young woman. I had no real way of knowing if my perception of his understanding was accurate or not, but my conviction in his power to understand allowed me to see myself and the whole experience differently. The power of his presence and the compassion in his eyes helped me to find sympathy for the young woman I had been.

So, sitting by the bay, I learned about the potency of the powerful listener. If he had talked a lot, even soothing or comforting words, he would not have had such an impact on me. It was his silence, his concerned eyes and my perception of him that were the key ingredients of my self-discovery. What does this tell me about teaching? What does this tell me about you?

It is important that my students see me as powerful. When new students are warned by the old pros that, "You gotta watch out for her, she'll shrink ya." I don't deny the allegation. I smile serenely. The new victim looks with apprehension at my Madonna-like smile. He fidgets with anxiety.

And as for you, I suppose your silent Buddha-like

presence implanted in my brain as I write letters to you, forces me to see myself and my students differently. Yes, you have two of the three key ingredients to be a powerful listener...silence and a powerful presence. What you are missing is Semmering's responsiveness. Not a sign of it for the past year. Consider yourself reprimanded.

Well, thanks again for sending him to us. I hope this enthusiastic response to him will leave you a teensy bit worried. A trade-in of the silent, reticent British model for the kindly, articulate American model did cross my mind. I hope that bothers you.

Thanks again,

Carolyn

REYNARD'S MIRROR

Early May, 1987

Chapter Eighteen

Expelled from Camelot

Dear Rey,

In spite of the fact that I've sacrificed and slaved here for 15 years, been abused by students, parents, school districts and administrators alike, put up with receiving a pathetic paycheck and then being begged not to cash it for a few days, and having to create my own curriculum for umpteen subjects from scratch by buying my own materials or dumpster diving in other school districts' trash bins, I was fired. On the other hand, my habitual tardiness, my inability to get paperwork in on time and my willingness to talk back and behave impetuously, may have contributed to the problem. However, my termination was not because of the aforementioned sins, but because I was caught trying to organize a protest for our union-free staff.

It all started when I came to work a couple of weeks ago and discovered that our accountant, an extremely kind-hearted woman, had been given an immediate dismissal and escorted off the premises. This was completely unexpected and she broke down in tears. This woman was a devout church-goer and a Sunday school teacher, for heaven's sake. She exuded earnestness and integrity. What happened to due process? What did this mean for the rest of the contract-free staff?

Now at the time, I didn't know that this was

customary when dealing with an employee who is responsible for money, but on the other hand, Paul was making no effort to let the rest of his nervous staff know what was going on. We were all living on the edge of poverty with basically nothing in the bank as a buffer. What if Paul suddenly pulled me in and fired me? I would be in a desperate situation. Nevertheless, fool that I am, I wrote a letter to the Board of Trustees complaining about the lack of due process. I circulated it, asking the staff to sign it if they were so inclined.

This wasn't the first time I had crossed Paul. Once when we were told that we were going to have to go another year with no cost of living increase, which basically meant a cut in pay, and Paul had made the mistake of having the Board of Trustees come to the school for an evening meeting, I decided to make a direct appeal to them. I had a speech all ready. I had practiced it with Adriane who appeared uneasy about my impulsive decision. When the time came, I stood up and lauded Paul, calling him a 'benevolent dictator', and described how the only reason I put up with such a low salary and my resultant poverty, was because of my enormous admiration for Paul.

I told them that I continued to be a loyal employee and was willing to work under such adverse conditions because of Paul's wisdom with kids and his willingness to be creative and spontaneous. I told them that the staff is a team, a tight family and we all continued to stay because of Paul's leadership. I would have thought that such effusive admiration would not have bothered Paul. We got our raise, but I'm pretty sure Paul was upset with my interference.

But back to being fired. One of my fellow employees ratted on me and my letter, my second attempt to reach the Board of Trustees, and I was called to Paul's office and immediately fired. Would I be immediately escorted off campus too? It would be nearly impossible to find work in the middle of a school year. I had no savings at all. I was overwhelmed at the thought of finding employment on such short notice.

Paul and I sat in his windowless brick-lined cube of an office, the scene of so many battles we had waged together, and we both stared at the floor. I could tell that although Paul was angry, he was not happy about having to fire me, but as he said, "I don't want to worry anymore about what you'll say or do next."

I looked at him and thought, he's uncomfortable about doing this. He won't look me in the eye. I think he wants to see submission. It looks like I'm going to have to cry. That is the only thing that could convince him. I can't afford to have my pathetic salary immediately cut off. So, in strategic self-defense to have enough time to find another job, I did what I figured he wanted. I cried, and promised to behave. I was genuinely upset and close to tears anyway. He backed off and said he would allow me to finish out the year if I really would behave myself. While I never know if good behavior is a real possibility for me, I told him what he wanted to hear. What other choice did I have?

To give him credit, this was probably the result he was hoping for from the beginning.

I had just turned 48. It was time to move on.

Probably the best thing Paul could have done for me was to fire me. I needed to get out of that exhausting pauperizing school. I am very grateful for what I learned at Mountainview. It was a magical place. I was very lucky that I was able to spend 15 years there. I felt no real anger at Paul. It was time for a parting of the ways...he to re-create Mountainview in a more acceptable public-school image, and me to find a more secure, better paying occupation.

A few days later, I went to a supervision session with Mitchell and told him about being fired. Mitchell can be so irritating at times. He grabbed my hand with tender compassion and said, "Well, he should have fired you! You deserved it and you needed to be fired."

Good ole Mitchell, always the provocateur with openers like that, something shocking to jangle the nerves and get my undivided attention. He continued, "Paul is the captain of a foundering ship and you are rocking the boat. The only thing he could do was throw you overboard."

"Of course he fired the accountant that way; otherwise she could do too much damage."

It was news to me that the boat was foundering. Why was now any different from the other 15 years' worth of foundering? I knew that Paul was trying to get money together to build a new school, closer to where most of our students live, and that the new location would be very near to a public school district office. He had become more distant and unapproachable towards my adolescents, who slouched about looking like stoners. Perhaps Paul was trying to impress donors, and the uncouth products of my classroom were not helping . If only I would shape up, and be more punctual, maybe my students would too. But we know how futile that would be, don't we?.

Well, after knocking me off my high horse, Mitchell became more sympathetic. "It's true; you have also been betrayed and mortally wounded by Paul. There was, in fact, a round table in Camelot. We all know that was the way Paul liked to run his school. It was a place to grow, be spontaneous and do some wonderful work with children, and that's been yanked away. The citizens of this state decided long ago that they would rather lock children up than put money into helping them, and Mountainview is suffering as a result." He told me that wishing Paul had been more transparent about the changing conditions was a waste of breath, "Paul had to do what he needed to do. It is unfair for you to think that he should be different."

Internally, I disagreed with this. If the staff had

had some power, as in a union, then more transparency might have been forced from Paul. More to the point, I would have had due process, but in a private school, with no contracts, I could be disposed of at will.

Mitchell continued, "You on the other hand, are very right to leave. You need to get out of there. You've been sucking at the teat for long enough. You don't need it anymore."

"What you need to do is find yourself a twenty-hour a week job. You could work in a clinic, do something that will provide basic subsistence. Then you could begin to get established in various offices as oh, an educational therapist charging maybe $30-$35 a session so that you can get yourself and your work known. If you take a full-time job teaching, you'll be just as burdened as you are now and you won't be able to get out from under the load." Then he began to make all kinds of offers of help: people he could recommend me to; office space; and letters of recommendation; saying, "You know you're a better therapist than most therapists."

His suggestions were bold and adventurous. Once again, I weighed teaching against becoming either an educational therapist or a regular sit-in-a-room-and-listen-to-your-troubles therapist. I decided that I needed to keep my options open and apply to public school districts for work while I explored his suggestions.

So there you have it, Rey. I am through at Mountainview. I have to move on. Since I am dubious about what a letter of recommendation from Paul might say, I wonder if you might consider writing one for me. I need three. I'm also asking Mitchell and a parent of one of my previous students.

Late May, 1987

Well, I received your letter of recommendation

today. I really appreciate the nice things you had to say about me. On the other hand, you may have doomed me. Think! How many administrators are going to want to hire the person you described in this paragraph?

"She is an outspoken woman and I should think that she does not suffer incompetence or insincerity in fellow workers very easily. I am sure that some people find her too full blooded or outspoken. Equally, however, I am certain that a creative director or creative staff would value a person with her mix of integrity, courage, intelligence and creativity."

While that last sentence was lovely, I really think you have no clue about the caliber of administrators in the public education world. This will terrify them. It will be a brave person who hires me after reading what you had to say about me.

Thanks, I think,

Carolyn

P.S. Kent dropped by last week! You wouldn't have thought that an unpleasant moment had ever passed between us, or that he had left in such a rejecting way. He just rushed in, hopped on his old desk, and beamed at me. Then he blurted out more about his life than he ever had shared in his entire time as a student. He has dropped out of high school, gotten a job and his own apartment which he shares with a roommate. He has plans of going to night school to finish his high school education. During most of the conversation I was in shock, but I sat and talked to him as though we always had such a chatty relationship. It was wonderful to see his tan dark-eyed cherubic face smiling at me like we were the best of old friends.

June, 1987

Chapter Nineteen

A Contrast in Summer Breaks

Dear Rey,

Well it is the last night of the school year, and apparently my last year at Mountainview. Now all I have to do is find a job while teaching summer school. I am celebrating, or is it a wake. I can't be sure. Besides being fired, my EX-partner, Brooke, has been wrenched away from me and assigned to another classroom for summer school by my unfeeling boss. She is out having dinner at an elegant restaurant. My buddy Adriane and her husband are enjoying the delights of a cruise through the Inside Passage in the Alaskan Panhandle. Julia is off doing Spartan churchy things. Most of my fellow two-income colleagues are taking exciting trips to Mexico or the Caribbean. They've been saving their pennies all year and planning for today. They have something to fill the gap and keep their minds occupied now that the vacation vacuum has arrived. I have great difficulty planning ahead. I am always preoccupied with the here and now and forgetful of the future.

So what am I doing now that I have achieved release from my adolescent charges? I'm sitting on my bed with my rented typewriter in front of me, indulging in eating potato chips and drinking pink champagne from a pickle jar. Two of my three dogs are sitting on the bed looming vulture-like over me. My sense of feeling at loose ends and left out of life in the fast lane, is alleviated by the rapt attention with which my two beauties are surveying me, tracking my slightest movement towards the potato chip sack. They quiver with expectancy at that most hopeful of all moments when I slip up and look them in the eyes. I inevitably get lost in their warm brown depths and cannot refuse them their most ardent desire, an onion sour-cream potato chip.

As an analyst you must experience similar feelings when a patient/client leaves you. You have the advantage of me. Hopefully yours do not leave until they're ready, and they don't all leave at once. Besides losing my place at Mountainview, I've just lost three of my students for good and my insensitive boss has taken my aide Brooke away from me for the summer as well. He justified this with petty reasons like budget costs and the needs of another despicable teacher. The woman has the nerve to have a much bigger summer school class of little five to seven year olds with penchants for hysterical tantrums.

If only Paul wouldn't wait until the last minute to make these changes. One moment my last summer at Mountainview was bright with promise, the next it was trashed. Brooke turned white when I broke the news to her. When she told the class today, they were outraged, even the ones who were leaving. They threatened to go on strike unless she was returned to the class in the fall. They do not know about me leaving yet.

Working at this school has been like being on a rollercoaster, the ups and downs are so precipitous and unexpected. Last weekend for example, I had the entire class, with the exception of Gillian, up at a resort on the eastern slopes of the Sierra Nevada. While we all had our moments, I think that this was one of the most satisfying groups I have ever taken away from home for four days. There was a tremendous sense of group unity. At one of

266

the stops we made in the Mojave Desert they spilled out of the three cars and swooped into the hapless business establishment, a small market. In that last bastion of civilization for the next 200 miles, Sonny, complete with mascara, black fingernail polish, black lipstick, and black leather jacket, commented to the alarmed manager, "You wouldn't think to look at us that we are all in the same family, but we are."

The following Wednesday, three of my totally unprepared babes were pushed prematurely out of the nest. Deborah, Gillian and Randy had enough credits. They were eligible for graduation, so out the door they went.

On Thursday, the toad took one of the best aides I've ever had away from me.

Today, Friday, I lost them all. Well, I shall get a reluctant five back in summer school – Sissy, Dawson, Nat, Charlie and Sonny. Kingsley managed to miss so much school that he will have to graduate at the end of summer school.

So I sit with my $2.89 bottle of champagne. Who can afford better on my pay? I fret over what to do with myself. I have no job interviews lined up, and it is getting very late in the year. Hoss, my 95 pound pussycat, just rescued me from my miserable reverie by poking his nose into my potato chip bag, taking matters into his own paws because of the inexcusable delay in the reinforcement schedule. Sigh.

When there are two adults in the classroom, the students usually sort themselves out into relating to one teacher more than the other. During the past year, Brooke has been paying special attention to Sissy who was well aware that I would not be enough of a mother for her. She knew Brooke would have more patience with her incessant moment-to-moment traumas she brought daily to class. Sissy has had three mothers, but none of them had ever taken much care of her. Sissy was still searching for someone to mother her. Regardless of Brooke's feelings, Sissy labeled her 'mom'. She could be seen poking her head intrusively into the teachers' lounge or peering under the doors of bathroom stalls seeking a beloved pair of feet. Her cry would echo in the hallways, across the playing fields, in the gym. "Where's mom? Don't any of you know where my mom is?" We grew used to hearing the rising crescendo of her voice reverberating throughout the school as her momentary problem of the day threatened to swallow her whole. Only Brooke could give her relief. The staff soon learned to keep track of Sissy's 'mom'.

In the classroom's intricate matrix of ties and connections, Brooke and I balanced and contained all its rampant energy. We were a great team, and now it's over.

Brooke and I went out to dinner last evening and I spent most of the time telling her that she really doesn't need me anymore, and trying to convince myself that I will be alright without her. I am going to miss that cool-headed sense of integrity and her witty sense of humor, and so will the kids.

It is hard, raising a student or an aide and then having to let them go. Year after year they leave, an endless annual marching of lost sons and daughters that disappear, never to be seen again.

I think I had really better think of something to do with myself, or else I shall really be bogged down in depression.

California Holiday Motel
King City, CA

I have decided to continue with the tale of how I am coping with the end of school and my time at Mountainview by writing about my final senior trip adventures as I go up the coast of California. I am finally off on a vacation of my own, not as exotic as a trip to the Caribbean or Alaska, of course, but it will serve the purpose of reorienting me to my existence.

Driving up in the dark, I was reminded of why I do this. As I watched the highway swerve back and forth in front of my headlights, the hypnotic white line sinuously leading me forward, I was struck by how similar life is to driving at night. We hang by a slender thread, racing ahead mindlessly, praying we won't meet disaster in a headlong rush. Trips by myself force me to once again concentrate on the pleasure of being alive in the midst of potential annihilation. Being alone on a fairly safe edge reminds me to relish what is mine. I've always felt that, in comparison to the rest of the world's population, I really hit the jackpot when and where I was born. I can vote, drive my aging VW up the California coast alone, and return to my leaky home. How many women on this planet have so much? Nevertheless, I intend to get my money's worth out of this carnival ride while being hurtled through space into oblivion.

As I drove up here, I remembered my final senior trip, taking my students up to Mammoth Lakes, a ski resort on the east side of the Sierra Nevada. That also had been in the middle of the night. We had three cars and I was leading the caravan in my VW bus while Brooke and Tony (the assistant coach I borrowed from the P.E. Department), drove their cars. Our route took us across the Mojave Desert on long stretches of road that were only two lanes, making us struggle to keep together, having to pass lumbering turtle-like cars in front of us while dodging on-coming heat-seeking missiles posing as trucks.

There were moments of real panic that dark night. I was crazy. What on earth was I doing taking this weirded-out batch of kids up to the mountains? Did I actually think I could control them? Hah! Did I think I could handle any mechanical breakdowns on the highway? Another hysterical notion. I was actually responsible for this entire bunch and I was leading them to a cabin resting right on the edge of a potential volcanic crater showing recent signs of seismic activity. When I called the rangers at the National Forest headquarters about the situation, I was reassured that the volcano was slated to erupt any time in the next hundred years. "Of course, the opening up of new fumarole vents and the daily earthquakes are of some concern, but don't let it ruin your vacation."

I muttered prayers to an alien being hopefully somewhere up in the heavens looking out for well-intentioned special ed. teachers, surely a group who need special monitoring. I chewed gum, drank coffee out of my thermos, hoping to stay awake but I only succeeded in making myself more jittery.

My only consolation, if you can call it that, was the blaring cacophony of adolescent music, raspy with speakers strained to the breaking point in little portable tape decks. A chorus of complaints accompanied this concert. Somehow the noise and the demands pulled me together. These were noxious irritants I was familiar with while visions of the possible vicissitudes of a malevolent fate caused me to feel as if I would fly apart into little bleating pieces.

Comforting were the cranky demands to satisfy their various yawning appetites. We had decided to start out at night to avoid the searing heat of the Mojave Desert, especially since my VW has no air-conditioning. For some reason my bus was the chosen vehicle of Dawson, Nat and Randy. They elbowed Kingsley out of the way and told him to find someplace else to ride. I didn't intervene. I needed to have some space from my shadow. As soon as Dawson got into the car, he told me he was hungry. Never mind that I had warned him in the parking lot at school to go to the bathroom and make sure he had something to eat because we wouldn't be stopping for the distance of one gas tank.

"Well how far is that?"

"About 250 miles."

"What! You expect me to wait that long?"

"I told you before you got into the car..."

"Listen, I get sick if I don't eat when I'm hungry."

"Well, I warned you that..."

"Come on Carolyn. When's the next city. You can stop there."

We were driving down the freeway through one of the longest stretches of neon-lit urbanization in the civilized world. They seemed oblivious to the fact that we had never left town and still had about two hours before we would finally leave the city behind.

Nat joined in to protect Dawson from any inroads I might make with reason and logic. "You can stop when we get to the next town. I'm hungry too. I can't wait that long."

Randy also joined in to support Dawson. With his slow country drawl, he offered, "Yep, Carolyn, you've got a carload of hun-n-gry boys on your hands. You're gonna hafta do somethin about it soon."

They browbeat me into making a stop 150 miles down the road.

We climbed back into the bus and the complaints started up all over again. It was too cold. The bus was too uncomfortable. They had to pee. They wanted to drive. They could drive better than I could. They wanted me to drive faster. They monitored my speedometer and were disgusted with me if the needle slipped down to the speed limit. As the journey progressed into the early hours before dawn and the drivers had to stop in order to stay awake, I could hear their groggy voices still complaining outside of Lone Pine as I jogged up and down the highway to restore circulation to my pins-and-needles brain.

"Where are we now?"

"Stopped again? What the hell is taking so long?"

Then they rolled over to snuggle down into a

snooze. Outside the bus, hopping from foot to foot, I looked through the windows at their limber adolescent bodies heavy in slumber in the back of my bus. I climbed back in to tackle more endless miles ribboning out before me. Dawn light at the foot of the Sierras brought a renewed sense of mastery and confidence in my ability to handle it all. We headed up Sherwin Grade, climbing into the grandeur of a rosy dawn bathing jagged, snow-capped mountain peaks.

Yes, their nagging helped to restore my sense of self. The familiarity of it all, even out in the blackest night in the Mojave Desert, helped a lot. When Dawson threatened to take a piss in the car if I didn't stop at the next hamburger joint, and I kept offering hip-high creosote bushes, which he finally accepted, he didn't know what a help he was being to me.

They must have had the same kind of fragmenting feelings themselves, taking on an unknown trip of such magnitude. Perhaps these panicky feelings were expressed in their nagging. The next day after we arrived in Mammoth, I was confronted with a wrenched leg that just had to lay on the couch the entire day (Charlie), a sore toe that had to be undressed and clucked over (Kingsley) and a hangnail that remained under my nose until I had done enough commiserating over the outrage of injury (Sissy).

I used to scoff at these little hurts, telling them to be tough and stop bothering me with such petty matters. Now I think they are testing me. Will I pay enough attention to them to keep them safe? Will I have the where-with-all to take proper care of them if they get sick or hurt?

It's hard going out into the world where no one cares. We must all face the stony indifference of life. I feel it tonight marooned in King City. I'm sure they felt it off in the wilds of a cabin in Mammoth with me. Well, I'm exhausted. I'd better try to sleep, although I don't want to turn out the lights in this barren motel room and lie here staring into the darkness with the winds of planets ringing in my ears.

Wednesday afternoon,
Point Lobos State Park

I am sitting at the end of Cypress Point. It is glorious here right now...sunny, cool, and breezy. The grass is a rich emerald green and has not turned yellow as it has down south. The grass is speckled with purple irises, little yellow blossoms and baby-blue daisies. The cliff walls below me are covered with the thick white rosettes of sea bluff lettuce and magenta bursts of ice plant. They look as if they have been designed by a Japanese artist. There are no sea otters in sight. The surging ocean is turquoise, white, and sapphire coated with fluxes of crystalline sparkles and foam. In fact, sparkles are everywhere, shiny leaves, crystal flakes in the granite cliff, spider webs, dandelion puffs. I love this place. I am completely at home here. I am going to move in regardless of what the state might say. Point Lobos and I are meant for each other.

Towards dusk, on my way back to my bus, I took the trail through the forest of Monterey Pine. On the leeward side of the peninsula it is dark and quiet. Few tourists hike this far away from the parking lot. I surprised a doe and her two fawns. She spooked and leaped off in a different direction from her babies. In order to get back to them she had to re-cross the trail. I stood perfectly still for about 15 minutes and had a marvelous time.

While her fawns forgot their fears and settled down to browse again, mother was uncertain about what to do with me. She moved out onto the path, taking delicate mincing steps towards me and moved her long neck about, craning this way and that while her over-sized rabbity ears twitched. She raised her muzzle and sniffed, but the wind was in the wrong direction. Finally, she began to approach me making loud stamps with her delicate hooves, one firm purposeful stamp at a time. Slowly, step by step she came to within 10 yards of me. Now I was beginning to feel spooked. It became an anxious stand-off. We stood and stared at each other until I politely looked to one side. Feeling she had me sufficiently cowed, she snorted loudly and bounded off, herding her fawns in front of her. I could hear her snorting as she disappeared into the forest. I followed her down the trail, noting with respect how much those deceptively tiny hooves had torn up the path.

If my class had been with me on this trip, they could not have stood quietly and appreciated the beauty of these deer. For them a deer or a sea otter is a moving target, a toy for one of their games, something to destroy with a gun in order to test their prowess and immunity from death. These students spend all their energies calming their fears and anxieties about themselves. Only the healthiest ones can enjoy the world around them, or the ones most symbiotically attached to me who must trail along and notice the landscape in order to keep my attention. The others run to their own society for safety and the rehearsal of old conversations and behaviors that provide a relief in alien places.

As I drove up to Mammoth with them, I found as I often do, that if I keep my mouth shut they seem to forget about my presence and begin to talk naturally about themselves. I heard a side of them that generally is kept secreted from me, and is depressing. Their conversation continuously revolved around anything that will stimulate them, sate their appetites or allay their anxiety about their potency.

When I hear them talk so frankly among

themselves, I understand how foolish my expectations are that they will ever be able to function like reasonable people. As we passed a gasoline tank truck, Nat joked, "Wouldn't it be rad if I could throw this soda bottle under the wheel of that truck so it would flip over and explode!"

Dawson and Randy agreed that this would be quite a sight.

"Imagine," Nat continued as the appeal of the image led him forward, "if it ran off the freeway and into the side of a house."

"Yep, there'd be a lot of people fryin', screamin' and runnin' around on fahr." Randy chuckled at the internal sight.

How could I get these kids to stand silently and observe a doe and her two fawns, enjoying the truths of her existence, tapping into her dapple-green, bird-piping, pine-scented life? How can I even get them to function in the act of learning unless I am pandering directly to their ravenous appetites for mindless thrills?

Who knows? Maybe this is how all adolescent boys think, and I am just being an alarmist. Still, I have to wonder what on earth I can offer these boys whose eyes light up at the thought of burning people fleeing disaster.

Thursday evening
Santa Cruz Mountains

I am renting the same cabin in the coastal redwoods that I had when I first moved here to begin my teaching career over 16 years ago. I am sitting in the kitchen and looking out through the glass-paned front door. I am resting my eyes on the green misty light filtering through the lacey needles of these wonderful ancient trees.

Today I went to Año Nuevo State Reserve.[6] There I lay in the sand for about 2 hours and hung my head over a sandy escarpment to watch an elephant seal herd about 6 feet below me. After being scrutinized by a young male with watery deep brown eyes, he gurgled a half-hearted challenge, blinked and stared, then blinked some more. Then he and I settled in to observe the machinations of herd life.

As I describe this, you must keep in mind that elephant seal siestas are continuously punctuated by the sounds of bugling challenge. It is a hard sound to capture, something between the roar of a lion and the emptying out of a stopped-up drain, a sort of a glug-glug-glug kind of roar.

We all lay in the warm sun, our ears peeled for the sounds of shushing sand; those tons of rubbery flesh can slide almost silently across that grainy surface. I shared their contentment as they lay soaking up the heat, flinging  cooling sand on their black backs and occasionally reaching an amazingly human-like flipper hand around to scratch delicately at an interfering itch. Some snored or seemed to have dreams. I was lying above two old scared vets who didn't move more than a flipper for over two hours until an immaculately coated youth lollopped his huge body over the top of both of them.

But back to telling you of my class' trip to Mammoth. The father of one of our ex-students had a

---

[6] This actual event occurred before a ranger station was established there, and no rangers or fences limited where a visitor could wander. Now, the clueless tourist is protected from such folly, especially during mating season.

cabin up there and was willing to let us use if for a four-day weekend. Probably the highlight of our trip to Mammoth was the spaghetti dinner. On the second afternoon, a planning session was held and my three passengers, Nat, Randy and Dawson, nobly volunteered to cook dinner. I knew what rank amateurs Randy and Dawson were as cooks so I heroically volunteered to clean up after them. After dinner we would celebrate Sissy's eighteenth birthday. It was still early in the day, a few hours before dinner needed to be started, so Brooke and I went into town, leaving Tony to keep an eye on the students. We needed to find a birthday present for Sissy. Today she was graduating into legal adulthood and at the end of summer school she would be graduating. Since she was so attached to Brooke, she was already mourning the loss of her school mom.

"You won't miss me when I'm gone," she told Brooke, "you'll just find somebody else and forget all about me." Brooke had decided to make things as special as she could for Sissy's birthday.

When we came back from our shopping, dinner was under way. There were five kids in the kitchen, the three boys who were supposed to be there, and the two self-appointed housemothers, Sissy and Deborah, who weren't. Deborah rushed out to me wailing, "I can't stand it! You should see what they're doing in the kitchen. I try to help them and all I get is abuse. You have to go in there and save our dinner. They'll ruin it if you don't!"

Calming her down, I sagely told her that it was the boys' responsibility and that as long as the girls took care of them, they would never learn to cook for themselves. I told her to leave them alone. Then I went into the kitchen. Only a fool would leave them alone.

The meal they had volunteered to cook was a relatively simple one, spaghetti, garlic bread and salad. Nat was making the sauce. He had spent most of his life fending for himself and knew his way around a kitchen.

Randy and Dawson were in charge of cooking the noodles, and making the salad and garlic bread. They both have doting mothers so they were lost and confused in a kitchen. This was a place where females belonged, not males.

As soon as I entered the kitchen, Nat began to yell at me for 'bailing' on cooking the dinner. "Where have you been? You were supposed to be one of the cooks! It's pretty chicken-shit of you to leave us with the work."

I gave him a piece of my mind for yelling at me and reminded him that I was on clean-up, not cooking. I sympathized with his frustration though. He was the only competent one in the kitchen and he needed help with the other two. I decided that Dawson was probably the worst cook of the bunch, so I offered to help him.

He was ineffectually ripping at the outside of a head of iceberg lettuce and tossing scraps into a bowl. I asked him if he had washed the lettuce. He looked at me blankly and then scowled. He carried the head of lettuce over to the sink where he passively held it under the tap as if the water running down and around the outside would somehow magically penetrate the interior. I took it from him, turned it over and started showing him how to spread the leaves apart so that water could get into the interior. He snapped at me, "Don't hold it for me like I'm a little kid!" He yanked it out of my hands and started back to the counter with it. About a pint of water poured out of the lettuce onto the floor. He looked down at the puddle on the floor and then up at me, his face radiating complete conviction that I was the cause of this and all the other afflictions in his life. I backed off and left him alone, feeling considerable anxiety as he savagely tore gobs of lettuce apart, chopped the tomatoes into quarters and the carrots into two-inch chunks and threw them all into the salad bowl. Much later in the evening, when hunger drove me to the salad, I found two inches of water standing in the bottom of the bowl.

Brooke interrupted me before I could offer to help a greatly depressed Randy with the mysteries of making garlic bread. She grabbed me by the sleeve and pulled me out of the kitchen. I found myself being offered the same advice I had just given to Deborah. "Now Carolyn, you've got to leave them to themselves. They're always being taken care of and they need to cope with this on their own. I think we should just leave the house and let them manage it as best as they can."

I felt relief pour through me, then guilt. I knew better than to leave them, but who wants to be yelled at for trying to help them? And then, I'm sure I wanted revenge. I wanted the pleasure of seeing them suffer. I remembered all those hours of abuse at their hands. I also wanted them to face the rock-hard fact that everything in life can't be done half-assed with mommy around to make it better when they throw a big enough tantrum. I knew I would pay for this, but what the hell, I wanted out of there.

However, before I left, I knew that I had better cover my tracks, so I went into the kitchen and concocted the best story that I could think of to legitimize my abandonment of them. I told them that I thought my hanging around was only making things worse. "I'm going to leave for a while, but before I go I want to make sure that things are under control and you know what to do." I reviewed the intricacies of making garlic bread and boiling water to cook noodles, then asked them, "Is there anything left to cook that you don't understand?"

No.

Offering a final feeble pep talk, I nervously repeated myself. "I'm going to go because you've done the hardest part which is making the sauce. All that is left is to cook the garlic bread and the noodles. I'm sure you can handle that, especially if we leave you in peace."

Good ole Randy, sensing that I needed absolution, rescued me. "Just go ahead Carolyn. We can handle it all by ourselves."

Having obtained permission, I fled joyously outside into the freedom of a sparkling Sierra night sky. Brooke, Deborah, Sissy, Tony and I went down to Mammoth Village. We found a restaurant, bought drinks, and were all very silly, exulting in having escaped the oppressiveness of smoldering adolescent boys discovering their incompetence. We laughed. We dawdled. But eventually there was nothing left but to go back to the cabin and eat our questionable dinner.

We returned to an ominously silent and darkened cabin. We climbed up the interior stairs to the living room. The fireplace stood empty and cold. Students sat slumped together, vague shapes in the gloom. In contrast, the light from the kitchen was glaring. I could just make out a confused jumble on the kitchen counter.

Tony asked, "Is dinner ready?"

We heard an assortment of mutters, "Yeah, sure. It's done. We've already eaten."

Deborah and Sissy rushed past me. I thought, oh dear, we stayed too long at the fair. I had known that they would get us somehow for leaving them. I had visions of everything being eaten up and no dinner left for us. I was to discover that once again, I was being optimistic.

I heard a squeal from the kitchen and my spirits sank. "Oh my God! Carolyn, come and look at this!" Deborah's voice, quavering with shock, called to me. "I've never seen a mess like this in my entire life!"

I stood frozen in the darkened living room, peering fiercely at the dusky huddled shapes in the gloom. I heard Randy's soft drawl, "Yep, it was all downhill after you left, Carolyn."

Deborah was right. I had never seen such a mess either. Overwhelmed by the enormity of it all, we forgot about the tremendous chore of cleaning it up. Females together, Brooke, Deborah, Sissy and I broke up into hysterics. United in our female superiority we laughed ourselves silly, pointing out highlights to each other with fresh bursts of guffaws. Understandably, this angered our three pathetic cooks. Dawson shouted at us from the dark of the living room, "Laugh it up, cause we're not on clean-up."

This sobering thought yanked us to a halt. Cleaning this up would take hours. Along one wall of the little kitchen a small, immaculate white stove had once held center stage. Now it was barely recognizable under blotches of red spaghetti sauce which coated its surfaces. More pots and pans than I thought the cabin contained lay everywhere. Spaghetti noodles stood at right angles to the strainer in hardened erect stands of columnar pasta. Oddments of vegetables and garbage lay everywhere on the counters. The sink was filled with dirty dishes. Paper towels, napkins, utensils, paper plates, ravaged baguettes of French bread and a soggy bowl of salad were strewn about on every available bit of counter space. Even the kitchen floor had not escaped. The portions not underwater grabbed at our shoes as Brooke and I tiptoed stickily back to the living room.

Tony turned on the light in the living room. My students blinked owlishly at us. Brooke and Tony were grumbling that there was no way the cleaning crew was responsible for this mess. Since I was on the cleaning crew, I heartily agreed with them. I began to organize us all for the next battle. "OK, we've got a lot to decide and..."

I was interrupted by another squeal from the kitchen. Deborah, ever the alert one, had found another problem. "Carolyn! They've ruined this pot!" I went back to the kitchen to find a blackened mass caked on the entire bottom of a shiny new aluminum pot. It was the pot Dawson had used to cook the noodles. My suspicious mind speculated about what they had been up to while this pot achieved such a thick layer of carbon. This was surely revenge for leaving them alone.

Facing them again in the living room, I told them, "Now I'm on the clean-up crew and I'm willing to help out, but when the cooks are as sloppy as this they must assume some responsibility for what they've done. Furthermore, if that aluminum pot can't be salvaged, they will have to replace it with a new one. Brooke and Tony both echoed agreement. Tony was really shocked at what they had done in an hour. "This is ridiculous," he said, shaking his head at the enormity of it all. He glared at the cooks.

As I have said, Tony is the assistant P.E. coach. He is young, dark and very muscular. He grew up in a very rough part of town and has survived many gang fights. If Tony wanted the cooks back in the kitchen to clean up, they would probably obey quite meekly. I told them we would all help, but they must clean up most of it because it was their fault.

They grumbled but did not resist with Tony staring stonily at them. Of course, this presented a secondary problem. Again, it was only Nat who could clean up. At one point I found Dawson swabbing down the spaghetti-blotched stove with the cabin owner's expensive velour bath towel. I lost it.

"What the hell do you think you're doing? Don't you know that towel costs a lot of money? Do you want to pay for both a new towel and an aluminum pot?" He looked down at the towel and back up at me, then he threw the towel down on the floor. I waited for him to stalk out of the kitchen, as he has done so often in school, but he did not. He picked up the towel and took it back to the bathroom. I was surprised at his self-control.

Evidently, they had had no supper either, except for chunks of French bread which they had sopped in the spaghetti sauce, the accomplishment of the only experienced cook among them. Spaghetti-sauce coated bread had been their meal. Poor babies, no wonder they were sitting in the dark waiting for us to come and rescue them.

Since we had a limited food budget we could not cook another meal. I also wanted to use this experience to present reality to them. For most people on this planet, if food is wasted, it is simply gone and hunger is the result. Deprivation would be a novel experience to these well-off California youths who expect all kitchens to be inexhaustible cornucopias.

After the kitchen was restored to its original condition, and Dawson remained behind, scouring the aluminum pot he had burned, we proceeded with the after-dinner plans. Brooke began to cook Sissy's birthday cake. Unfortunately she forgot to compensate for the fact that we were at nearly 9,000 feet of altitude. Such an elevation requires adjustments in the recipe, especially when baking. The cake was another disaster. As Brooke attempted to plaster icing on its caved-in and crumbling surfaces, we all sat around and laughed at her. Poor Sonny, starving from a day on the toboggan slopes, kept sticking his finger in the icing and licking it off. He said it was worth getting his knuckles rapped with Brooke's wooden spoon.

Finally, about midnight we served up the only real meal of the evening, ice cream and cake. We turned out the lights, lit the candles which were sitting askew upon the cake's hummocky surface, and Tony went downstairs to the girls' room for the birthday girl. He reappeared carrying a radiant bundle in his arms. Sissy was protesting loudly with a huge grin, "I'm busy reading my book! Don't bother me!"

She was elated, blowing out the candles, reading each card with deliberation and opening her presents with tedious precision to avoid tearing the wrapping paper. She was oblivious to her guests who looked funereal as they waited in the flickering candlelight for their sugar-laden dinner. I shouted encouragement to them as I trotted around their periphery taking pictures. "Listen, someday you'll look back on all of this and laugh. Everybody is doing fine. You missed your dinner and had to face an awful clean-up, but you are really doing very well." I was ignored. They ate their lopsided cake and ice cream in silence, which was only punctuated by complaints that there wasn't enough ice cream.

Well enough of this. After my day of lounging with elephant seals, I have returned to my cabin. There are wonderful redwoods outside my door; they are huge, dark shadows against the night sky. There is also a huge, dark half-dollar sized spider I've just found in my bed, captured and abandoned to the hardships of life on the porch. I told the landlord about it and he complained about my not killing it, saying, "Thanks a lot! In a week there'll be 500 little offspring clamoring to get inside."

Tomorrow I shall start back down the coast. I will stop off at Point Lobos again. There are a few trails left that I haven't hiked. Perhaps I shall see some sea otters.

Friday evening
California Holiday Motel
King City

I spent the day at Point Lobos again. I had a wonderful time. I found a small cove where two sea otters were napping in the kelp. I climbed down into the cove and took up a post on some nearby rocks. The otters had wrapped themselves in kelp fronds and were curled up like kittens into brown balls. The kelp cradled them in place as they rose and fell while underwater waves rolled through the crystal clear submarine garden to splash mildly on the rocky shore.

More interesting was a quartet of sea lions

competing for space on the rocks nearby. The biggest of the bunch held the dry portions. The rocks jutted out into the cove and captured the incoming swells, which poured over the top and around the edges of the sea lion lounging area. I watched one in particular who kept fidgeting. Waves would wet his belly and this was clearly aversive after having achieved a warm, dry tummy. He inched closer and closer to another sea lion only to be threatened with growls back to his former damp spot. He was very aware of my presence and would periodically stare at me, trying to estimate how much interference I would cause him during his afternoon nap.

Finally, a very large wave swept into the narrow neck of the cove and washed my poor sea lion right off his perch. As soon as he re-surfaced, he looked right at me. He swam over to a cranny where he could climb back up to his former spot. He surged out of the water into the cranny, but slipped back into the choppy water. He turned and looked at me. Finally he went to another rock. I watched him push his body up onto a six-inch wide ledge inclined at an angle of about 45 degrees. Amazingly the undulations of his belly allowed him to climb up that narrow, barnacled and mossy slope. He finally came to a halt on a flat surface not much bigger than the palm of my hand. He scooched himself around until he was facing the water and closed his eyes to the warm sun, flippers and head held high in the air. Observing these aquatic mammals has produced an uneasy sense that they really are four-legged animals trapped in streamlined bodies. At times, I could see the outlines of shoulders, elbows and arms straining for freedom, for release from their containing flesh.

I sat in the sun at the edge of a crystal tide pool dotted with purple sea urchins and ate my red cherries and green grapes fresh from the Salinas Valley and pondered the afternoon of a sea lion with satisfaction. As I continued to watch my sea lion arch his body to the rays of the sun, I began to feel sympathetic aches in the back of my neck. I finished my lunch and left my sea lion and otter post and headed back the long way across the peninsula to my VW. I wandered through cypress groves and pine forests, their branches heavy with moss. I found grassy glades unencumbered with poison oak that beckoned me to come and take a nap. Sea mammals understand the importance of a nap in the middle of the day.

Tomorrow I must try to get my aging bus back down to the streets of urban California. Wish me luck! It's sounding a little rocky on the timing; at least I hope it's the timing and not a valve ready to break off and rocket about the inside of my engine casing.

It's sad to be at the end of my trip, but it is also very satisfying. Assuming that I make it tomorrow without any problems, I will have accomplished an adventure on my own. My backbone will have been propped up by an exercise regime of independence and assertiveness. I can descend again into the pit of special education summer school with my head held high, and even without Brooke, I'll be ready to give the little buggers a dose of what they need.

After we arrived home safely from our class trip, Brooke, Tony and I compared notes about what had happened in our cars during the drive home. It's clear to me that the kids were having the same feelings I'm having tonight. They had survived. They were going home to a familiar kind of safety. Their spirits were bubbling. A lot was accomplished on that eight-hour trip back home.

I haven't said too much about Tony, the third adult helping to manage my class. As I mentioned before, he had a very tough childhood. He was a person who never lost his temper. The lessons of his youth had taught him just what was worth losing your temper over. Kingsley, probably because he had been separated from me once again and had to ride with Tony, managed to transform Tony from his low-key, soft-spoken self into a fuming, tight-lipped stranger. I knew the feeling well.

While filling up my gas tank at a lonely outpost in the Mojave, I noticed with mild interest that Tony was replaying a scene with Kingsley similar to the one I had shared with you. I'd never seen Tony so angry, yelling at Kingsley with clinched fists. Then he stalked over to me and said, "You'd better get Kingsley out of my car because I'll kill him if you don't." I looked with alarm at his enraged face. "Anything you say, Tony." This was certainly not a rift that could be patched up.

My threesome refused to relinquish their spaces and urged me to ship him home on the Greyhound bus, a proposition with considerable merit, I thought. After toying with abandoning Kingsley to the coyotes, Brooke made the sacrifice of stowing him in the back of her VW Bug with Sonny. Deborah, by virtue of her pleasant verbal skills had won the front seat.

Deborah had been avoiding the fact that she would soon be leaving us. "So," she would tell me, "what's the big deal?" During the last month of school she kept finding appointments, job interviews, and all sorts of more important matters to keep her out of the classroom as we neared the end. When I confronted her with this, she told me, "I don't want to talk about leaving. If you keep it up you'll make me cry. I think you won't be happy until you get me to cry."

In spite of her mother's apathy, Deborah had salvaged herself. I knew we meant an enormous amount to her. I was afraid that if she did not face her loss it could turn into depression and Deborah had already made one suicide attempt in her young life.

As she rode home with Brooke she began to relive her years at the school. She told Brooke how important we had been to her and that if she ever became rich she would endow us with a huge sum of money.

Since Deborah had only been in our class for a short time, Brooke wanted to know how she felt about our approach in the classroom. Deborah thought that Brooke and I made a great team. "You use a lot of psychology on us and I think it does a lot of good."

"Do you think we teach enough academics?" Try as we might, we can never get enough academics into each day's work.

"I think that by the time you get these kids, if they haven't learned anything, they aren't going to. They're going to be out in the world soon. It's more important that they understand themselves than learn some more facts. You challenge us and make us face ourselves. It's what we need."

Kingsley and Sonny, wedged in the back of Brooke's car, were listening. Eventually, they too, began to volunteer what they had gotten out of their time with us.

In Tony's car, Charlie and Sissy, freed from Kingsley's infuriating presence, were telling their life stories.

In my car, things were going a bit differently. My threesome were confessing their petty crimes to me. This has happened to me more than once. When we are heading home and the students are feeling effusively happy, they begin to tell me what they have done behind my back. I am always upset by this. I feel guilty for not being a better supervisor. I even feel complicity, as if by not being more alert, I have contributed to it all somehow.

I ranted and fussed about how none of this had better happen again. I laid out lists of threats and punishments. I acknowledged their prowess by being shocked, worried and upset, while secretly being relieved that none of their behaviors had risen to the level where I had to turn them in. They felt better about confessing and made empty promises about the future.

288

In the late afternoon we pulled into a hamburger oasis at Four Corners, a crossroads in the middle of the desert, with students full of clean consciences and good spirits. My three renegades were broke, having dissipated their finances early. They were willing to sit stoically in the car rummaging through the remaining supplies for whatever potato chips, dry breakfast cereal and bread that was left while the rest of us ate, but in the midst of such good feelings and camaraderie, I couldn't abandon them to this lesson in frugality and forethought. I offered them a total of five dollars for all three of them if they would wash the bugs off my windows, mirrors and headlights.

Randy gave me a wide freckle-faced grin and said, "Well for five dollars, Carolyn, we'll wash the whole damn car!"

I handed over the five dollars and went to get myself some food at an outdoor taco stand. This desert stop became one of the peak moments of the whole trip. The class had accomplished the impossible and survived four days together. They were bursting with good feelings about themselves and life. Jokes flew, good-natured antics were pantomimed. Most miraculous of all, no one was rude. We could have been a church youth group on a Sunday outing. Sissy teased Dawson by snatching his black leather jacket from under his arm, putting it on, and getting him to chase her all around the taco stand. Locals silently observed them with interest. As the descending sun turned the desert into orange glory, I sat down at a sticky taco-sauce splattered picnic table and ate my 75 cent bean burrito while I contemplated the three-ring circus whirling around me.

In darkness, I headed back to my bus to find it was missing. My resourceful passengers had taken it out of gear and pushed it across the highway to a gas station where they made good their promise to clean my windows. They gleamed and sparkled, reflecting the neon lights of our oasis. I gloried in the precious moments when my adversaries became my allies, even in the face of the damage they might have done to themselves or my bus. Bellies full of burritos and soda, we headed home.

Two days later, in back of the school on the grassy lawn, Brooke and I graduated our three babes, the class of 1987. Randy, Deborah and Gillian were sent out into an inhospitable world much too soon.

I led a toast, standing on the steps of my trailer, looking down on the audience sitting in folding chairs on the grass. I spoke to my graduates, "As we have tried to  teach you, we have also learned from you. We will always carry a part of you with us. And if you have learned from us, you will carry us with you as you go out into the world. Remember, in every ending there is a new day. Farewells are also beginnings." In a toast, we all raised our clear plastic cups filled with soda pop and embossed with a lime green advertisement for real estate. Deborah solemnly cut the ribbons which held three helium-filled balloons. Intertwined, they soared up into the California skies above our heads.

Then school was out for the summer, the students poured out of the halls, the teachers went home to their already packed bags and left town. I belatedly took my solitary trip up the coast to re-orient myself to existing without my focus, my treacherously unbalanced stabilizing point. Each year while I was at Mountainview, it became increasingly important for me to spend that week alone, doing something mildly adventurous. As the daily stimulation which each of those kids brought to me is stripped away, I must rediscover my own solitary capacity for living. This year, my last year, it resided in the shaky reliability of my VW bus and in brown-eyed animals who were willing to let me share the sunshine of bright sparkling California days with them.

Carolyn

REYNARD'S MIRROR

June, 1987

Chapter Twenty

Charlie's Goodbye

Dear Rey,

Summer school has resulted in disaster. We were all so close when we took our trip to Mammoth, and then everything fell apart. Summer school began with the remnants of my old class, Dawson, Nat, Sissy, Sonny, Kingsley and Charlie. I was lucky, probably because I had no aide or possibly because the school was cutting back on accepting older adolescents. Anyway, administration did not transfer new intruders from the younger grades into our class. Even with this small boon from administration, as the students approached the end of summer school, they fell apart. Dawson became more oppositional. His family had decided to leave the state so he was going out in style, mean and bullying. Kingsley had kept his promise to not have any more fights with me, but he was playing sick and forcing his mother to let him stay at home. Sissy, without Brooke, turned surly towards me. Nat was going surfing once or twice a week, and Sonny was becoming obscene again. But the worst of all was Charlie. He attempted suicide.

Our consulting psychoanalyst, Mitchell, reminds me that it is often difficult to experience good endings with adolescents who have been abused or neglected. He calls it turning passive trauma into active victory. When Kent left, he stole or trashed every memento I had of him. Perhaps he was turning the tables on the childhood injury of his mother's abandonment of him. Maybe Shaun's ending was a rehearsal for separation from his doting mother and absent father. However, I don't know if I can consider Charlie's suicide attempt an effort to control his ending with us. Mitchell tells me I must not assume so much self-blame for Charlie's unpredictable behavior and he also says that I must give up my need for syrupy Hollywood endings.

I was totally unprepared for the news awaiting me when I arrived at school. Paul stopped me as I checked in with the "Prove You're not Tardy" sign-in sheet that Monday morning.

"First, I want you to know that Charlie will be all right, but he attempted suicide last night. He overdosed himself on pills. They took him to the hospital, and he's home now."

Normally, I do not respond quickly to shock and this time was no exception. At first, I reacted to this news as if it were just another hassle Charlie was putting me and his grandmother through. Then I began to get mad. I didn't understand my anger, but there it was.

Brooke had a more understandable reaction. She broke into tears. Her response only made me feel worse about my own inappropriate feelings. I began to wonder if I'd been doing this kind of work for too long. Sensitivities that should be tender had become callused through years of being abused by these kids.

A few days later I went to my evening supervision session with Mitchell. All I can say is, thank God for Mitchell. This man has made such a difference. I simply would not have survived without his help.

I almost didn't bring up Charlie's suicide attempt during supervision. It was Adriane's turn to present a case, and I didn't want to intrude on her time but the group does have an understanding that emergencies take precedence over the schedule. With Adriane's encouragement, I decided that Charlie's behavior certainly qualified as an emergency. I knew Mitchell would have something valuable to say. I especially wanted to bring up my odd reaction to it all. Why didn't I feel terrible instead of angry? What was wrong with me? Should I get out of teaching?

I found myself talking quite heatedly as I progressed through a description of Charlie's history. Evidently I was still angry at him. I described his compulsive lying, his inability to present a sincere face to anyone. He was in flight from self-discovery, avoiding depression through drugs.

Mitchell warned me that I was discounting my reaction too easily. "I wouldn't be too quick to disregard your anger. Perhaps your reaction was more accurate than anyone else's. Why does it bother you so much."

I told him, "There seemed to be an expectation by the other staff members that I should be very upset and guilty. They kept trying to comfort me, and my feelings are just too out of kilter with what the situation should elicit. I remember one well-intentioned teacher turning her sorrowful eyes on me and attempting to console me with..."and how are you doing? This must be very hard on you."

With the sensitivity I had come to expect from Mitchell, he expressed what I really wanted to say to my kindly colleague. "You should have said to her, 'Fuck off!'"

"Damn right!" I agreed.

"You knew what he did was chicken-shit!"

"Exactly!" To my surprise I snatched up one of the pillows on the couch and beat at it with my fist to emphasize my hearty agreement with him. This was very unusual behavior for me. My voice grew louder. "That's exactly how I felt about Charlie. He talked and acted so macho. He was busy convincing everyone of this fact, but I knew damn good and well that he was a frightened kid under all that posturing." I was pounding with both fists now. "He injured his classmates very badly. You can't imagine the energy it took to hold myself and the rest of the class together after what that little creep did. I had worked and worked to keep him from fleeing from himself, but he beat me!"

After venting my anger for a while, I turned dutiful again. I said I felt guilty because I hadn't given Charlie more of my time. Putting more energy into working with him probably would not have paid off, but merely increased his flight reaction. I haven't written much about Charlie, mostly because I was leaving him in peace. Even now, I believe if I had been more determined to work with him, I doubt he would have been accessible. Suddenly, Mitchell interrupted my description of Charlie. "What you're saying reminds me of something in one of Rey's last manuscripts." He jumped up and left, returning with one of your chapters from your new book. "I think this will help us to understand this boy." He began to read to us.

Across half the globe your words came to offer me advice and comfort...finally. Through your writing I remembered that Charlie was only alive with shining eyes when he was lying. When he was creating a fantasy world in which he thrived, he made eye contact. In fact, a good measure of whether he was lying or not was how animated and alive he seemed. Otherwise, he was dull and listless. Charlie could not bear reality, nor could his grandmother. It was Charlie's grandmother who had raised him from infancy. Charlie had learned that he must keep her safe from reality. He had explicitly warned me that if I told her the truth about him when he misbehaved at school, she

296

would disintegrate. She had to be protected and that was Charlie's job. The few times I had pushed too hard in my zeal to make him face reality he had turned into a wilting, drooping lad who would run from the classroom to sit in the little weedy green alley behind my trailer. Yet he was eloquent to the point of being domineering when he expressed some ideology he had bonded with.

Most importantly, you talked about the effect of working with such a person. What does it do to the therapist who is faced with this situation? Charlie frustrated me enormously. I never knew what was real and what wasn't. I was unable to grasp who he was. He forced me to construct my own Charlie. I saw him as a fragile person hiding behind bravado. Very likely, my construction of him gave me an excuse to dismiss him and escape from the hopeless and powerless feelings he created in me.

I constructed my Charlie, while Julia, his therapist at school, constructed her Charlie. These two Charlie's did not match and it was very rare that she and I did not have the same view of a student. We battled over which one of us was insightful enough to see the real Charlie. In the aftermath of his suicide attempt, all of us – students, staff, parents, off-campus friends – sat together and shared our perceptions of him. We were all shocked. He had been using more drugs and alcohol than we thought. He was more aggressive and sexually active as well. I guess Julia saw him better than I did. On the other hand, maybe I was right too. Maybe I intuitively knew he was not up to such an intense life. He was in over his head and my surprise was a good indication of how far he had let his life get out of whack in order to maintain his constructed image.

My response to Charlie was normal and reasonable. I avoided him because he was upsetting to me. His need to lie, to create a reality to live in, left me feeling at odds with my sense of him. When I tried to work with him I always felt muddled and unmoored. And because he could not present a reliable picture of himself, he forced me to construct my own version of who he really was.

Your words suggested that Charlie placed me in the infant position. My feelings about Charlie might well be his experience of his grandmother, waxing and waning, never firm or concrete, always elusive. As I created my Charlie in order to have a real person at the other end of the relationship, so perhaps did he have to cut and paste together his grandmother, the world and himself. I suddenly had a sense of that lad's daily battle...to have spent 17 years wandering in a fog which was only lit by the spotlight ephemera of his own creativity was truly terrifying. My image of his struggle filled me with compassion for him and my anger at his suicide attempt simply drained away.

I continue to feel guilty because I did not seek supervision with Mitchell about him earlier. Mitchell would have given me some direction, some clue as to how to work with him. Even now, I am convinced that this boy would be very difficult to help. His grandmother has sent him away to a school where he will be under surveillance for 24 hours a day. There he will learn a new catechism about drugs and alcohol. As long as he bonds to that reality he may be all right, but it will still be a construction to cling to in the hope that if he practices at it long enough it will become real. Who knows, perhaps it will.

I sure wish you weren't so far away. I know, I know, I can't expect you to be able to give me supervision from such a distance. All I can say is, "Thank God for Mitchell...and your writing, of course."

Carolyn

July, 1987

Chapter Twenty-One

The Teacher as Therapist: The Battle Within

Dear Rey,

I am in the middle of summer school. We are still recovering from Charlie's loss, but I am really looking forward to escaping the harsh taskmaster of teaching at Mountainview. I need more than four weeks that's left after teaching summer school to recuperate from a year of working with my little sweethearts, and I am really looking forward to earning enough money so that I won't have to teach summer school any more.

Kingsley and Sissy will be graduating soon. Remember when Kingsley and I had a showdown about a year ago? I described it in one of the first letters I sent to you. It was the worst encounter we ever had. I warned him then that if he ever hit me I would be finished with him. I also told him that we had to stop the pendulum swing of our relationship from affection to rage and manage to live with each other in the middle ground. I was sure that we would have more problems, but we never did.

But now, just before he is about to graduate, he is becoming difficult again. I took him aside for my customary so-how-are-you-going-to-end-your-time-with-us chat.

"Look Kingsley, I know that you are not ready to

299

leave yet. Your school district, however, refuses to pay for you to attend here any longer. You have enough credits, so you must graduate. Your temper and your unpleasantness is your way of telling us that you don't want to go."

"We have no choice Kingsley. It is time for you to become an adult. How do you want to leave, with everybody here hating you and glad to see you gone or with all of us pleased and happy for you? I especially want you and me to have a pleasant ending so we will have good memories of each other."

He looked down and studied the stained orange and yellow shag carpet, a frown claimed his chubby sunburned face as he thought it over. Then he looked me in the eye and said, "You're right. You and I shouldn't have to do this to each other."

I sighed inwardly, irked once again by his suggestion that I was partly responsible for his sour and cranky behavior. That discussion was two weeks ago and he seems to be determined to end his time on a positive note. That showdown of a year and a half ago was a crucial point for both of us. I will miss my shadow when he is gone.

The last time you were in town I asked you if what I was doing in the classroom had any relationship to psychoanalysis. I know it's a farfetched thought, but somehow it seems more closely related to psychoanalysis than it does to other forms of therapy, and I do think therapeutic work is happening in this class. You said something about regression to dependence. It's interesting that I just can't remember your answer well. Later on, I demonstrated my ignorance about what you had explained, and you barked at me, a stimulating experience to be sure, but one which is prone to blast the mind into imbecility for a few minutes. During those minutes, you re-explained it all to me and I missed it again.[7]

On the other hand, I'm not sure I even care if you can tell me what it is that I do. Oh, it would be nice to have it all wrapped up in a tidy pink theoretical bow. It might even be useful insofar as I could have a more powerful perspective on it all. I think though, that Kingsley and Dawson have done a better job of illustrating what, if anything, is happening therapeutically in my classroom.

After summer school, Dawson and his family will be moving away. He will not return to Mountainview in the fall after all. I am shocked at how upset I am about losing him. He used to be the most hateful boy in the whole school, yet as you told me a year and a half ago, I have learned to love that boy. That, I think, is the point.

When I first started teaching, I was just like all those beginning therapists I sit with in supervision. I wanted to love students to health and well-being. Therapists are really at a disadvantage because they do not have to make their clients produce. Teachers are supposed to make their students 'learn'. Society expects us to set limits and control bad behavior. Our 'clients' come to us against their will; their parents make them come. We have captive 'clients' who can't leave and must be made to perform. As a result, teachers have the advantage of experiencing hatred in their classroom. Therapists have a much more difficult time recognizing their own hatred, and that of their client's. In fact, it may be that the adversarial role between a teacher and student actually

---

[7] Later I asked Mitchell to explain it to me and he told me it was a phrase from Donald Winnicott. A patient regresses in the therapeutic relationship to the state of dependency he or she experienced as a child before being forced to conform or develop defensive techniques to cope with parental or societal demands. In therapy the patient has a chance to begin again, to build behaviors which are more consistent with the 'true self' which do not result in 'maladaptive behaviors'.

gets the participants to a quicker manifestation of transference than talk therapy does.

Hatred is a useful tool, unpleasant and exhausting to be sure, but important if the teacher/therapist knows how to recognize and use those countertransference feelings.

My students are hateful. If I deny the ugliness they elicit in me, I am denying them. I have not truly seen them.

Today, Aaron, a 12 year-old student I am working with in supervised individual counseling, rushed up to me in the hallway to use me as a defense against his tormentor. His bully screamed at Aaron, "Nobody at school likes you. Nobody!"

Big dark eyes looked imploringly at me. "Carolyn likes me, don't you?"

"Sometimes," I said honestly. "A lot of the time I don't."

His challenger hooted in satisfaction and walked off. I reached out, gently grabbed Aaron's chin, and said, "It's that mouth of yours. That's where the problem is. If you could just manage to stop being so mean, I'd probably like you all the time."

By acknowledging my frustration with him, he knows I have truly seen him. This is the starting point, the place from which we might both grow. If I can learn to coexist with him where no one before me has, then we might progress out of the mire, the place where he is stuck. It is important that he sees I can grow to care for him in spite of his hateful words. To deny its existence, and to offer him false affection only, is to join him in a lie.

The intensity of his stare told me I had been right. I had captured him for a moment. Like a small squawking fledgling that has been tamed, he sat calmly and gazed at me from the palm of my hand.

These kids are very sensitive to who has the strength to love them in spite of their hatefulness and who doesn't. I vividly remember one of the psychologists at Mountainview telling me that he never worried about yelling at me because he knew I was strong enough to take it. That is probably one of the reasons I settled on you to pester with all my stories.

You would not be appalled when I described myself chasing an escaping student across the parking lot, screaming at him to come back. Unprofessional to be sure, but you would understand how I was driven to this state. In fact, you would chuckle in amusement.[8]

You have never been put off by my distressingly unprofessional behavior, but other therapists were. They either rejected me through criticism or looked away from me as if I were too distressing a sight. I remember sitting across from you during someone else's supervision session when one of the therapists asked you, "What do you do about those patients who you really don't like?" Hah! I

---

[8] This event was caused when I unforgivably sided with a new male aide instead of one of my students. Furious, the student stormed out of the classroom planning to climb on his motorcycle and tear off down the crowded California streets. While he paused to put on his helmet, I caught up with him, climbed on his motorcycle and refused to move. Overcome with frustration, and, because he was very fond of me, he couldn't push me off the bike, so he walked away. I raced to the teachers' lounge and got a wrench out of the toolbox under the sink. I hurried back to the bike and removed the spark plug. When my student returned for his bike and found it inoperable, he was forced to sit down with Paul and myself to resolve the problem.

thought. I know the answer to this one. I knew you had the strength to find a way to care for them all.

You explained that you had learned to care for all but one of your patients no matter how miserable a creature they were. You probably did not hear the internal shout of "Eureka!" blasting through me. You had validated my thoughts about you and how I must deal with the adolescents who evoke hatred in me. The battle is not with them, it is within myself. If I cannot find the strength for my internal battle, if I emotionally walk away from them, they will not progress. I must see them in all their wretchedness and I must be strong enough to contain and learn to care for them.

Writing to you allows me to see the small child in myself. On the wall above my rented typewriter I have a picture of myself when I was about six years old, a first grader in Louisiana. The photos of my platinum hair in braids, my blue eyes, and my small sweet face reflects many moods – pensive, spirited, happy, open and transparent, with perhaps a hint of anticipation. It is like looking past my eroded and scarred surface into the crystal within, pure and clear with its pattern already set.

I must find that same child in my students. When Dawson draws me into battle with him I must recognize that powerful spirited little individual who would not let his family and the school system crush him into oblivion.

This year I watched Dawson bounce a preschooler on his knee in delight, rescue and bathe a lost puppy, entice the school director to play with him, scowl at me and tell me, "Do you have any idea how fucked you are?", burst into tears when Paul assured him that he would not be thrown out of school for coming to school drunk, terrorize old ladies at the mall, and refuse to back down when a highly defensive mall cop was threatening to arrest him.

How could I not love this boy. Look at what a bright many-faceted jewel he is. Such an intense spirit. He is a precious commodity in our society.

I must give up my supremacy. They must be able to surpass me. They must feel their stature and their vitality. It must all be appreciated. Is that not what a good mother must do? To value and enjoy, to confront and fight... those interactions establish the stature of the other as a functioning equal.

And speaking of being a functioning equal, let me tell you a story about an experience I recently had at a dinner gathering of psychoanalysts and their students. I was sitting next to a woman who was in the process of finishing her dissertation for her Ph.D. We had talked the entire evening about her, her dissertation and the therapy she was doing. It has always amazed me how many people who want to be therapists are unable to be interested and listen to the other person in a conversation...maybe it's a reaction to the nature of their work. But finally, in a vain attempt to interject a little reciprocity, I elbowed my way into the conversation and mentioned that I was a special ed. teacher.

"What!" she gasped in disbelief. "Well, what are you doing here? What on earth can _you_ get out of these meetings?"

You might guess that she made me mad. I found myself saying, "Learning about analysis helps a lot in my teaching. Actually, between the two professions, there is no doubt in my mind that the more difficult and demanding profession is special education. What you handle for an hour with one person or perhaps an occasional group, I do for six hours a day, five days a week, usually with a group of twelve. I know I could do what you do, but I'll bet there's damn few of you who could handle my job."

She excused herself and went to the restroom.

I believe what I said. In spite of the greater difficulty of being a special ed. teacher, our society deems the therapist to be more valuable. In 1987, my dinner partner has the potential to earn from between $80 to $150 an hour. At Mountainview, I earn much, much less. Something is very wrong, don't you think?

Yes, I long for the day when special educators drive luxury cars and psychologists come to us for advice. Perhaps I might even allow one into a supervision group, if she can fork over enough money.

Only three more weeks until summer vacation and the I leave Mountainview for good. I can't believe this is the end!

Carolyn

August, 1987

Chapter Twenty-Two

Reynard's Mirror

Dear Rey,

Well, Zane and I decided we needed to get away before making any decisions about the future. We loaded up our bus with dogs and gear and headed north to British Columbia. I am still reeling from the fact that Mountainview is no longer a part of my life. I need time and distance to mull it all over.

We have arrived at Port Hardy at the northern end of Vancouver Island, in British Columbia, Canada. We are waiting for a British Columbia Ferry to come and take us to Prince Rupert. It is raining and the three dogs, Zane and I are all jammed into the VW bus together. The dogs are wet and dampening everything they touch. The windows keep steaming up. Once we get on board the ferry, Zane and I must rush upstairs to the heated open-air rear deck to claim our semi-reclining deck chairs, for it is there that we will spend the night. We can't afford a cabin, but they do have public showers. I cannot wait to experience dry air once again, and hot water, and showers. What bliss!

I could not believe that you would come to

California in the summertime. It is fortunate that you caught me at school when you did. I just happened to be there to clean up my classroom before leaving for good. I almost didn't answer the phone.

It was only five days ago that I spent a whole hour with you over coffee. I am in another world now, one populated mostly by mosquitoes that seem to find me a particularly tasty morsel. I already have over a 100 bites on my body. Last night I felt delirious.

I am still reeling from your determination to get me to write a book. "Look," you said, "your life cannot move forward until you write that book. You must get it done so that you can decide what you will do next, continue teaching or become a therapist. First, however, you must face the fact that you can be a writer!" You kept pushing the word at me, trying to get me to change my retiring view of myself.

I said to myself, this man has no objectivity at all. I have simply struck some common chord with him. He cannot say so many good things to me about my writing in one intense sixty minute compliment. My mind just goes blotto beyond the first five minutes.

Even though it was mid-day when you left, I stopped at the corner market on the way home and bought a bottle of pink champagne. Arriving at my housing tract hovel I notified my husband that we apparently had a hatchling writer in the family and he was going to have to toast the moment with me, regardless of his feelings about cheap sweet champagne at two in the afternoon. I poured the raucous pink liquid into two window-pane thick goblets and we offered me a toast.

"Well, I'm glad you'll listen to Rey. You never believed me," Zane said.

After the toast, the question to be pursued was what to do with myself. Packing for the trip or household cleaning would be too banal. TV would be maddening. Other writers would derail me. Notice how I phrased that.

Ah! I know! I'll read me!

So I got out the copies of my letters I've written to you over the years... (I hope this won't be a shock to you that I kept copies. I was not about to send my chicks off into the ether without making copies.)...and I turned on my new age writing music, gulped my champagne and fell asleep among the pages of my fetal book.

Ten days later

Unhappily, we are on our way south now. After exploring the wilderness of northwestern British Columbia, we are now camped by a lake northwest of Prince George. We have returned to the fringes of civilization. Summer cabins abound here. We've found a large field next to the lake and just discovered a small herd of horses that have come out of the dusk to size us up. We hustled our oblivious dogs into the bus before they noticed our equine visitors. The horses stared at us expectantly, as if we should be giving them treats. I pulled out some carrots and after Zane demonstrated that it could be done without injury, I put my carrots into a bowl and took them into their midst.

That was an experience! Just me and my vulnerable toes surrounded by skittish, whirling, nickering, enormous animals circling around me. Their naked hides rippled over muscle as they jostled and shoved each other, muzzles reaching for carrots. They had sweet colts among them. They also had demanding, pushing noses with snapping, yellowed teeth. They were wild flowing power. I could see why the psychiatrist in the play Equus came to agree with his patient that they were God. They became bored with me when I ran out of my offering of carrots, as gods are wont to do. They left me feeling enormously deprived as they disappeared into the darkness. A loon cried on the lake.

The dogs, trapped in the bus, greatly upset that they were prevented from their rightful sport of being kicked in the head, were released from captivity. They have calmed down now, but once it became really dark they retired to the safety and comfort of the bus. As I told you before, no reasonable dog lays on the cold hard ground next to a fur-singeing campfire when there are comfy blankets and safety from creatures of the night to be had.

Zane and I are sitting by the campfire. We both have candles sitting in glass jars, our versions of lanterns. He is reading science fiction. I am dealing with your insistent pushy memory.

You came to town and astonished me by paying special attention to me and by your kind words about how much you enjoy receiving my letters. I know you told me at the beginning that you wouldn't comment on my letters. Silence, just silence, was your response.

It seems to me that a possible explanation for your silence is the witchdoctor theory. When you, the shaman, tell me I should write, it's as if you have truly transformed me. Zing! Zap! My body chemistry shoots into overdrive. You shake a rattle at me filled with bear's teeth and wolf knuckle bones and synergistic explosions of creativity blossom in my brain. I become driven, compulsive about writing.

If I knew that you couldn't cure your own heartburn, that you are ineffectual and clumsy when changing a tire, and that you get lost on Interstate 5, your shaman's wolf totem mask might slip and I would see the ordinary human behind it.

When I told you that I might like to use my letters to you as a basis for a book, you liked the idea. Then I asked you whether I should use your real name or not. I was touched when you looked me firmly in the eye and said you would leave it entirely up to me. Such courage!

I offered to use another name and you leaned

310

forward with enthusiasm. "Yes, then the reader will have to experience the psychoanalyst as an unknown, which is the actual case, isn't it?" You grinned wolfishly at me from behind your beard.

I looked at you in delight, then I felt fury. You son-of-a-bitch! You are being silent on purpose! I hate you! Is this a plan? Is this an exercise in transference? You are keeping silent so I will create you in my own image. How wonderful! Look at how much you are enjoying this! I have decided that I hate you. Then I decided that a partnership in silent separation held an odd appeal.

I refuse to discuss this any further.

Five days later

Dear Jules,

I think Jules is what I will call you now that you are to become an unknown. It works, don't you think? You are such a gem.

I am sitting along the Selway River in northern Idaho with an iced gin and tonic at hand, experiencing the joys of la vie primitif. Zane has just returned with some trout and he is presently scraping the innards out of the poor little things. The dogs, calmed at last from their vigilant despair over his absence, are peacefully dozing

311

around us. The Selway fills our ears with its incessant rush and chatter.

When you and I had coffee, you asked me if I had given any more thought about whether or not I wanted to become a therapist. I think I have made my decision.

I wish I could communicate to you the peace and contentment that being in the backwoods of northwestern British Columbia offers a mentally bruised special ed. teacher. No, that's not quite right. Northwestern British Columbia is an alternative existence, so vast and magnificent, so welcoming and threatening that the mind cannot contain it. To understand the dimensions of the universe, to grasp the meaning of death and eternity, these reside in the menacing relentless power of a glacier, in the aloof and harsh indifference of mountain peaks, and in the anonymous marching ranks of endless miles of spruce and pine.

In contrast, to walk through the delicate glowing emerald undergrowth in a light mist, to build a teepee shelter and start a fire in spite of the rain, and to sit by a campfire looking out over a glowing ember of a lake at sunset...these feel like home.

Resolution, closure about what life is really all about, lie just around the bend, downstream, in the next valley. Truths of existence are possible to glimpse up here, perhaps only tiny piping snatches of truth but nevertheless, they are far more accessible than is possible in the contrivances of urban life.

You in your exile in Great Britain might dream that there is plenty of space in the woods of Washington, Oregon, or even northern California. To seek a place to pull off the road on the coast of northwestern United States is doomed to failure. Barricaded roads, barbed wire and no trespassing signs will herd you back into prescribed camping sites where county, state and federal laws demand obedience and tied-up dogs.

But in northwestern British Columbia blessed

logging roads abound. It's true. I am ashamed to admit this but I have come to love the logger. He is a trailblazer for my VW bus, carving roads for me and my husband into the wilderness where secret lakes and rivers await, unmolested by crowds. Still, it takes time to come to terms with elbow room, silence, enough privacy to bathe in murky waters, and the eeriness of an evening chorus of wolves.

Wolves are benign, shy creatures in comparison to the grizzly, who as luck would have it, likes to hang out in British Columbia too. In fact, the day we purchased our 'bear bell' off the rack of basic and essential fishing gear in Stewart, B.C., we were told that the area we had just camped in the night before probably had the highest density of grizzlies in the province. Evidently grizzlies see eye to eye with us in preferring to reside in thickets of alders along streams frothing with salmon flailing their way back to their birthplace to achieve orgasm and lingering death in one fell swoop.

It takes time to come to terms with living with churlish, nearsighted grizzlies and orgasmically suicidal salmon.

I have come to the decision that immersing myself in wilderness holds a very high priority for me and it is one that requires lots of time. Therefore, I do not want to become a therapist. I have finally realized that I prefer the job description of a teacher's lot in life.

Poverty alarms me, but not having privacy and free time terrifies me. Teachers can manage decent vacation schedules, and hopefully if they have saved enough money over the year, they can actually travel somewhere. Furthermore, they are not expected to wrangle with the predictable and implacable intrusions of clients whose lives go out of whack in the middle of the night.

No, I like the action of teaching. I like working with ideas, bundling students up into my old VW and dragging their unwilling little minds through a factory or a museum. I love taking them to perhaps the last steel foundry on the west coast to show them molten steel being rolled into bars or to a factory to see miles of little wheat crackers flowing past us on a conveyor belt. The thought of being cooped up with somebody in an office for an hour at a time makes me feel claustrophobic.

These kids are very special. They are not appreciated nearly enough. They represent the inability of our society to herd large groups of children together and normalize them. They could not be made obedient like the others. I think our society needs disobedience. I like their gumption, their spontaneity and effervescence. I like the surprise of them. I will never be bored.

Five days later
Near Twin Falls, Idaho

Dear Raoul, (That has more panache, don't you think?)

I am at my mother-in-law's now, a wonderful woman. Have you ever read the Fellowship of the Ring? Do you know the part where the Hobbits reach the elven court in Rivendell after overcoming many tribulations. Well, that's what coming to my mother-in-law's is like. Suddenly there is blessed hot water that simply flows from the tap. Food, hot complicated food, of amazing quantity and variety appear magically on the table three times a day. Not for another year will I do all of my eating out of one bowl. I get to stretch out instead of battling with three dogs and a husband for the right to both turn over and keep the covers. I am clean! But the most wonderful blessing of all is that the bugs are outside, banging away at the window in a futile attempt to get at me. My body is now safe.

Now for a change of topic. As you may have noticed, I've been thinking a lot about what I will call you in my book. What a wonderful opportunity! A chance to name you. You will be happy to know that I have finally decided. When I write my book I shall change all the salutations and your real name shall not be known. I shall call you Rey, for Reynard the Fox. I think that captures your sly, crafty psychoanalytical soul quite well. It isn't a perfect fit, and I must apologize to you for that, for Reynard was a savage fellow who was more than willing to eat his opponents. However, Reynard's magical mirror, the third gift to his king and queen, captures what these letters are all about.

In case you've forgotten the fable, Reynard the Fox had been summoned for trial by King Nobel the Lion. His many crimes had caught up with him. In fact, he had already been tried and pardoned once, but here he was again waiting for judgement at his second trial. To calm his angry sovereign, he began to describe three non-

existent treasures he had sent to the king and his wife, the Queen. He told King Nobel that he was to receive a ring of three jewels, and each stone had magical powers. The queen was to receive two presents. The first, horribly enough, was a comb made of a living panther's shoulder blade and the second gift was an amazing magical mirror. Reynard's mirror was of such virtue that men might see in it all that they would wish to know. You'll be happy to know that Reynard was pardoned for a second time and resumed his life of outsmarting and eating his opponents.

Reynard, and you, of course, are cunning fellows. The ring of three magical jewels, the comb, and the mirror were nothing but figments of Rey's imagination, a ruse to deflect retaliation from an angry king. If there were such a thing as Reynard's mirror and I held it before my eyes, all I would see is me...but that is what these letters have been doing all along...showing me myself.

Like a small child, I write to you as if you have the answers. You do not. You have your own set of answers, a carefully woven silken tapestry of answers perhaps, but not necessarily the 'right' answer, or the only answer. Like the poor queen, I will never find the boon of certainty because it's illusionary.

Over the years these letters have become a reflection of myself, a collection of the tales of my life, stories I needed to share with the writer in yourself. The image I discovered in the letters is not too different from the photograph hanging over my desk. I see a platinum-haired child smiling at me through the years of my life. I like the image I see in my letters. I like the answers I have found and I must thank you for your wiliness and your silence. I think. Maybe. Perhaps.

But the reflection I have created with you, is the same task my students have with me. I must mirror their reflections as best as I can. "Is this you?" I ask. They let me know if I am on the right track with a change in their behavior...a smile, a joke, cooperation. Then we move forward to the next event and I must hold the mirror up to them again and we progress onward in mutual cooperation to find the personal mythic image that we all create for ourselves. It is my job to not throw them away, to survive them, and to hold the mirror up, continuously exploring with the child, "Is this you?"

Oh yes, there is *one* other reason I named you Rey. A minor one, I'm sure. My father's name was Roy. You have given me the opportunity to share conversations with you that I couldn't have with him.

Thank you,

Carolyn

P.S. Also, I don't want to hear any more twaddle about me being the fox. I know that some of my fox drawings could be me or they could be you, but let's be clear here. It is you who is the sly, cunning fellow, not me. Like Nat, when he took the 'Good Guy' badge away from me and gave it to lovely Diana...I am telling you, "Here, the fox is you and don't go changing it around anymore."

Epilogue

It was October, when the aspen turns gloriously gold and Zane and I, with our three rapturously happy dogs tried to hike up to an alpine lake lying near 9,000 ft. After pulling our aging bodies up over yet another hump of rocky glacial moraine, we turned and looked down onto a grand vista, the azure waters of a land-locked lake and the purpling slopes of volcanic craters.

The trail rose in a series of benches and at the top of each one thickets of aspen were revealed, white-barked with fluttering leaves of lemon, gold and lime. The sheer granite walls of the eastern crest of the Sierra Nevada loomed over us, prematurely blocking out the light of the sun. An impending dusk was insisting that we turn back before we reached the alpine lake at the end of the trail.

I pleaded with Zane, "Just to that bend in the trail. I must walk through that grove of aspen. Just a little further." Before he could tell me no, I rushed and gasped my way up the path carpeted with golden aspen leaves. My dogs bounded and cavorted ahead of me.

"Look!" I shouted back to my sensible husband, who was checking his watch and frowning at the plummeting sun, "I can see the glint of water beyond those trees. It's a brook in a meadow. We can't go back yet, I've got to see that meadow."

"C'mon Carolyn," he sighed, "the sun will be setting soon. Do you really want to hike back down this trail in the dark? We can always come back after work tomorrow. It's only half an hour away."

Oh, right, I keep forgetting that we live so close to it all now."

We raced the darkness down the slope. We won but just barely.

Afterword

By Paul, Director of 'Mountainview'

It has been some 30 years since Carolyn left Mountainview to begin a new part of her life as a special education teacher in public school, living east of the Sierras in northern California. Shortly after leaving our small private school, Carolyn wrote a letter to me asking to assist her with some necessary paperwork she needed for her new position. In her letter, Carolyn thanked me for my support and in addition referenced the many positives she acquired during her teaching days at Moutainview. She also complained about how restrictive public school policies are, and how much she had to rein herself in.

I hope in part we can take some small amount of credit for what Carolyn learned here at Moutainview. However, it is more important to focus on how Carolyn took what she learned and truly became a master special education teacher with an amazing ability to understand and integrate therapeutic approaches while working with her students.

Along with her teaching at Mountainview, Carolyn also became a "student" herself who was willing to learn some hard lessons from her high school students. She learned about the feelings of being manipulated, being the target of hurtful and hateful remarks and being left with the question of, "Why are you teaching us anyway?" These reactions have frightened many out of the field with no wish to return. Carolyn, as tired and frustrated as she sometimes felt, had the energy, willingness and understanding to accept the trials her students presented. She had no problem sharing her issues and failings with fellow staff members at our weekly meetings with our consulting psychologists and she was able to incorporate much of what she learned back to her classroom.

Her response to her students was directed by the journey that they were on and not her journey, thus enabling her students to see her as a trusting ally. For some of these students this was the first opportunity to have this kind of a relationship with an adult, let alone a teacher. Her understanding of her students' past experiences, its impact on their present lives and her ability to get her students to 'let her in' is why Carolyn has been so successful. I hope others reading this book of Carolyn's 'front line' experiences will gain insights from a teacher who knew she had to become a "student" again in order to be a better and more accessible teacher.

Appendix

Possible Helpful Thoughts

ABOUT THE AUTHOR

I can trace my Scottish Crawford family as far back as 1810 in North Carolina. We took the southern route through Georgia and the Civil War. My family continued through to Oklahoma, Kansas, Louisiana and Texas. We finally made it to California where I graduated from UCLA with an MA in Geography. This was before Reagan got his teeth into the California University system, and tuition was only $50 a semester. I was able to work my way through college in the student book store and later, for the Geography Department as a staff cartographer. While I was at it, I picked up an elementary teaching credential. I went to work at Mountainview for 15 years and added a secondary teaching credential, a special ed. certificate and an M.A in Psychology from California State University at Long Beach.

I gave up private school deprivations, and excellent administrative and psychological support to become a proper, well-behaved special ed teacher in the public sector. Perhaps unwillingly, public school offered me a decent salary, resources, training, a pension and medical insurance that belonging to a union provided. I now live in a community of about 300 people. I taught special ed. for another 21 years in grades K through 12; teaching primary and elementary school in the morning and high school after lunch. I helped my students progress from decoding phonics to deciphering Shakespeare (not one of my strengths). These students no longer left me after a few years. I was able to watch them grow from childhood, become adolescents, and finally now as 30 and 40 year-olds, they greet me with warm smiles and their children.

I had to learn there was no Paul or Nick in public school administration. In my 21 years of teaching here we had about 15 different principals, most were using our little remote district as a stepping stone to larger and better paying districts. Many, but not all, were hopeless. I found that if I could handle my student's behavior problems without involving administration, my existence as part of the staff seemed to disappear from their minds. Twice, I took a misbehaving adolescent to the principal's office, and was appalled at the way the situation was handled. I never took another student, but of course the students here had <u>far</u> fewer problems.

I'm retired now, but I can't give up teaching. Most years, I try to volunteer with the little ones, although sitting in those little bitty chairs is a bit of a challenge. The kids I like best are still the scrappy oppositional ones. I made the right choice; teaching, not therapy was my game.

Made in the USA
San Bernardino, CA
22 September 2018